THE CHRISTMAS LACE BOOK
Christine Springett

GW00645061

INDEX

ACKNOWLEDGEMENTS

I would like to record my sincere and heartfelt thanks to the members of my family and the workers who make up the Springett 'team' who have alternately encouraged and bullied me into putting together this collection of Christmas projects. Without their help, so generously given, it would not have been possible, so thank you one and all.

ISBN 0 9517157 1 2

EQUIPMENT

BOBBINS. Although it is possible to economise and use substitutes for many of the other items on this equipment list I think most lace teachers would agree that there is no substitute for bobbins. Always buy the best that you can afford, inexpensive plastic bobbins or the cheapest wooden bobbins will get you started, but whichever you choose make sure that the head shape is well defined and smooth enough to allow the thread to slide easily without snagging.

BEADS. English lace bobbins are usually weighted with a ring of beads at the end of the shank, and because weight is important it is essential to use glass beads for the 'spangle', plastic beads will not be satisfactory. The spangle usually consists of a single larger bead with several smaller ones on each side which you may like to arrange in diminishing size so that the smallest are situated on each side of the bobbin.

WIRE. The glass beads of the spangle are traditionally threaded on brass wire which can be purchased from lace equipment suppliers.

PILLOW. Lace is traditionally made on a straw pillow, but many lacemakers today buy the very inexpensive polystyrene pillows which can be padded with several layers of carpet underfelt or an old woollen blanket to prevent the surface breaking up so readily. A simple round pillow 16"-18" (40-45cm) in diameter is fine to begin with. It is possible to use a thick piece of polystyrene insulating material but it is not so easy to make lace on a completely flat surface, so try and shape the top to make a slight dome.

COVER-CLOTHS. Whatever shape or material your pillow the surface should always be covered by a fabric which can be removed and washed when necessary. You should choose a fabric in a plain colour, most lacemakers choose dark green or blue. The fabric itself should have a smooth finish and should be pre-washed to make sure that neither colour nor loose fluff or 'lint' will be transferred to your lace thread as the bobbins are moved over it. A plain woven cotton or 'drill' fabric is best. You will need not only a cover for your pillow, but also at least two square cover cloths with which to 'dress' your pillow once the pricking is pinned in place. These will ensure that your bobbins always move over a smooth surface. One cloth should be kept to place over your pillow whenever you stop working, this will help to keep your lace clean. Dark coloured men's handkerchiefs can be used as cover cloths.

PINS. Traditionally brass pins are used for lace and these can be purchased from lace equipment suppliers. Obviously it is possible to use ordinary dressmaking pins if nothing else is available. Children need fairly sturdy pins as fine pins are easily bent.

PATTERN OR PRICKING. There are two ways of making a pricking. Firstly you can use the more traditional way of transferring the pattern onto a piece of special pricking card. For this you will need a photocopy of the pattern, the pricking card, a cork pricking board and a pricker. Place the photocopy over the card and place both on the pricking board. Anchor them in place with a pin at each corner and using the pricker (a needle held firmly in a wooden handle or 'chuck') make a hole wherever there is a dot. Remove the photocopy and copy the markings onto the card. It is very important to take care in both steps as your lace can only be as good as your pricking, a poor pricking can never allow you to make good lace. Many lacemakers today prefer to photocopy the pattern directly from the book onto a piece of ordinary card. You should put clear or blue matt film over the pattern to make sure that none of the marking comes off on your thread. You can then prick the pattern before you start, or you can make the holes as you go along. With children it is much more accurate to prick the pattern first. As children don't usually want to repeat the same pattern time after time the second method is probably quite acceptable.

PINLIFTER. This is a very useful gadget which does precisely what its name suggests - lifts pins which have been pressed all the way down into the pillow by means of a small forked metal prong.

CROCHET HOOK. I use a .6mm hook for a variety of tasks such as making 'sewings' or joining together work at the finish.

LAZY SUSAN. Another useful little tool which can be used instead of a crochet hook. Basically it consists of a needle mounted in a wooden handle so that the eye of the needle faces outwards.

STITCH HOLDER. To keep the bobbins in order whilst the pillow is being moved, or when the lace is moved up the pattern, you can use a knitting stitch holder, or a piece of ribbon or tape which is threaded through the spangles of the bobbins.

THREAD. Where a fine glittery thread is required you can use:-
Mez Effektgarn, Madeira 40 or DMC Metallise.
Where a medium thickness glittery thread is required use:-
DMC Fil Argent Clair (silver) or DMC Fil Or Clair (gold)
Alternatively you can use a double thickness of Madeira 40 or DMC Metallise.
Where a thicker glittery thread is required use:-
Twilley's Gold Dust or Madeira in the 20m flat packs.
Where an even thicker glittery thread is required use Twilley's Gold Fingering.
(When using these thicker threads with children it is wise to tie a simple knot at the ends of the cut length to prevent it unravelling as the bobbins are wound.)
Where I have used white thread you may find the following equivalents useful:-
36/2 Brok cotton or DMC 30 Retors d'Alsace Brillante.
100/3 Brok cotton or DMC 50 Retors d'Alsace Brilliante.
DMC have recently re-named some of their threads:-
DMC Fil a Dentelle is now DMC Special Dentelles.
DMC Retors d'Alsace and DMC Brilliante are now DMC Broder Machine.

GLUE. To mount many of these projects I have used glue such as Bostik, Uhu, Copydex and just plain paper gum such as Gloy. Always use glue extremely sparingly and with appropriate caution.

Published by C & D Springett
21 Hillmorton Road
Rugby
Warwickshire
CV22 5DF

If you have enjoyed the ideas in this book you may like to know that there are other Christmas projects and a wide range of similar pieces for other occasions in 'Lace for Children of All Ages' which is also available from C & D Springett.
If you have any problems obtaining any accessories for these projects write to:

C & D Springett, 21 Hillmorton Road, Rugby, Warwickshire, CV22 5DF. Tel: (0788) 544691.

Printed by Apex Printers
1 Avon Industrial Estate
Butlers Leap
Rugby
Warwickshire
CV21 3UT

A GLOSSARY OF TERMS AND TECHNIQUES

CLOTH STITCH. Also known as 'linen' stitch or in the UK as 'whole' stitch. Number the positions of the four bobbins from the left, lift 2 over 3 (also called a 'cross'), now lift the bobbin in position 4 over 3 and 2 over 1 (also called 'twists') and finally lift 2 over 3 to complete the stitch. N.B. It is the POSITIONS not the bobbins themselves which are numbered, and the positions are ALWAYS numbered from left to right.

COLLECTING KNOT. I always use a 'collecting knot' to bring a large number of threads into a tight group. Take the two outside threads, one from each edge, and tie the first part of a reef knot with an extra twist (see below), pull it tight and then, lifting the bunch of centre threads, pass the knotting thread from the left underneath to the right, and the righthand thread underneath to the left. Now tie a reef knot on top, again putting an extra twist on the first half of the knot.

COVERING A PIN. A pin is 'covered' when a stitch is worked immediately underneath it. In Torchon lace the stitch beneath the pin is usually the same as the stitch used above it.

CROSS. Is made by lifting the lefthand bobbins over the right - the opposite of a twist. It is usually made the centre two threads of the working group of four.

DOUBLE HALF STITCH. Often used at one end of a row of half stitch. Simply make two half stitches with the workers and the edge pair before putting up the pin. The next row is started with a similar stitch. A double half stitch is exactly the same as a cloth stitch and twist if you prefer to think of it that way.

FAN. A triangular area with a curved side making an attractive headside for Torchon edgings. 'Open fans' and 'French Fans' fill a similar triangular shape at the edge of a pattern.

FOOTSIDE. The usually straight edge which is mostly on the right (in the UK) of an edging.

FOOTSIDE EDGE PAIR. The old worker pair which was left at the footside edge at the end of the previous row.

FOOTSIDE PASSIVE PAIR. The passive pair which runs straight down immediately to the left of the footside pins and to the right of the ground pins.

GIMP. A thick thread outlining part of a pattern.

HALF STITCH. Number the positions of the bobbins from the left as usual. Lift 2 over 3, then 4 and 2 over 3 and 1 in the normal way.

Left: Hanging on 'astride' or 'open'
2nd 1st 2nd

Left: Hanging on in order
1st pair 2nd pair

HANGING ON. There are two ways of hanging on two or more pairs around a pin to start a piece. To hang pairs on 'in order' push the first pair to the left and hang on the second pair to its right. The bobbins of each true pair will then lie next to each other. To hang pairs 'astride' or 'open' hang the first pair with the bobbins close together, the next pair sits astride this pair with one bobbin outside each as shown below.

HEADSIDE. The curved or shaped edging usually on the left (in the UK) of an edging.

INTERLINKING. When starting a piece it is useful to interlink two pairs when they are hung from the same pin. This is done by hanging the first pair around the pin and pushing it to the left, the second pair is placed to its right and the two centre threads are twisted twice right over left as usual. This brings all the bobbins back to their true partner, but means that when the starting pin is removed the starting loops of each pair will be interlinked which will give a much neater effect.

JOINING. At the end of a piece of work use a crochet hook or lazy susan to bring one thread of the finishing pair through the corresponding starting loop, remove the bobbin so that the thread can be pulled all the way through, replace the pin and tie off with a reef knot.

KISS. A Bedfordshire lace technique used to link two adjacent trails. The workers are brought to the inside edge of both trails, twisted at least twice and pins placed as usual. Make a cloth stitch with the two worker pairs, twist them at least twice again and cloth stitch them through the trail they are nearest. The workers have now changed trail.

MAGIC CHAIN. A chain stitch effect made by two pairs of thicker thread running down the centre of a cloth stitch trail.

PASSIVES. The pairs which go more or less straight down through the work at right angles to the workers.

PICOT. A decorative loop formed to one side of a plait or on the outer edge of a band of cloth stitch. Made by adding 3 or 5 twists (depending on the thickness of the thread) to the picot pair before the pin, and two twists with the same pair after the pin. Restart your plait with a cloth stitch.

PLAIT. A basic feature of Bedfordshire lace giving a closely woven bar which is often decorated with picots. Always start a plait with a cloth stitch and continue with a series of reversed half stitches (ie. twist and cross) tensioning well between each stitch. Never make a plait too long, if you are in any doubt as to whether you need the last twist and cross you should undo it. A plait which is too long will form a curve between its starting and finishing pinholes instead of forming a nice straight line.

PUTTING UP A PIN. Pins should be pushed far enough into the pillow to prevent them wobbling when the threads around them are tensioned. Pins in the centre of the work should be upright or lean slightly backwards, they should NEVER slope forwards. The pins at the edges of a piece should lean slightly outwards. Pins can be pushed right down into the pillow to prevent them getting in the way at a later stage.

A reef knot

A reef knot with and extra twist on the first half.

REEF KNOTS. Make an ordinary reef knot by passing the threads left over right and under and then right over left and under. This can be tied without removing the bobbins, in which case always hold the bobbins so that they can be passed spangle first through the loop. It is sometimes difficult to prevent the first half of the knot slackening whilst the second is made, to ensure that you do not lose the tension of the first part of the knot put an extra twist on the first half ie. left over right and under, over right and under again before pulling it tight.

ROSE GROUND. A decorative filling stitch used in Torchon lace. It is made up of two preparation stitches before the four pinholes at the corners of the diamond marking which are followed by two more preparation stitches which could more aptly be called 'conclusion' stitches at this point. I have used a cloth stitch and twist as my preparation/conclusion stitches and a half stitch, pin, half stitch for the four diamond pinholes, but there are many other types of Rose Ground which you can substitute if you prefer.

SEWING. 'Making a sewing' is a technique used to link two adjacent areas of work, usually two trails. The first trail is worked in the usual way, the second trail will share pinholes with the first so bring the worker pair to the shared pinhole and remove the pin. With a crochet hook or lazy susan bring ONE of the worker threads up through the loop formed by the workers at the edge of the first trail, pass the OTHER worker through the loop formed by its partner and replace the pin without splitting any of the threads. Tension the workers carefully before continuing.

SPIDER. A small cloth stitch oval with twisted pairs radiating out from it.

TENSIONING. It is vital to tension your work at the end of each row before proceeding with the next row. To do this pull the worker tight and then tension each passive bobbin in turn so that all the threads lie smoothly and are evenly spread. Poor tensioning will spoil the appearance of your lace so its importance cannot be over-stated.

TORCHON GROUND. There are several different combinations of stitches and twists which can be used to make up the more open net-like appearance of the background sections of the Torchon pieces. I usually choose half stitch, pin, half stitch and twist, but you can easily substitute your favourite version if you prefer.

TRAIL. A narrow band or tape usually of cloth stitch.

TWIST. Always lift the righthand bobbin over the left to twist a pair. The worker pair is usually twisted two or three times at the end of every row.

WEAVER'S KNOT. If you break a thread and need to use a knot to rejoin it this knot will enable you to trim the ends off very closely so that the knot is barely visible. Make a loop with the bobbin thread as shown, and pull a second loop through it, pass the broken

end through the second loop and hold the two ends level. Now pull on the bobbin so that the bobbin thread tightens and forms the knot. Leave the ends as they are for as long as you can, trimming them short just before the knot goes into the work. Alternatively, having rejoined the broken thread, hang on a new bobbin and work it with the broken thread for 1/2" or so then throw out the knotted thread so that the knot does not actually go into the lace.

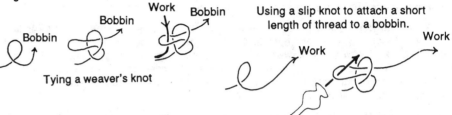

Tying a weaver's knot

Using a slip knot to attach a short length of thread to a bobbin.

WINDING BOBBINS. Where I have given specific lengths of thread to use for projects it is obviously vital to wind half of each length onto each bobbin. To do this fold the length in half and trap the thread at the midpoint between the pillow and the pin by leaning the pin backwards at a very acute angle. Alternatively you can make a simple slip knot loop, placing the pin through that loop. Do not be tempted to put the pin through the thread to anchor the midpoint to the pillow, as this will weaken the thread which may cause it to fray or break. Wind the thread by holding the bobbin in your left hand and winding AWAY from yourself. To make a hitch on the top of the bobbin wind the thread in the same direction twice around your left thumb. Place the tip of that thumb on the top of the bobbin and slip the loops down onto the head. Do not remove your thumb until you have tightened the thread to hold it securely around the head of the bobbin. When you are using a very short length of thread you can attach it to the bobbin by making a simple slip knot and passing the head of the bobbin through the loop before pulling the thread tight. When you wish to remove the thread simply pull on the short end and the loop will grow large enough to allow you to slip the bobbin out.

WORKERS OR WEAVERS. The pair which zigzags from side to side of a cloth stitch or half stitch area.

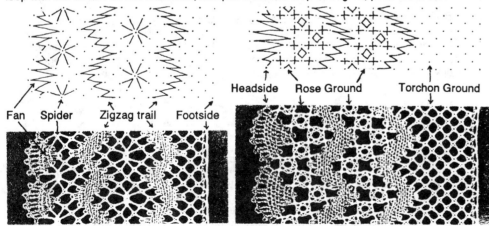

Fan   Spider   Zigzag trail   Footside

Headside   Rose Ground   Torchon Ground

Lace and the pricking required to make it showing some of the basic features of Torchon lace.

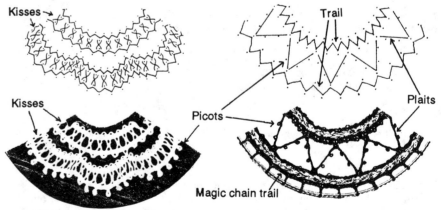

Kisses   Trail   Plaits

Kisses   Picots   Magic chain trail

Lace and the pricking required to make it showing some of the basic features of Bedfordshire lace.

SIMPLE BORDERS FOR CHRISTMAS CARDS.

There are four variations in stitch and shape for these borders. You can choose to use either a cloth stitch or a half stitch edging for a round or an oval shaped border. Both use mainly thick threads and can be successfully completed even by a less experienced or younger lacemaker. The thread lengths required are the same for both the round or oval border.

CLOTH STITCH BORDER

For the cloth stitch round or oval border:-

4 pairs of Twilley's Gold Dust as passives. Cut 4 x 54" (135cm) lengths.

1 pair of DMC Fil a Dentelle as workers. Cut 1 x 5yd (5m) length.

For the sample border I used green thread on a red card background with a Christmas tree motif mounted in the centre of the oval cut out.

WORKING INSTRUCTIONS

Hang one passive pair from each of pins 1, 2, 3 and 4 and the worker pair from pin 5. Cloth stitch the workers through the first three pairs of passives then twist the workers twice before cloth stitching through the outside passive pair. Twist the workers twice at the end of the row and put one twist on the outside passive pair. Put up pin 6 and tension each pair carefully. You are now ready to work back across the row. Cloth stitch through the outside passive pair and tension both pairs by swinging them apart, gently pulling on each thread as you do so. Now twist the outside passive pair once and the workers twice before cloth stitching through the three passive pairs to the end of the row. Twist the workers twice as usual before putting up pin 7.

Continue in this way taking care to remember to twist the worker twice between the outside passive and the group of three passive pairs, and twice at the end of each row. The outside passive pair is twisted once each time the worker cloth stitches through it.

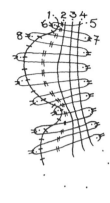

Above left: Working diagram for the round or oval cloth stitch border.

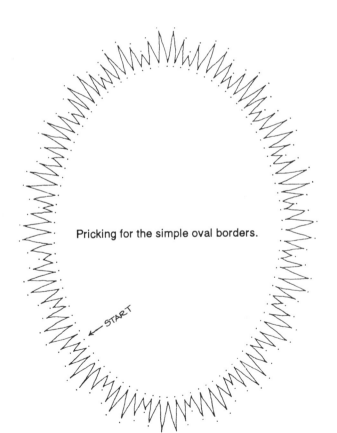

Pricking for the simple oval borders.

START

Left: Cloth stitch border mounted on a small card with an oval cut out.

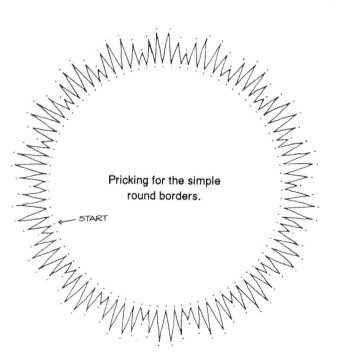

Pricking for the simple round borders.

START

Tension all the pairs carefully at the end of each row making sure that the outside passive stays close to the pins throughout the curve of each scallop and that the group of three inner passives are pulled up well so that they lie quite flat and smooth. By easing the tension on the outermost pair of this group of three passives you can achieve a slight curve which will complement the curve of the outside passive pair.

To complete your border you must join each pair to its corresponding starting loop. Cut off one of the worker bobbins leaving a 6" (15cm) length to bring through the loop at starting pin 5. Remove the other worker bobbin and tie a reef knot putting an extra 'over and under' on the first half of the knot so that it doesn't slip as you tie the second half of the knot in the usual way. Each passive pair is joined to its starting loop in the same way, but as the Gold Dust thread is so much thicker than the Fil a Dentelle of the worker pair, and there is much less strain on the passives, there is no need to add the extra over and under to the reef knot. You can now remove all the pins and trim the surplus thread away close to the knots.

The oval border is glued to the small size card with an oval cut out. The inner edge of your lace will follow the impressed line 1/4" (5mm) away from the cut out. The round border is also designed to fit on the small sized card, but the inner edge fits right up to the edge of the cut out. Use your glue very sparingly to attach the lace, applying it to the wrong side of the inner group of three cloth stitched passives. Choose your motif to decorate the centre of the card and glue it into place. Alternatively you can use a picture from the front of an old Christmas card or calendar, or even an appropriate photograph.

HALF STITCH BORDER

For the half stitch round or oval border:-
4 pairs of Twilley's Gold Dust. Cut 4 x 2yd (2m) lengths.

For the sample I used green thread on a dark green card with a Christmas bells motif mounted in the centre of the oval.

WORKING INSTRUCTIONS.

Hang one pair of passives from each of pins 1, 2, 3 and 4. The pair on pin 4 starts as the 'workers', so use them to make the first half stitch with the pair from pin 3. Continue in half stitch through the remaining two pairs. At the end of the row twist the 'workers' twice more, this will give you a total of 3 twists on the lefthand pair because the final half stitch has given the 'workers' one twist already. Put up pin 5. You will need to work another row or two before the pairs are steady enough to tension effectively, so continue working across the second row making a series of three half stitches before adding the extra two twists needed at the end of the row. This will bring you to pin 6.

Continue in this way taking care to make no mistakes in your half stitch which will spoil the regularity of your border. Keep looking back to check your previous work, and if you spot a mistake then it's worth going back to put it right. Always undo half stitch back to the beginning of a row and make sure that each of your passive pairs is twisted once before you restart. It is also important to remember to add those two extra twists at the

end of every row as this will ensure that you start the new row with a different 'worker' thus allowing the thread from each bobbin to be used evenly. If you add only one twist you'll find that it is the same thread which runs backwards and forwards across each row and it will soon run out.

To complete your border bring the 'worker' back to the inner edge, and join it to the starting loop at pin 4 by bringing one thread of the pair through the loop and tying a reef knot. Now join each of the passive pairs to the corresponding starting loops and tie a neat reef knot to secure each pair. Remove the pins and trim off the ends close to the knots.

The border can now be mounted on a small sized card in the same way as the simple cloth stitch edging described previously. Add the finishing touch with a motif or commercial greeting, alternatively Christmas wrapping paper can be a useful source of illustrations suitable for mounting inside the cut out area of the card.

Below: Half stitch border mounted on a small card with an oval cut out.

Below: Working diagram for the round or oval half stitch border.

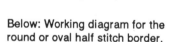

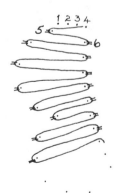

6

MORE ADVANCED BORDERS FOR CHRISTMAS CARDS.

FINE HALF STITCH BORDER

Here are four different borders which can be used to trim a small sized card with either a round or an oval cut out. They are all worked in finer thread than the previous borders.

For the half stitch borders you will need:-

Round Edging:-

5 pairs of DMC 30 Brilliante as passives. Cut 5 x 80" (210cm) lengths.

1 pair of DMC Fil Or Clair (gold) or Fil Argent Clair (silver). Cut 1 x 1 1/2yd length.

Oval Edging:-

5 pairs of DMC 30 Brilliante as passives. Cut 5 x 2 3/4yd (265cm) lengths.

1 pair of DMC Fil Or Clair (gold) or Fil Argent Clair (silver). Cut 1 x 1 3/4yd (160cm) length.

In my example I used green DMC 30 with a gold outside passive to make a circular border for a Merry Christmas motto in red and gold. Two red silk flowers and two green fabric leaves add the finishing touch - and hide the join!

Below: Working diagram for the fine round or oval half stitch border.

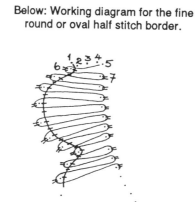

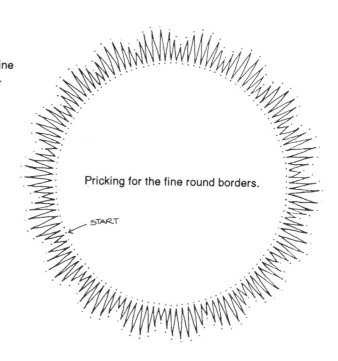

Pricking for the fine round borders.

Left: Fine half stitch border mounted on a small card with a circular cut out.

WORKING INSTRUCTIONS.

Hang the gold or silver pair of passives from pin 1. Hang one pair of DMC 30 passives from each of pins 2, 3 and 5. Hang two pairs 'in order' from pin 4. The pair from pin 5 start off as your 'workers' and half stitch across the row through the four pairs of passives to the left. Now you come to the metallic outside passive; make one half stitch with the workers and the metallic pair, followed by a second half stitch worked with exactly the same four bobbins. If you like you can call this a 'double half stitch', or if you prefer, you can think of it as a cloth stitch and twist, which is exactly the same.

At the end of every row you will add two more twists to the outside pair, which will make a total of three twists on this 'worker' pair. These extra two twists will ensure that the 'worker' changes on each row so that the thread from each bobbin is used evenly. Put up pin 6 and you are ready to start the next row. Make a 'double half stitch' with the workers and the outside metallic pair and before going any further tension both pairs carefully. It is much easier to tension this double stitch now than to wait until you reach the far end of the row. Then half stitch across the row and add two more twists to the outside pair before putting up pin 7. Tension each pair carefully at the end of every row. Continue the work in half stitch remembering to make a double half stitch every time you come to the outside metallic pair and to add two extra twists to the 'worker' pair at the end of every row.

When you have completed the border each pair must be joined into its own starting loop and secured with a reef knot. Try and make the join as neat as you can, but if you like you can disguise it very effectively by choosing a type of decoration which overlaps the lace as shown in my example!

Using your glue very sparingly glue the lace into place on your card, select your trimmings and when you are satisfied with their arrangement glue them onto your card.

FINE CLOTH STITCH BORDERS

For both versions of the cloth stitch borders you will need:-

Round Edging - With DMC 30 Brilliante or DMC 80 Cordonnet Special cut:-

1 x 7yd (7m) length as workers.

2 x 1yd (1m) lengths as inside passives.

1 x 1¼yd (110cm) length as the middle passives.

1 pair of DMC Fil Or Clair (gold) or Fil Argent Clair (silver) as the outside passives. Cut 1 x 1½yd (135cm) length.

In my example I used red DMC 30 Brilliante with a gold outside passive pair for the first cloth stitch version. Three medium sized red ribbon roses, and some gold fern leaves with a red and gold Greetings motto complete the card.

Oval Edging - With DMC 30 Brilliante or DMC 80 Cordonnet Special cut:-

1 x 8yd (8m) length as workers.

2 x 1¼yd (110cm) lengths as inside passives.

1 x 1½yd (135cm) length as the middle passives.

1 pair of DMC Fil Or Clair (gold) or Fil Argent Clair (silver) as the outside passives. Cut 1 x 1¾yd (160cm) length.

In my example I used white DMC 80 Cordonnet Special with a gold outside passive pair to make an oval border for the second cloth stitch version. A Christmas lantern motif makes an attractive centre piece.

Left: First version of the fine cloth stitch border mounted on a small card with a circular cut out.

Right: Second version of the fine cloth stitch border showing the use of additional twists between the inner two passive pairs.

WORKING INSTRUCTIONS.

Both versions of the cloth stitch edging are started in the same way. Hang the worker pair on pin 5, the two inside passive pairs on pins 3 and 4, the middle passive on pin 2 and the outside passive pair in the contrasting metallic thread on pin 1.

With the workers from pin 5 cloth stitch through both of the inner passives, twist the workers twice and cloth stitch through the middle passives, twist the workers twice and cloth stitch through the outside passive pair. Add one twist to the passive pair and two twists to the workers, put up pin 6 and tension all the pairs carefully. Begin the next row with a cloth stitch through the outside pair, it's a good idea to tension this stitch before continuing across the row as the metallic thread is harder to tension well than the smoother cotton threads. Now add one twist to the outside passive pair and two twists to the worker. Cloth stitch through the middle passive (NB this passive is NOT twisted), twist the workers twice and then cloth stitch straight through the final two passive pairs before adding the usual two twists to the worker at the end of the row. Put up pin 7. Work the two following rows in exactly the same way until you reach pin 9. Now you must decide which version of the cloth stitch borders you are going to work.

For the first cloth stitch version continue working with this same twist pattern throughout the border. Take care to keep both the outer and the inner passive pairs close up against the edge pins. If you allow the second of the two inside passive pairs to be tensioned a little less vigorously you'll find that it echoes the curve of the outer scallop quite effectively. With careful tensioning you should be able to guide the middle passive into a gentle curve half way between the outer passive & the inner two passives.

The second cloth stitch version has a slightly more complex twist pattern as you can see from the working diagram. After putting up pin 9 cloth stitch the workers through the first inside passive pair, then twist the workers once before cloth stitching through the second inside passive pair, complete the row in the normal way and put up pin 10. Work back across to pin 11 again twisting the workers once between the two inside passive pairs. For the next four rows increase that one twist to two, this will bring you to pin 15. On the next two rows return to twisting the worker just the once, and from pin 17 until pin 9 of the following repeat there are no twists at all between those two innermost passives.

The extra twists in this second version emphasise the curve of each scallop and is particularly effective when worked in white thread and mounted on a dark background card.

Both versions are finished in the same way, each pair being joined to its corresponding starting loop and tied with a reef knot. These ends can be trimmed close to the knots once the pins are removed.

It's now just a matter of choosing a motif, commercial greeting, group of flowers or leaves to provide the finishing touch. All are carefully glued into place making certain to take full advantage of the camouflaging qualities of any part of the decorations which overlap the lace border, which can then be positioned so that the join is completely hidden!

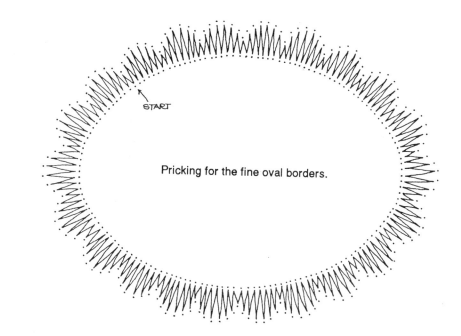

START

Pricking for the fine oval borders.

Below: Working diagram for the first version of the fine cloth stitch border.

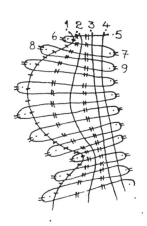

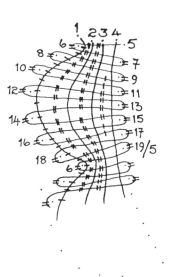

Above: Working diagram for the second version of the fine cloth stitch border.

COMBINATION BORDER

The final border in this series is a combination of both cloth stitch and half stitch, an arrangement which provides an interesting challenge!

This combination border can be worked in either DMC 30 Brilliante or DMC 80 Cordonnet Special. You will need:-

Round Edging:-
2 outside passive pairs. Cut 2 x 11/2yd (135cm) lengths.
2 inside passive pairs. Cut 2 x 1yd (1m) lengths.
2 pairs 31/2yd (350cm) long.

For the example I used DMC 80 Cordonnet Special to make a white border which was mounted on a small red card with a circular cut out. For a little added sparkle I put a piece of red paper-backed tinsel behind the cut out to form a background for the Christmas candle motif.

Left: Combination border
mounted on a small card
with a circular cut out.

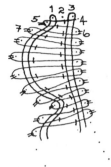

Right: Working diagram for
the combination border.

Oval Edging:-
2 outside passive pairs. Cut 2 x 2yd (2m) lengths.
2 inside passive pairs. Cut 2 x 11/2yd (135cm) lengths.
2 pairs 41/2yd (450cm) long.

WORKING INSTRUCTIONS.

Hang the two outside passive pairs 'open' on pin 1. Hang the two inside passive pairs 'open' from pin 3. Hang one of the remaining pairs on pin 2 and the other from pin 4.

Taking the pair from pin 4 as your worker cloth stitch through both of the inner passives and twist the workers once. Half stitch through the passive pair on pin 2 and cloth stitch straight through the two outer passive pairs before twisting the workers twice at the end of the row. Put up pin 5, and smooth all the pairs gently because at this point they will not be steady enough to tension firmly.

Start the next row by cloth stitching through the outer passives, then twist the workers once before making the half stitch with the middle passive and cloth stitching through the inner passives to the edge where the workers are twisted twice as usual. Put up pin 6.

Continue with the same stitch pattern not forgetting to add that vital twist immediately BEFORE making the half stitch with the middle passive (there is no need to twist after the half stitch as you will find that there is already a single twist on each pair at this point). It is also important to twist the correct number of times at the end of each row to ensure that the 'worker' changes each time which allows the thread to be used evenly.

To join the border at the end bring the workers back to starting pin 4 and using a crochet hook or a Lazy Susan bring one worker thread through that starting loop. Now tie a reef knot with the worker pair using an extra 'over and under' on the first half to prevent it slipping as you tie the second half of the reef knot in the usual way. Because two of the starting pins had two pairs hanging from them the best way to join the cloth stitch passive pairs is to bring one thread from each pair through the starting loop at the same time and then tie a reef knot with each true pair. This can be done more easily with a Lazy Susan than with a crochet hook. The middle passive pair is joined to the starting loop at pin 2 by bringing one thread through that loop and tying a reef knot. Remove all the pins and trim off the ends close to the knots.

Again it may be possible to cover the join completely with the decoration you choose to complete your card, so position the lace border accordingly as you glue it into position.

FRENCH FAN BORDERS.

I have designed a variety of cards using a basic French Fan edging, by varying the shape of the border and the colours of the threads you can achieve an eye-catching result which is easy and quick to make. You can have great fun experimenting with a variety of trimmings to complete your card. Needless to say the borders can be used to trim cards to celebrate many other events as well as Christmas.

THE BASIC FRENCH FAN BORDER.

Oval Edging:-
1 pair of workers. Cut 1 x 5yd (5m) length.
4 pairs of passives. Cut 4 x 1 1/2yd (135cm) lengths.

Round Edging:-
1 pair of workers. Cut 1 x 4 1/2yd (4.25m) length.
4 pairs of passives. Cut 4 x 1yd (1m) lengths.

Small card showing oval basic French
Fan border worked entirely in white.

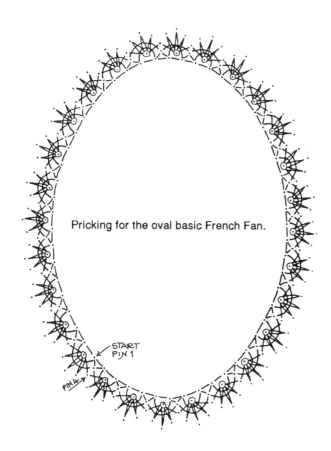

Pricking for the oval basic French Fan.

For the dark green card with the oval cut out and the oval paper 'Merry Christmas' garland I used all white threads in 36/2 Brok, you could use DMC 30 Brilliante if you prefer.

For the cream coloured card with an oval cut out and 'A Merry Christmas' garland I used DMC 30 Brilliante in red for the workers and three pairs of passives. The outer pair of passives running along the curved edge of the fans was a gold metallic thread DMC Fil Or Clair.

For the dark green card with the round cut out I used white 36/2 Brok for all the pairs with the exception of the outside passives which again were DMC Fil Or Clair.

For the dark green card with an oval cut out and a lace candle in the middle I used red DMC 30 Brilliante for all of the passives and the DMC Fil Or Clair for the workers.

These are only some suggestions, you can create your own combinations and enjoy experimenting with different effects.

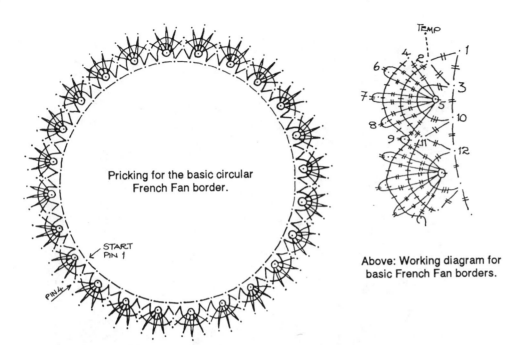

Pricking for the basic circular French Fan border.

START PIN 1

PIN 4

TEMP

Above: Working diagram for basic French Fan borders.

WORKING INSTRUCTIONS.

I think it's a good idea to start borders like this a little bit off centre, as I believe this makes the join less conspicuous than it would be if it was right at the centre of one of the curves. For the circular edging I always turn the border until the join is at 4 or 5 o'clock, rather than being on the more obvious quarter points of 12, 3, 6 or 9. However if you prefer you can easily start the borders elsewhere, it's up to you!

Hang 2 passives pairs from pin 1 and interlink them. Twist both pairs twice. Put in a temporary pin somewhere above pin 2 and hang the third pair of passives from it, placing the new pair to the left of the pairs on pin 1. Now take the lefthand pair from pin 1 and make a half stitch with the new pair, put up pin 2 and cover the pin with another half stitch. Add two twists to each pair. Now remove the temporary pin and tension both pairs so that they rest snugly round the pin. Taking the righthand pair from pin 2 make a half stitch with the remaining passive from pin 1 and put up pin 3. Again cover it with a second half stitch and two twists.

Hang the outside passive on pin 4, then hang the worker pair from the same pin but put the bobbins down to the right of the passive pair. Twist the centre two bobbins (of the four hanging from this pin) twice so that these two threads are interlinked around pin 4 with the workers on the right. Twist the outside passive pair once and the workers twice if you are using ordinary cotton thread for your fan workers. If you are using a metallic thread it may be best to only twist the workers once between the passives as this will make it easier to tension the threads at the end of the row. Cloth stitch through the passive from pin 2, then twist the passive once and the worker twice (or only once if you're using DMC Clair as your worker) before cloth stitching through the lefthand pair of passives from pin 3. Twist the workers twice because it is the end of the row, but do not twist this last pair of passives at all. Put up pin 5 and tension all the pairs carefully.

Now work back towards the outside of the fan starting with a cloth stitch through the inner passives. Remember not to twist that pair, but to add two twists to the workers before cloth stitching through the middle passive. Twist this passive once and the workers twice. Cloth stitch through the outer passives, twist them once and the workers twice at the end of the row. Put up pin 6 and take your time in tensioning the workers whilst you position the threads carefully so that the outside passive stays close against the outside pins, the inside passive stays close against the circled pivot pin (pin 5) and the middle passive follows a nice smooth curving pathway between the two.

Work back across the row using exactly the same twist sequence and slip the workers behind pin 5 once more at the righthand end of the row. Do not remove pin 5 to do this, simply lift the worker bobbins and guide the threads behind the pivot pin. Tension each pair and then work back to pin 7. Repeat these rows until you arrive at pin 9. You will now have used the pivot pin 5 four times so you will find that your threads quite naturally rise up that pin, so take care with your tensioning. This is the method I have used in most of the French Fan projects, but this is not the only way of making a French Fan, so you may prefer to use an alternative eg. you can remove the pivot pin so that when you tension the inner fan passive the worker loops at this end of the row disappear. NB. Do not pull on the worker once the pivot pin has been removed until you have completed the three ground pins.

Left: Small card showing the oval basic French Fan border worked in red with gold outer passive.

Having completed your first fan you must now turn your attention to the three pins which form a triangle of ground between each fan. First of all you must put two twists on the middle passive and three twists on the inner pair of passives as they leave the fan. Now take the inner passive and work a half stitch, pin, half stitch and two twists with the pair from pin 3. Take the lefthand pair from this pin (pin 10) and make a similar stitch with the middle fan passive at pin 11. Repeat the same stitch with the righthand pair from pin 11 and the pair remaining at pin 10 to complete pin 12. Make sure each stitch is smoothly tensioned before going back to the outside edge to pick up the worker which you left at pin 9 to start the next fan.

If you follow that simple sequence of fan followed by the triangle of ground you should find these patterns quite straightforward, but do check that you have fully completed the fan before turning to the ground, make sure that you have got all the way to pin 9, and that you haven't stopped one pin too soon. Also don't forget to twist the passive pairs as they come out of the fan before you start the ground.

You should find that you make good progress around your border, then it's a matter of joining it as neatly as you can, so complete your final fan and join the workers into the starting loop at pin 4 and tie them off with a reef knot. The outside passives do not have to be joined into the starting loop as the worker, now that it is well secured, keeps them firmly in their place, so I just tie a reef knot with the outside passives at this point. Don't forget to twist both the middle and the inner fan passives as usual before joining the middle pair into the starting loop at pin 2. The inside fan passive and the edge passive pair will both join into the starting loop at pin 1. This can best be done with a Lazy Susan which enables you to bring both threads through the loop together, and they can then be tied in separate reef knots to the other thread of their original pair.

Once you have removed all the pins you should trim off the ends as close to the knots as you can, as despite the knots, you may prefer to use this side as the right side of your lace if you have not removed the pivot pin before tensioning the inner passive at the end of each fan. This allows the peak of threads from the pivot pin to add a more 3-dimensional look to the border, and it will also allow you to mount your lace more easily onto the card background as it will lie flatter this way. Take care not to stretch the edging once it is off the pillow as it will be easily distorted, so it's a good idea to glue it onto your card as soon as possible. To do this put a touch of glue behind the densest part of each fan and glue down just four or five fans at a time. The circular edging fits right up to the cut out on the small sized card, and the oval borders follow the impressed line a little way in from the edge of the cut out.

For the circular card I glued a piece of pale green card behind the cut out and arranged three small red ribbon roses with three tiny green holly leaves (from a paper 'holly triangle') and to pick up the gold outside passive pair in the lace I used three gold coloured metal leaves, but if you cannot find these, then small gold sequin leaves would make excellent substitutes. Take your time gluing these items into place as it's important to get the positioning right first time, there's nothing worse than smudges of glue which cannot be removed or disguised.

Small card showing the basic circular French Fan border worked in white with a gold outer passive.

THE SMALL CANDLE.

I used a combination of the same red and gold threads I used for the edging to make the small candle in the centre of this card. It is started at the top by the flame and is worked downwards so that all the finishing ends can be easily hidden by the gold holly leaves and the small red ribbon rose.

2 pairs of workers in red DMC 30 Brilliante. Cut 2 x 1½yd (135cm) lengths.

6 pairs of outside passives in red DMC 30 Brilliante. Cut 6 x ½yd (45cm) lengths.

4 pairs of inner passives in DMC Fil Or Clair. Cut 4 x ½yd (45cm) lengths.

WORKING INSTRUCTIONS.

Put up pin 1 and hang the six pairs of red passives across the pillow above that pin making sure that all the bobbins are kept in order so that none of the threads are crossed. Place the two red worker pairs across the pillow in the same way below pin 1. Turn your pillow so that the righthand set of bobbins are available for you to work with comfortably. The 2 worker bobbins will be on your left and the 6 passive bobbins will be on the right. The bobbins on the other end of these threads must now be anchored securely so that you can start work with the bobbins nearest to you. You can do this by putting a large pin through each spangle, or by getting a friend to hold those bobbins down firmly against the pillow until you have worked the next few rows to keep those bobbins steady. Twist the worker pair twice and then cloth stitch through the three pairs of passives on the right, twist twice at the end of the row and put up pin 2.

Now put a temporary pin in pin 14 and hang the four gold passive pairs 'open' around it. Secure the lefthand four bobbins leaving the righthand four free to work with. Pick up your workers from pin 2 and cloth stitch through the three pairs of the outside trail. Twist the workers twice before cloth stitching through the two gold pairs. Twist the workers twice and put up pin 3. Work back to the outside of the candle remembering to twist the workers twice between the gold and the red passives. Put up pin 4. The next two rows are worked with the red passives only which will bring you to pin 6. The following row works through both sets of passives, but again the groups are separated by two twists on the workers. Put up pin 7 and return in the same way to pin 8. Work the next two rows through only the red passives, and the following rows through both red and gold passives. Leave the workers at pin 12, remove the temporary pin from 14 and return to pin 1.

You are now ready to start work with the second set of bobbins. Follow the same sequence using the working diagram to help you reach pin 19. Leave your workers here whilst you cloth stitch the gold passives through each other to make the crossing which will give the chain effect down the centre of the candle. To make the crossing take the righthand pair of the two passives making up the lefthand trail and cloth stitch it through both of the gold passive pairs from the righthand trail. Go back and take the remaining pair from the original lefthand trail and again cloth stitch it through the two pairs from the righthand trail. You will now find that the two pairs of bobbins which were on the left are now on the right and vice versa.

Pick up your workers from pin 19 once more and work the next four pin holes cloth stitching through both groups of passives, twisting the workers twice at the end of every row and twice between the red and the gold passives. Do the same on the other side from pins 24-27 and you'll be ready to cloth stitch the two pairs of gold passives through each other in the same way as before.

Continue working in this way until you reach the bottom of the pattern. There's no need to stand on ceremony at the end as the holly leaves do such an excellent job of hiding it all, just tie a reef knot with each pair and cut off the ends. The candle is glued into place down the centre of the cut out and the holly leaves positioned to cover the ends. Cut a small flame out of gold paper-backed tinsel with an even smaller red paper tinsel flame glued on top. (Be careful to use a glue which does not affect the tinsel finish.) A red ribbon rose adds the finishing touch.

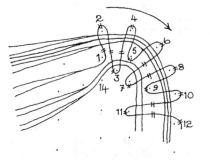

Above: Working diagram showing the start of the small candle.

N.B. The single lines to the left of pin 1 represent single threads, those to the right indicate a pair as usual.

Below: Working diagram showing the construction of the small candle.

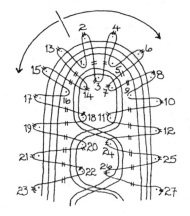

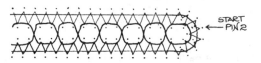

Below: Pricking for the small candle.

Below: Small card showing the oval basic French Fan border worked in red with gold fan workers. The small candle is also worked with red and gold threads.

14

CHRISTMAS CARD WITH CANDLE II.

As a variation on the previous project you might like to try a slightly finer border which can be worked entirely in metallic thread. The candle is worked all in white with a twisted rope of trails down the centre.

For the frame you will need:-
1 pair of workers in Mez Effektgarn - you can use similar metallic threads, but they are more likely to stretch, so I would recommend the Mez thread for this particular project. Cut 1 x 8yd (7.5m) length.
1 pair of outer passives in DMC Fil Or Clair or Fil Argent Clair. Cut 1 x 2yd (2m) length.
2 pairs for the middle and inner passives. Cut 2 x 1½yd (135cm) lengths.

For the candle you will need:-
2 pairs of workers in 36/2 Brok or equivalent. Cut 2 x 1½yd (135cm) lengths.
10 pairs of passives in the same thread. Cut 10 x ½yd (50cm) lengths.

Below: Small card with oval border and lace candle II.

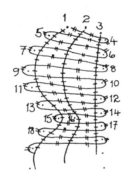

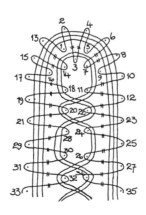

Below: Working diagram for the start of the oval border.

Left: Working diagram for small candle II.

For the sample I worked the border in gold and mounted it on a small dark green card with an oval cut out. The candle was worked in white thread and trimmed with a gold and red tinsel flame, two tiny gold holly leaves and an embroidered motif to give the impression of holly berries.

WORKING INSTRUCTIONS.

Hang the outer passive pair on pin 1 and hang the worker pair to its right from the same pin. Interlink these two pairs by twisting the centre two threads twice, now twist the passive pair once and the worker twice. Hang the middle passive pair from pin 2 and the inner passive pair on pin 3. The twist pattern is very easy to remember. The worker is twisted twice after every cloth stitch and at the end of every row. The passive pairs are always twisted once after each stitch.

Take care with your tensioning encouraging the middle passive pair to make a nice curve which will echo the shape of the scalloped edge. To help you create that curve I have added one extra pinhole at the V of each scallop, so complete the row as usual and leave the workers at pin 15, whilst you put up pin 16 between the outer and the middle passive. Now continue working the next scallop.

To join the piece simply tie the workers off into its starting loop at pinhole 1. Once these are securely knotted you can just tie off the outer passives. The middle and inner passive pairs are joined to their starting loops at pins 2 and 3 respectively. Remove the pins and trim off the surplus thread.

This shape will follow the impressed line on the small sized card with an oval cut out. Attach it to the card using just a touch of glue behind each scallop.

The candle is started in exactly the same way as the candle in the previous project, but as you can see from the photograph of the finished card the two inner trails cross through each other much more frequently. Just use the instructions for the candle described above and follow the pattern markings carefully. Whenever the lines which indicate those inner trails cross through each other then leave your workers at the outside pinholes and cloth stitch the trail passives through each other using the 'half spider' process. At the bottom of the candle just tie each pair off with a reef knot and trim each thread close to the knot.

Position the candle in the centre of the oval leaving enough room at the top for a flame cut out of red and gold tinsel. The knots of the finish will be covered by two tiny holly leaves (cut from a holly triangle) and an embroidered motif which resembles holly berries. All are glued into place.

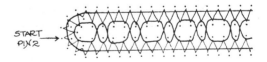

Above: Pricking for small candle II.

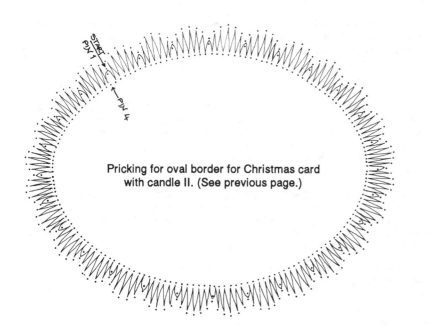

Pricking for oval border for Christmas card with candle II. (See previous page.)

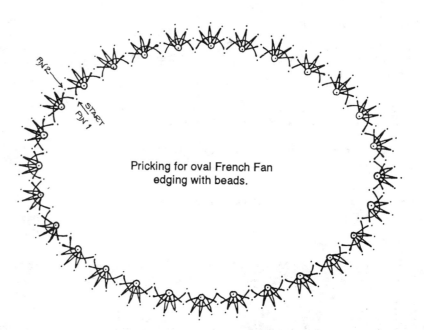

Pricking for oval French Fan edging with beads.

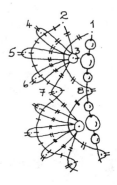

Below: Working diagram for the French Fan edging with beads.

Below: Small card with an oval French Fan edging decorated with beads.

OVAL FRENCH FAN EDGING WITH BEADS.

This edging is made up of a very simple French Fan, but the row of beads along the inner edge give it a special sparkle!

You will need:-

1 pair of 36/2 Brok, DMC 30 Retors d'Alsace or DMC 30 Brilliante as fan workers. Cut 1 x 5yd (5m) length.

1 pair of the same thread as passives. Cut 1 x 2yd (2m) length.

1 length of the same thread with sewing needles (fine enough to go through the beads you are using) threaded on to both ends. Cut 1 x 2yd (2m) length.

1 pair of DMC Fil Or Clair (gold) or DMC Fil Argent Clair (silver) for the outside fan passive. Cut 1 x 1½yd (135cm) length.

28 gold or silver beads 3mm in diameter.

56 gold or silver beads 2mm in diameter.

I used plastic beads rather than the metal ones I use when spangling bobbins, there is then less chance of sharp edges fraying or cutting the threads. You can use other types of beads, but you must make sure that there is room between the edge pins to accommodate whatever combination you choose to use. It is important to test out your beads at the more tightly curved parts of the oval as this is where the distance between the edge pins is smallest. For the sample I used all white threads with gold beads to match the gold in the paper "Merry Christmas" motto. A piece of red paper-backed tinsel set behind the oval cut out of a small red card gives a very festive finish.

WORKING INSTRUCTIONS.

Hang the passive pair with bobbins onto pin 1 and push it to the left. Now place the thread with needles at each end around that same pin so that the mid point is positioned at the pin. Interlink these two threads in just the same way as you would if there were four bobbins on the end instead of two bobbins and two needles. Twist the bobbin pair twice. There is no point in twisting the needle threads at any point as these threads will be completely hidden by the beads.

Hang the outside passive pair on pin 2. Hang the fan worker pair from the same pin to the right of the previous pair and interlink them. Twist the passive pair once and the worker twice. Cloth stitch the worker through the bobbin pair from pin 1 which will be hanging to the left of the needle pair. Twist the worker pair once around pin 3 which will be your pivot pin for the fan. Work back out to pin 4 twisting the workers twice, but do not twist the inside passive pair at all. Tension each pair carefully at the end of every row keeping the outside passive pair close to the edge pins and the inner passive close to the pivot pin. Continue in this way until you reach pin 7 where you must leave the worker whilst you add the beads to the needle pair, but first twist the inside fan passive pair twice as it leaves the fan. This is very important as an untwisted pair here can spoil the appearance of this border, so don't forget!

To add the beads I found it best to thread all three beads onto one needle in order - small, medium, small, push these onto the thread and place your lefthand index finger underneath the beads so that they are forced upwards. This should keep the thread at the bottom of the holes whilst you push the second needle through the same set of three beads from the same direction. This I hope will enable you to pass the second needle through without splitting the first thread, but if you do find that you have sewn through it with the second needle, then push the beads up towards the pin and unthreading the second needle pull the thread back, so that once again the threads are quite separate, then replace the needle.

Once the beads are threaded onto both threads you make a cloth stitch with the needle pair and the pair which has just left the fan (the old inside fan passives). Put up pin 8 and twist the bobbin pair twice. Cover the pin with a second cloth stitch and twist the bobbin pair, which should now be on the left of the needle pair, twice. You can now make the next fan following the instructions for pins 2-8 once more.

Now you should tension the needle threads. When the threads are pulled tight the beads should sit snugly between the two pins. However, be warned, do not be tempted to pull on these passive threads too heavily in case you break them, and a breakage close to the work would mean disaster.

This border is completed by joining each pair to its corresponding starting loop. Tie each pair off securely (particularly the needle pair to make the beads safe) with a reef knot, and once the pins are out, trim off the ends. Now do take care once the pins have been removed as the weight of the beads can easily pull the border out of shape, transfer it gently onto your card and glue it down straight away, carefully lifting a small section at a time so that you can glue three or four fans into position each time. The line of beads should fit just inside the impressed line on the small card with an oval cut out. You can complete the card with a commercial paper Christmas greeting which I glued onto a background of tinsel mounted behind the cut out, but remember if you are gluing onto tinsel you must use a glue which will not dissolve the tinsel's shiny finish, so experiment on a small piece first.

FRENCH FAN WITH CLOTH STITCH TRAIL.

This edging pattern is very versatile. Here I have used it to make two rectangular shapes as a border for two paper Christmas robins.

For the smaller rectangle you will need:-
In 36/2 Brok cotton, DMC 30 Retors d'Alsace or DMC 30 Brilliante in white:-
1 pair of workers for the fan. Cut 1 x 6yd (6m) length.
1 pair of workers for the trail. Cut 1 x 2yd (2m) length.
2 pairs of passives. Cut 2 x 2yd (2m) lengths.

In DMC Fil Or Clair (gold) or DMC Fil Argent Clair (silver):-
1 pair of outside passives for the fan. Cut 1 x 1 1/2yd (135cm) length.
2 pairs of passives for the trail. Cut 2 x 1yd (1m) lengths.

For the larger rectangle you will need:-
In 36/2 Brok cotton, DMC 30 Retors d'Alsace or DMC 30 Brilliante in white:-
1 pair of workers for the fan. Cut 1 x 7yd (7m) length.
1 pair of workers for the trail. Cut 1 x 2 1/2yd (225cm) length.
2 pairs of passives. Cut 2 x 2 1/4yd (210cm) lengths.

In DMC Fil Or Clair (gold) or DMC Fil Argent Clair (silver):-
1 pair of outside passives for the fan. Cut 1 x 1 3/4yd (160cm) length.
2 pairs of passives for the trail. Cut 2 x 1 1/4yd (110cm) lengths.

I worked both samples in white with the trail passives and outside fan passives in gold to pick up the gold in the paper motifs. I mounted both on green cards.

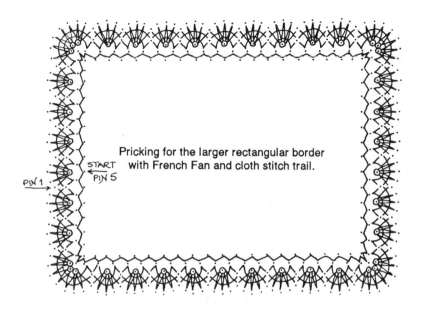

Pricking for the larger rectangular border with French Fan and cloth stitch trail.

PIN 1

START
PIN 5

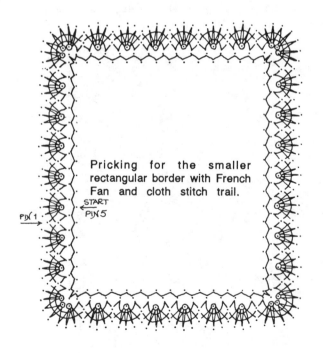

Pricking for the smaller rectangular border with French Fan and cloth stitch trail.

PIN 1

START
PIN 5

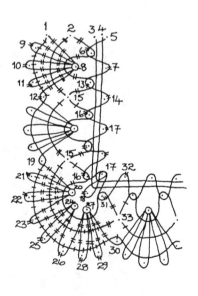

Above: Working diagram for French Fan with cloth stitch trail.

WORKING INSTRUCTIONS.

To set up this border hang the two pairs of white passives on pin 2 and interlink them in the usual way. Twist both pairs twice before leaving them to set up the inner trail. Hang the trail workers on pin 5 and the two trail passives on pins 3 and 4. Take the workers and cloth stitch them through the two trail passives and the righthand passive pair from pin 2. Twist the workers twice and put up pin 6. Tension all the threads before cloth stitching the workers back across the row. Put up pin 7 after twisting the workers twice as usual. Leave the trail workers here while you start the fan, but before you leave the trail add two twists to the white pair of passives at the lefthand edge of the trail so that they are ready to become part of the fan as the inner passive pair.

Hang the outside fan passive on pin 1 and push the bobbins to the left, now hang the fan worker around the same pin and put the bobbins down to the right of the outside passive pair. Twist the middle two bobbins twice to interlink the two pairs. Twist the outside passive once and the worker twice. Cloth stitch through the passive hanging from pin 2 (the middle passive of the fan) and twist the passive once and the worker twice. Cloth stitch the workers through the white pair which has just left the trail and check that it hasn't lost its two twists in the meantime. Now twist the workers once and put up pin 8 in the circled pinhole which will be the pivot pin of your fan. Pull the workers tight and tension each pair of passives very carefully guiding the passives into the correct position - the outside passive close to the outside pins, the inner passive close to the pivot pin and the middle passive midway between the two.

The pivot pin of the fan will be used three times more and each time the worker pair will be twisted once behind it. Continue working the fan following the twist pattern set out in the working diagram. Just to remind you, the workers are twisted twice between each passive pair and at the outside edge of the fan, but only once behind the pivot pin. The outside and the middle passive fan pairs are both twisted once each time the worker cloth stitches through them. The inner passive is not twisted at all until the fan is complete. Take care with the tensioning at the end of every row and don't continue unless each passive is pulled up tight and lies in a nice smooth curve.

The fan is complete when the worker has reached pin 12, leave it here and add one twist to the middle passive pair and two twists to the inner passive pair to give both pairs a total of two twists as they leave the fan. This is only too easy to overlook, so take care that you do not forget these twists. If you like you can remove the pivot pin now and pull on the inner fan passive to make the worker loops disappear. This will give you a flatter fan.

Now go back to the trail worker at pin 7 and cloth stitch it across through the two regular trail passives and the next white passive pair (ie. the inner passive pair which has just left the fan). Twist the workers twice, put up pin 13 and tension all pairs. Work back across to pin 14, twist the workers twice and tension all the threads. Twist the white passive pair at the lefthand edge of the trail twice and then use it to work a half stitch with the middle fan passive pair having checked that it has retained its two twists. Put up pin 15 between these two pairs and cover the pin with a second half stitch. Twist both pairs once more to give a total of two twists on each pair. Cloth stitch the trail worker from pin 14 through both trail passives and then through the righthand passive from pin 15, twist the workers twice and put up pin 16. Cloth stitch back across the trail to pin 17. Leave the workers here and twist the lefthand passive pair twice so that it is ready to join the next fan as the inner passive pair. You are now ready to start the next fan. Continue in this way until you reach the corner.

18

At the corner work pin 16 in the usual way then cloth stitch the workers back to pin 17, twist the workers only once before putting up pin 17 as you will need to use this corner pinhole twice. Cloth stitch through both trail passives, twist the workers twice and put up pin 18. Work back across the trail to pin 17. This time twist the workers twice, remove pin 17 and put it up again in the usual way - but do not try to put it through the previous worker loop. Before putting any tension on the worker pair pull the inside trail passive pair taut, then gently pull up the workers. Leave the workers here whilst you work the corner fan which has three pivot pins. Pick up the workers from pin 19 and use pivot pin 20 three times (outside pins 21-23), use pivot pin 24 twice (outside pins 25 and 26) and pivot pin 27 three times (outside pins 28-30). You may remove the first pivot pin once you start work on the second, and the second pivot pin once you start work on the third.

Above: Card showing small rectangle of the
French Fan edging with a cloth stitch trail.

The final pivot pin can be removed on completion of the fan. Twist the middle and inner passive as they leave the fan as usual. Work pin 31 to bring the inner fan passive into the trail and out again, but be gentle when tensioning the trail worker because of the back stitch at pin 17. Leave your worker at the edge of the trail at pin 32 and work the usual half stitch, pin, half stitch and two twists with the two white passives at pin 33. You are now ready to continue the edging by following the instructions for pins 5-15 as before.

To complete the edging each pair is joined to its corresponding starting loop. The two white passive pairs will both join into starting pin 2 and each will be tied off with a separate reef knot. The fan worker will finish at starting pin 1 and be tied off with a reef knot, the outside passive can be knotted off here without bringing it through the starting loop. Remove the pins and trim off the ends close to the knots. Try and keep the finishing as neat as you can as this may be the right side of your lace when it is mounted on the card.

Because these two borders do not fit around the rectangular cut outs of the commercially produced cards I have mounted them on a piece of ordinary card 7 1/8" x 4 5/8" (182mm x 117mm) which I folded in half to form a finished card 3 1/2" x 4 5/8" (91mm x 117cm).

Glue your lace into position using the bare minimum of glue behind each fan. It is wise to glue just three or four fans down at a time, rather than attempting to do more in a hurried fashion before the glue dries. Add your paper robin and, for the card with the smaller piece of lace, a Christmas greeting.

SIMPLE TORCHON FAN AND GROUND CIRCLE.

This very simple circle pattern is made up of two very basic elements of Torchon lace - a cloth stitch fan and a triangle of ground. It is therefore a good practice piece to help a less experienced lacemaker consolidate these basic skills. I have made this pattern in two sizes. The smaller of the two fits nicely inside the circular cut out of the small size card, and the larger fits inside a bangle to hang on your Christmas tree.

For the Christmas card you will need:-
1 pair of fan workers in Twilley's Gold Dust. Cut 1 x 3 3/4yd (350cm) length.
1 pair of passives for the outer edge of the fan in the same Twilley's Gold Dust. Cut 1 x 1yd (1m) length.
1 pair of passives for the inner edge in Twilley's Gold Dust. Cut 1 x 24" (60cm) length.
5 pairs of 36/2 Brok cotton, DMC 30 Brilliante or DMC 30 Retors d'Alsace. Cut 5 x 30" (75cm) lengths.

For the sample shown I used silver Gold Dust with white passives. I mounted the lace on a small green card with a piece of green tinsel behind the circular cut out. A small embroidered red and green motif glued in the centre completes the project.

WORKING INSTRUCTIONS.

Hang the outer fan passive pair on pin 1 and push it to the left. Hang the fan worker from the same pin and put it down to the right of the previous pair. Interlink the two by twisting the centre two threads twice, making sure that each returns to its true partner when that interlinking movement is complete. Now hang one pair of ordinary white passives from each of pins 2, 3, 4, 5 and 6.

You are now ready to work the fan, so take the workers and cloth stitch them through the pair from pin 2, twist the workers twice and put up pin 7. Now cloth stitch back to pin 8 through both pairs of passives, twist the workers twice as usual and put up the pin. Tension all the pairs you have worked through carefully. You are now ready to work the next row taking in one more pair at the righthand end of the row because the fan is continuing to widen. Work pins 9-16 in this way remembering to twist the workers twice at the end of every row and to tension the work so that all the passives lie flat and smooth before continuing with the next row.

The row which lies between pin 16 and pin 17 is shorter than the previous row, so you now have to start leaving out a pair at the righthand end of every row, so push that last passive (which has in fact only just joined the fan at pin 15), to the right and ignore it whilst you cloth stitch the workers through the remaining four pairs of passives, put up pin 17 and tension all the pairs. Work back to pin 18 and again ask yourself if this next row is longer or shorter than the previous row. Again the answer will be that it is shorter, so once again you must push the righthand passive pair away, and work the next two rows with only three pairs of passives. Continue 'decreasing' in this way until you reach pin 24. Leave the worker and the outside passive pair here. Now add two twists to each of the five pairs of white passives which have just come out of the fan.

Hang the final pair of passives (the short length of Twilley's Gold Dust) on a temporary pin somewhere above pin 25. Now take the white pair from pin 15 and make a cloth stitch with the inner passive pair, putting up pin 25. Twist the white pair twice, but do not twist the inner passive pair at all. Cover the pin with another cloth stitch and again twist only the white pair twice. Remove the temporary pin and pull gently on the inner passives until the starting loop rests snugly around the white threads just before pin 25. You are now ready to start the triangle of ground.

It is very important to work this area of ground in complete diagonal lines, so taking the white pair from pin 25 work a half stitch with the pair from pin 17. Put up pin 26 and cover it with a half stitch and twist (i.e. twist both pairs once). Push the righthand pair to the side and take the next pair from the left (from pin 19) and work the same stitch sequence again. This half stitch, pin, half stitch and twist is one of the best known forms of Torchon ground. Again discard the righthand pair after pin 27, and taking the new pair from pin 21 you can work pin 28. Pin 29 will be worked with the lefthand pair from pin 28 and the new pair from pin 23. Tension the row looking closely at the threads as you do so, you should find that the pair on the left after your final pin is exactly the same two threads which you brought from pin 25, and that each new incoming pair has crossed straight through that original pair. If you find that any threads do not pull accurately along that diagonal line, but have been diverted onto a new pathway around any pin, then you have made an error and you must go back and correct your mistake.

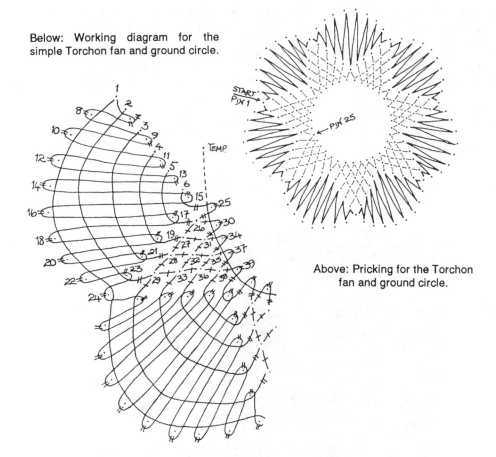

Below: Working diagram for the simple Torchon fan and ground circle.

Above: Pricking for the Torchon fan and ground circle.

You are now ready to go back to the inner edge and start a new line of ground pins. To start each row you will take the righthand white passive pair and cloth stitch it through the inner pair of Gold Dust threads, twist the white pair twice, put up the pin and cover it with another cloth stitch. Twist the white pair twice as it leaves the inner passive pair and work a new series of ground stitches at pins 31, 32 and 33. Now return to the inner edge and work the white pair from pin 31 through the inner passive pair, around pin 34, cloth stitching back through the inner passive pair and twisting it twice before making ground stitches at pins 35 and 36. Again go back to the inner edge and work pin 37 before making a ground stitch at pin 38. It is absolutely vital not to think that you have now completed your triangle of ground, there is still one more very important pinhole to work, so again take the white passive through the inner edge pair and work pin 39 in the usual way. Only then is the area of ground complete and you can turn your attention to working the next fan. If you fail to work that final pinhole you'll find that you get out of step with the pinholes along the inner edge, and the star shape formed by these open areas of ground between the more solid cloth stitch areas, is much less effective. So take great care to work this area accurately.

Work six more fans and areas of ground in exactly the same way and you will find your circle complete. Now join each pair into its own starting loop. You will have had to push the starting pins well down into the pillow in order to work the final fans, now carefully remove one at a time and using a Lazy Susan or a fine crochet hook, bring one thread from each pair through the correct starting loop and tie a reef knot. Cut the threads off about 4" (10cm) away from the work and remove the pins. Trim the threads close to the knots and your lace is ready for mounting.

I put a piece of green tinsel behind the cut out area of the card and glued it carefully into place making sure that the glue did not 'melt' the tinsel. Paper backed tinsel is less affected by glue, but you must still avoid getting any on the right side of the foil as it will take off the shiny finish. This means you have to be very careful when you glue the lace into place. Use the barest minimum of glue and only behind the dense area of the cloth stitch fans. An embroidered motif in red and green glued into the centre gives the finishing touch.

Above: Simple Torchon fan and ground circle mounted on a small card with a circular cut out.

CHRISTMAS CARD WITH TORCHON SPIDER AND FAN GARLAND.

This pattern combines the basic Torchon skills of fan and ground with a spider and a cloth stitch trail. It is worked in slightly finer thread than the previous project and the pinholes are a lot closer together, making it a considerably more challenging piece.

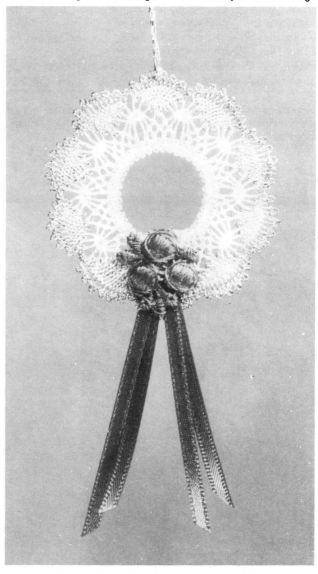

Above: The spider and fan garland made into a Christmas tree decoration.

You will need:-

1 pair of fan workers in DMC Fil Or Clair or Fil Argent Clair, alternatively you can use a double thickness of DMC Metallise or fine Madeira. Cut 1 x 3yd (2.75m) of DMC Clair or 1 x 6yd (5.5m) of the finer metallic thread which is folded in half to give a working length of 3yd (2.25m).

1 pair of passives for the outside edge of the fan in the same metallic thread. Cut 1 x 1yd (1m) length of Clair or 1 x 2yd (2m) length of the finer metallic thread which is folded in half to give a working length of 1yd (1m).

1 pair of workers for the trail at the inner edge in 36/2 Brok or 30 DMC Retors d'Alsace or Brilliante. Cut 1 x 1½yd (135cm) length.

7 pairs of passives in 36/2 Brok or equivalent. Cut 1 x 1¼yd (110cm) lengths.

2 pairs of passives for the inner trail in 36/2 Brok or equivalent. Cut 2 x ¾yd (70cm) lengths.

I worked it in silver and white for the card and gold and white for the Christmas tree decoration. Both combinations look effective, particularly with the addition of a red and green embroidered motif and short lengths of narrow red and green ribbon. The motif and ribbon completely cover the join which is a big advantage!

WORKING INSTRUCTIONS.

From pin 1 hang first the outside fan passive and then the fan worker to its right, and interlink them in the usual way. Twist both pairs once. Hang a white passive pair on each of pins 2, 3, 4 and 5. Now work the fan in the usual way always twisting the worker once between the outside metallic passive and all the white passive threads. Twist the outside fan passive once each time the worker cloth stitches through it and twist the worker twice at the end of every row. Take care with your tensioning as the threads are close together in this fan and if you don't tighten both workers and passives sufficiently at the end of every row your fan will not be smooth and flat. Leave your workers at pin 19 at the end of your fan.

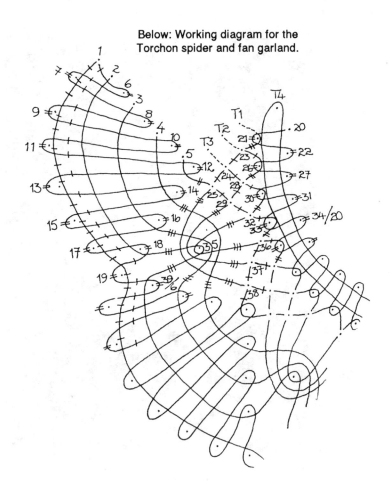

Below: Working diagram for the Torchon spider and fan garland.

Left: Torchon spider and fan garland decorating a small card with a circular cut out.

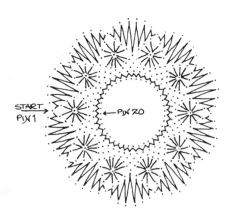

Above: Pricking for the Torchon spider and fan garland.

22

Hang the three longer remaining pairs of white passives from pins T1, T2 and T3. Hang the two short pairs of passives "open" from T4 and the inner trail worker from pin 20. Cloth stitch the workers through the two pairs of passives from T4 and also the pair from T1. Twist the workers twice and put up pin 21, return to pin 22 cloth stitching through all three pairs of passives. Twist the workers twice now, and at the end of every row. Leave the workers here, remove temporary pins T1 and T4 and tension all the pairs. Twist the outer pair of trail passives twice (originally from T1) and work a half stitch with them and the pair from T2, put up pin 23 and cover it with another half stitch followed by a twist on both pairs. Work a similar Torchon ground stitch (half stitch, pin, half stitch and twist) at pin 24 using the lefthand pair from pin 23 and the new pair from T3. Continue working along this diagonal row making another ground stitch at pin 25. To do this you will need to take the passive pair which left the fan after pin 12 and twist it twice. Now you can work pin 25 using this pair and the lefthand pair from pin 24.

Now remove pins T2 and T3, pull gently on the pair coming away from pins 23 and 24 to take out the slack. You can now return to the trail bringing the worker across from pin 22 to pin 26 taking in the pair from 23, before returning to pin 27. Don't forget to twist the edge passive pair twice as it comes out of the trail before working a Torchon ground stitch at pin 28. Again you will find it less confusing if you continue to work along that diagonal until the row is complete. In this instance it only needs one more ground stitch at pin 29 to finish the row. The pair from pin 28 is now taken into the trail at pin 30. Leave the worker at pin 31 and twist the outer passive pair twice so that it is ready to go into the ground. Now make the final ground stitch at pin 32. Take the righthand pair from this pin into the trail at pin 33, return the workers to the inner edge (pin 34) and twist the outside passives twice as they leave the trail after pin 33. You are now ready to work the spider.

Each leg of the spider needs to be twisted a total of three times. So you must add three twists to each of the three passive pairs leaving the fan after pins 14, 16 and 18. The three legs joining the spider from the right (from pins 25, 29 and 32) already have two twists on them as part of the torchon ground, so just add one more twist to each. Now take the pair from pin 14 and cloth stitch it through the three pairs from the right, then cloth stitch the pair from 16 through the same three pairs, and finally do exactly the same with the pair from pin 18. Put up pin 35 in the centre so that the three pairs of passives which started on the left are now sitting on the righthandside of the pin and vice versa. Complete the spider by taking the passive pair lying immediately to the left of the pin and cloth stitching it through the three pairs lying to its right. Take the next pair from the left and work it through those same three righthand pairs, and finally do the same with the last pair of passives from the left. The three pairs will now have changed sides yet again, and will in fact be back on the side that they started from. All six legs of the spider are now twisted three times. Go back to the pair which left the trail after pin 33 and make a diagonal row of torchon ground stitches at pins 36, 37 and 38. You are now ready to make the next fan, picking up the fan workers from the left of pin 19 cloth stitch them through the outside passive and twist both pairs once, cloth stitch the workers through the first spider leg, twist the workers twice and put up pin 39. This pin corresponds with pin 6 of the previous fan so you can go back and follow the detailed instructions from that point if necessary.

Do complete the whole fan before leaving the worker at the last pin (pin 19), then you will have all the pairs necessary to work the small triangle of ground. You will need to work the trail at the same time, so follow the instructions for pins 20-34. Again concentrate on completing this one area before thinking about the spider (pin 35) and the short row of ground (pins 36-38) which will bring you back to the next fan.

When you have completed the circle you must join the trail worker into its starting loop at pin 20, and the fan worker into its starting loop at pin 1. Secure both pairs with a reef knot. If you are planning to use this circle as a garland on a Christmas card or as a Christmas tree decoration where you can effectively use an embroidered motif to cover the starting and finishing section there is no need to join any of the other threads into their starting loop. Just tie a reef knot with each pair around its final pin because the embroidered motif you will add to the garland completely covers this whole area. When you have tied off each pair remove the pins and trim off all the surplus thread. Position the lace circle in the centre of the circular cut out of a small size card and glue it down using a touch of glue behind each cloth stitch fan. Make sure that the finishing point is at the bottom, so that your embroidered motif will cover the join. Cut two 3 1/2" (9cm) lengths of narrow ribbon, one red and one green, fold them in half at a slight angle and glue them into place, now glue on the embroidered motif to complete your card.

If you prefer you can use this pattern to make a small decoration to hang on your tree, but remember that to hide the join you will need to glue a second motif onto the other side of the lace, so that it looks just as neat from both sides. Add a doubled length of thread at the top of the circle to make a hanging loop.

CHRISTMAS CARD WITH FAN AND ROSE GROUND TORCHON EDGING.

This card is decorated with a rectangle of a simple torchon edging, it is a little out of the ordinary because the fans make up the inside edge of the rectangle, rather than being on the more usual outer edge.

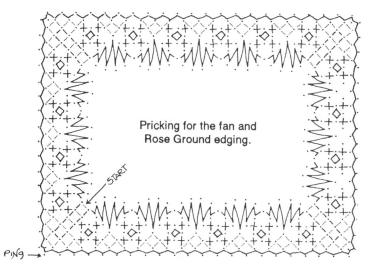

Pricking for the fan and Rose Ground edging.

1 pair of workers for the outer edge trail in DMC 30 Brilliante, DMC 30 Retors d'Alsace or 36/2 Brok. Cut 1 x 2½yd (225cm) length.

4 pairs of passives in the same thread. Cut 4 x 1¾yd (160cm) lengths.

1 pair of workers for the fan in DMC Fil Or Clair (gold) or DMC Fil Argent Clair (silver). Cut 1 x 4yd (3.75m) length.

1 pair of passives for the outer edge of the fan in the same thread. Cut 1 x 1¼yd (110cm) length.

2 pairs of trail passives in the same thread. Cut 2 x 1¼yd (110cm) lengths.

I worked the example in red and gold threads which echoed the colours of the commercial 'Greetings', the leaf and red ribbon rose gave the final touch. The leaf is strategically placed to completely hide the join in your lace edging!

WORKING INSTRUCTIONS.

Hang the outside fan passive pair on pin 1, the ordinary passives on pins 2, 3, 4 and 6, the fan worker on pin 5 and the trail worker on pin 7. The two trail pairs should be hung "open" around pin 8.

Cloth stitch the trail worker from pin 7 through the two passive pairs from pin 8. Twist the workers twice as usual and put up pin 9. Cloth stitch the workers back through both passive pairs of the trail and the next passive pair from pin 6. Twist the workers twice and put up pin 10, tension all the pairs and work back across the trail and put up pin 11. Leave the workers here for the moment.

Take the ordinary pair of passives from the righthand end of the trail (which were taken into the trail at pin 10) and twist them twice, now cloth stitch them through the fan worker pair hanging from pin 5. Put up pin 12 and cover it with a second cloth stitch and twist both pairs twice. Continue along this diagonal row of pins making a half stitch, pin, half stitch and twist with the fan worker and each ordinary pair of passives hanging from pins 4, 3 and 2 (pins 13, 14 and 15). Cloth stitch the fan workers through the edge passive pair from pin 1 and put up pin 16. Twist the outside passive once and the worker twice. Leave both pairs here whilst you return to complete the triangle of ground which has to be done before you can start the fan.

Go back to the trail workers which you left at pin 11 and work them across the trail and through the ordinary passive pair from pin 12. Twist the workers twice and put up pin 17. Take the workers back across through all three pairs and put up pin 18, twisting the workers and tensioning all the pairs as usual. Don't forget to twist the ordinary passive pair twice as it leaves the trail after pin 17. Work an ordinary Torchon ground stitch at pin 19 (ie. half stitch, pin, half stitch and twist). Now go back to the trail workers and complete two more rows of the trail taking the lefthand passive from pin 19 into the trail at pin 20 and twisting it twice as it leaves in exactly the same way as you did at pin 10 and pin 17. Leave the workers at pin 21.

Now you are ready to make the two 'preparation stitches' required for the Rose Ground diamond which is placed between each fan. I have chosen to use a cloth stitch and twist preparation stitch, but you can use a different version if you prefer. So take the two passive pairs from pins 19 and 20 and make a cloth stitch and twist. Do the same with the two pairs from pins 14 and 15. You will not put up any pins during or after these two special 'preparation stitches'. Now spread those four pairs out neatly on the pillow so you can see each pair clearly. Take the two centre pairs (originally from pins 15 and 20) and make a half stitch, pin, half stitch, putting up pin 22. Now take the two lefthand pairs

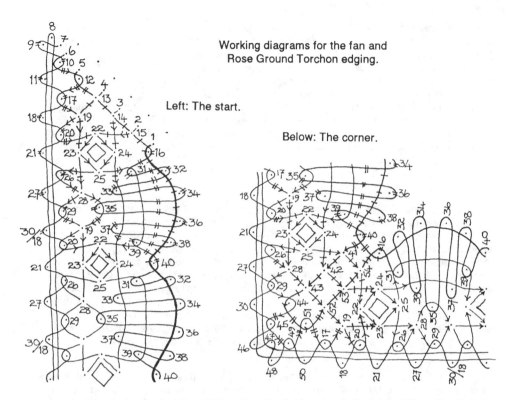

Working diagrams for the fan and Rose Ground Torchon edging.

Left: The start.

Below: The corner.

(one originally from pin 19 and the other the lefthand pair from pin 22) and make the same half stitch, pin, half stitch around pin 23. Do the same at pin 24 with the two righthand pairs (one from pin 22 and the other originally from pin 14). Complete the diamond with a half stitch, pin, half stitch around pin 25 using the two centre pairs (one from pin 23 and one from pin 24). To complete the Rose Ground you must finish in exactly the same way as you began, and that is with two preparation stitches, so take the two lefthand pairs and make a cloth stitch and twist with them, then repeat the same stitch with the two righthand pairs. Again no pins are required for these two preparation stitches. It really is vital to remember these preparation stitches both before and after the Rose Ground diamond. This is the danger point for the inexperienced lacemaker, so keep a sharp eye open for errors in this area, as forgetting any of the preparation stitches will spoil the whole appearance of your lace.

Continue with two more rows on the trail taking the passive pair (originally from pin 25) into the trail at pin 26. Twist that passive twice as usual before using it to make a Torchon ground stitch at pin 28. The lefthand pair will now go back into the trail at pin 29, don't forget to twist it twice as it leaves the trail immediately after the pin 29. Work one more row and leave the workers at pin 30 as you are now ready to work the fan.

Pick up the fan workers at pin 16 and cloth stitch them through the edge passives. As you are working with a metallic thread as your workers it's a good idea to tension these pairs immediately after this cloth stitch by swinging the pairs apart and pulling gently on each thread at the same time. Twist the worker twice and the edge passives once before cloth stitching through the incoming passive pair from pin 25, put up pin 31. At the end of every row the fan worker will be twisted twice and all the pairs must be tensioned well. Complete the fan in the usual way taking in new pairs before working pins 33 and 35, then leaving the lefthand fan passive out after completing pins 35, 37 and 39. The passive leaving the fan after pin 35 is twisted twice, and those leaving after pins 37 and 39 are twisted once. Leave the workers at pin 40 on completion of the fan and repeat the instructions from pin 20 until you arrive at the corner.

Leave the trail workers at pin 30 as you approach the corner, and go back to the fan workers which you left at pin 40 at the end of the previous fan. Cloth stitch the workers through the edge passive, tension them and twist both twice, now work Torchon ground stitches at pins 41, 42, and 43. This will bring the fan worker down along that diagonal line, but at pin 44 you must change its direction and to do this you make a cloth stitch, pin, cloth stitch, instead of the Torchon ground stitch. Twist both pairs twice. Bring the trail worker from pin 30 across the trail passives and take in the ordinary passive from pin 44, putting up pin 45. The next three trail pinholes (46, 47 and 48) are worked with only the two trail passives, but at pin 49 bring in the ordinary passive which must be twisted twice as it crosses the corner line between pin 45 and 49. Twist it twice as it leaves the trail at pin 49 and work a cloth stitch, pin, cloth stitch with the fan workers at pin 51, so that once again the fan workers change direction. Twist both pairs twice after pin 51. Use the fan workers to make simple ground stitches at pins 52, 53 and 54 so that once more they arrive at the start of the fan, cloth stitching through the edge passives and twisting in the usual way before putting up pin 16.

The corner is now complete so you can go back to pin 11 and follow the instructions through until you reach the next corner. When the rectangle is complete each pair is joined neatly to its own starting loop and tied off with a reef knot.

You can now glue your lace to a small card putting touches of glue behind each fan and along the outside trail. Ensure that the corner with the join is correctly positioned so that it can be hidden behind the leaf and ribbon rose. A commercial paper greeting completes the project.

CHRISTMAS CARD WITH TRAILS AND KISSES.

This is a very much more challenging project requiring a good working knowledge of traditional Bedfordshire 'kisses' which link the parallel trails, and picots which I have used on some of the outer edge pinholes. When complete it is a very pretty piece which fits into the circular cut out of a small card.

Above: Christmas Card with fan and
Rose Ground Torchon edging.

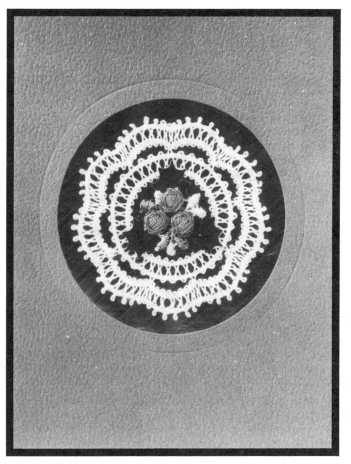

Above: Christmas card with trails and kisses.

25

For the Christmas card with trails and kisses you will need:-

4 pairs of passives for the two circular trails in the centre in 36/2 Brok or equivalent. Cut 4 x 1/2yd (50cm) lengths.
2 pairs of passives for the outermost trail. Cut 2 x 1yd (1m) lengths.
2 pairs of passives for the inner scalloped trail. Cut 2 x 1 1/2yd (135cm) lengths.
2 pairs of workers for the innermost trails. Cut 2 x 1 1/2yd (135cm) lengths.
2 pairs of workers for the outer scalloped trails. Cut 2 x 2yd (2m) lengths.

I used white Brok thread throughout, but you could work it in one of the DMC 30 threads which are available in a wide range of colours. I mounted my lace on a small red card against a background of red paper-backed tinsel. I added a dark green holly leaf triangle with an embroidered motif glued to its centre.

WORKING INSTRUCTIONS.

Start this piece by getting the two inner circular trails going. Hang one pair of inner workers on pin 1 and the other on pin 2. Hang two pairs of the shortest passive threads 'in order' on pins T1 and T2. The two trail workers now come together to make a traditional 'kiss', so cloth stitch both workers through their two pairs of passives, twist the workers twice and put up pins 3 and 4. Now make a cloth stitch with the two worker pairs and add two twists to each pair, then cloth stitch the righthand worker pair through the passives on its right, twist them twice and put up pin 6. The lefthand worker cloth stitches through the two pairs of passives to its left before being twisted twice at pin 5. Remove pins T1 and T2, tension all your threads and the first 'kiss' is complete. So you see that this is not a very complicated process, but be warned, it is only too easy to forget to put up pins 3 and 4, so make sure that the cloth stitch row is complete with both pins correctly placed before getting on with the 'kissing'! You'll notice that the workers have now actually changed trails, and they will do this at every pair of inner pinholes - this is marked with a cross on the pricking, so you can see why this technique got its name. Leave the workers at pins 5 and 6 whilst you get the outer pair of trails under way.

Hang one pair of outer workers on each of pins 7 and 8. Hang the two pairs of shorter outer passives on pin T3 'in order'. Do the same with the remaining two pairs of passives at pin T4. Complete pins 9, 10 and 11 in exactly the same way as you started the inner trails, making a kiss between pins 9 and 10 and leaving the outer worker at pin 11. Before you can bring the workers to pin 12 you must exchange one of the inner passive pairs with the worker waiting at pin 5. To do this simply take the inner passive pair from pin 8 (originally the righthand pair from T4) and cloth stitch it straight through the worker from pin 5, twist the old passive twice to cover the pin and it now becomes the new inner trail worker. The old worker from pin 5 now takes its place and becomes the new inner passive on the scalloped trail. This neat little exchange links the two sets of trails quite securely. You can now bring the worker from between the two outer trails to pin 12, twisting it twice at the end of the row in the normal way.

The inner trail continues making a kiss each time the workers arrive at the inner pinholes. You will need to leave the outer of these two pairs of workers at the equivalent of pin 5 at each repeat whilst you work on the scalloped pair of trails. You will then exchange the worker at that pin for the inner passive in order to link the two pairs of trails at the V of each scallop. To make a more attractive edge to the outer trails I made picots at five consecutive pinholes starting at pin 15. I twisted the worker pair five times before placing the pin and twice afterwards.

Below: Working diagram for the trails and kisses motif.

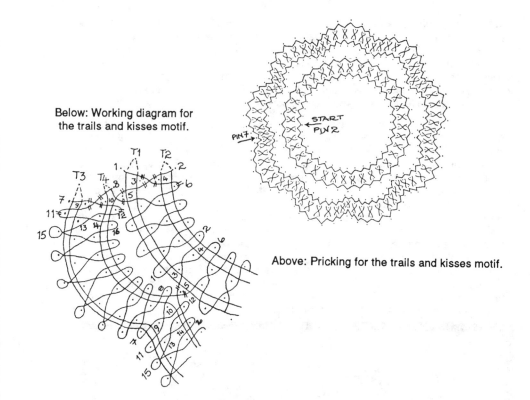

Above: Pricking for the trails and kisses motif.

To complete the circle I made a sewing with the outer worker of the scalloped trail into its own starting loop. I then cloth stitched across the trail to pin 9 where I tied the workers in a reef knot. The two passive pairs were also tied off with reef knots. This will give you a small overlap, but because of that sewing the whole circle will keep its shape when it is lifted from the pillow. Work a similar overlap with the inner of the scallop trails using pins 8 and 10 for a second time. There is no need to do a sewing on this trail, just use a touch of glue to keep the overlap in place once the lace is off the pillow. Do the same with the two inner trails, making a sewing into pin 2, working back across the trail and twisting the workers twice around pin 4 and making a cloth stitch with the first pair of passives before tying off both pairs of passives and then finally the worker. Work a small overlap on the outer of the two circular trails, but there is no need for a sewing. Tie off all the pairs neatly, remove your pins and glue the overlaps into place making sure that the neater starting edge of each trail completely hides the finishing overlap and its knots.

I used a small card with a circular cut out which I backed with a piece of red tinsel. Make sure that you are using a glue which does not spoil the surface of your tinsel and glue your lace into place positioning it carefully so that the join on the inner two trails is hidden by the little triangle of holly leaves which provides a nice backing for the embroidered motif added to its centre.

CHRISTMAS GIFT TAGS.

SNOWFLAKE GIFT TAG.

This is a miniature version of the snowflake-shaped decoration worked inside a bangle to hang on the Christmas tree. The two cloth stitch trails are easily worked and the addition of the beads between the trail presents no difficulties. The pricking is quite fine and therefore the pinholes are rather close together, so this may prove a problem for a less experienced worker, but if you take care to follow the markings and don't miss any pinholes it's quite straightforward.

1 pair of **Mez Effektgarn** as workers for the outside trail. Cut 1 x 1½yd (135cm) length.
1 pair of the same thread as workers for the inner trail. Cut 1 x 1yd (1m) length.
2 pairs of the same thread for passives in the outer trail. Cut 2 x 1yd (1m) lengths.
2 pairs of the same thread for passives in the inner trail. Cut 2 x 3/4yd (70cm) lengths.
18 tiny metal, glass or plastic beads approximately 2mm in diameter.

I worked this piece entirely in silver Effektgarn with tiny silver beads, which when mounted on a green tinsel background in a silvery card gift tag, looked most effective.

WORKING INSTRUCTIONS.

Hang the longest pairs of passives 'in order' from pin T1 and the longer pair of workers from pin 1. Cloth stitch the workers through the passives and twist the workers twice before putting up pin 3. Remove the temporary pin T1 and tension all three pairs carefully. Cloth stitch the workers back to pin 4, twist them twice as usual and put up the pin. Leave them here whilst you start the second trail.

Hang the inner workers from pin 2 and the two pairs of passives 'in order' from pin T2. Work two rows of cloth stitch in just the same way removing the temporary pin T2 after the first row, and twisting the workers twice at the end of every row. You are now ready to add the first bead.

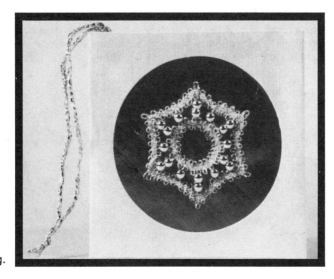

Right: Snowflake gift tag.

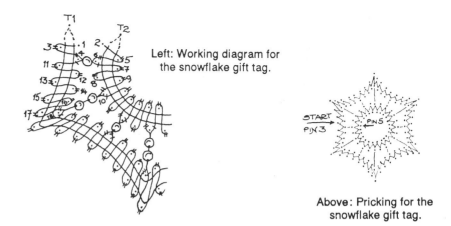

Left: Working diagram for the snowflake gift tag.

Above: Pricking for the snowflake gift tag.

Use a crochet hook or a lazy susan to bring one of the worker threads from the outside trail through the bead to make a loop through which you will pass one of the worker threads from the inner trail. Pull the threads tight and the bead will slide up to the work, twist the worker pairs once and then proceed with the trails until you reach pin 10 on the inner trail and pin 18 on the outer. You must then add two of the small beads using the same method as before. As you work round the point of the 'snowflake' don't be too heavy-handed when tensioning the outermost passive pair as this will pull it away from the point leaving an ugly elongated worker loop, a more gentle tensioning will encourage it to stay closer to the point pin and will give that part of the design a much more pleasing, solid appearance.

Continue working round the snowflake adding beads each time you reach the straight line which links the two trails. Press the starting pins down into the pillow as you complete the last two sections of the project to enable you to work more comfortably. To complete the piece I didn't try to hook the finishing threads through the starting loops, as the pins were so close together and the beads were rather an obstacle. Instead I worked a short overlap by continuing the trails using the previous pins, simply lifting them one at a time as I completed that row. I used five pins in each trail for a second time (ie. pins 2, 5, 6, 7 and 8 on the inner trail and pins 1, 3, 4, 11 and 12 on the outer trail). This brings the workers to the inside edges of the project where they can be tied off with a reef knot. The passives are also tied off in this way. Trim the threads fairly close to the knots and remove the pins.

Once you have removed the last pin you must handle the snowflake very carefully as if you have used glass or metal beads, the motif will be surprisingly heavy and will easily be pulled out of shape, so it is best to have prepared your gift tag in advance, then you can turn the piece over so that the neater starting ends of the trails lie on top of the knots of the finish. Gently lift the first section of each trail and with a touch of glue fix the overlap into place. To attach the lace to your card use a very small amount of glue behind the outside trail, the inside trail I left completely free of glue as it tends to be lifted by the beads, so is best left to find its own level. Remember that if you do choose to use a tinsel background for your snowflake to take great care gluing it into place as some glues will spoil the surface of the tinsel, so if you apply too much glue and it oozes out beyond the edges of the trail, it will spoil the clean outline of your snowflake.

STAR AND OPEN FAN.

This project is very quick to make with six triangles of cloth stitch forming a star shape between the open fans which are worked in gold to add an eye catching sparkle.

1 pair of DMC Clair Or or Clair Argent for the fan worker. Cut 1 x 2½yd (225cm) length.
1 pair of 36/2 Brok as the cloth stitch worker. Cut 1 x 2yd (2m) length.
4 pairs of 36/2 Brok as passives. Cut 4 x 1yd (1m) lengths.
1 pair of 36/2 Brok as the inside passive. Cut 1 x ½yd (50cm) length.

For the sample I chose a white and gold colour scheme which I mounted on a green gift tag with a red and green embroidered motif in the centre.

WORKING INSTRUCTIONS.

Hang one of the white passive pairs on pin 1 and push it to the left, hang the fan worker from the same pin and put the bobbins down to the right of the previous pair. Now twist the centre two bobbins twice to interlink the pairs, then add one twist to both pairs. Hang one pair of passives on each of pins 2, 3 and 4. The short passive is hung on pin 5 and the white worker pair on pin 6.

The fan is worked throughout with a cloth stitch and twist sequence, so start by taking the worker through the passive pair from pin 2, twist both the worker and the passive pair once, then cloth stitch the worker through the pair from pin 3, and again twist both pairs once. Cloth stitch through the pair from pin 4 and twist the passive pair once. The worker will be twisted twice here as it has now reached the end of the row, put up pin 7 and tension all the pairs. Work back to the outside of the fan using the same cloth stitch and twist that you used before. At the end of the row twist the worker twice and put up pin 8. On the next two rows you will only work through three pairs of passives, the passive from pin 7 will be omitted. On reaching pin 10 tension the worker and all of the passives carefully, guiding the passives so that they are evenly spaced across the row. Another passive (the one from pin 9) will be left out of the next row, so you will only have two pairs of passives as you work to pin 11 and back to pin 12.

On the next row you will work all the way down through the four fan passives (keeping to the cloth stitch and twist pattern) and you must now share pin 13 with the white worker. First cloth stitch the white worker (from pin 6) through the pair from pin 5 (the inside passive pair) and twist the worker once but do not twist the passive at all. Now cloth stitch the fan worker and the white worker together and twist both pairs once before putting up pin 13. Cover the pin with another cloth stitch and again twist both pairs once before bringing the fan worker out to the outer edge with the usual cloth stitch and twist. Put up pin 14 at the end of this row.

For the second half of the fan you will slowly increase the number of passives in the fan. The first two rows (to pins 15 and 16) will have two passives, the next two rows (to pins 17 and 18) will have three and the final two rows of the fan (to pins 19 and 20) will have four pairs of passives. When your worker has reached pin 20 your fan is complete, so leave the worker here whilst you work the cloth stitch area of the inner edge.

Pick up the white worker pair from where you left it at pin 13. It should have one twist on it. Cloth stitch it back across through the single inner passive to pin 21, where it is twisted twice before working back through the inner passive and the passive which left the fan after pin 19. Twist the worker twice and put up pin 22. Cloth stitch back across the row, add two twists to the worker and put up pin 23. Continue to work the cloth stitch triangle taking in one more passive at the lefthand end of each row (ie. just before pins 24 and 26). The passive which has only just come into the cloth stitch at pin 26, leaves immediately after that pin, and at pins 28 and 30 the lefthand passive will be left out of the next row, so that when you reach pin 31 there will only be the inner passive pair remaining. This is exactly as you started at pin 6, so continue to work the next five repeats following the instructions from pin 6-31 each time.

When the circle is complete the white worker is joined to its starting loop at pin 6 and tied off in a reef knot. The inner passive joins with its starting loop at pin 5. Three of the white passives will join their respective starting loops at pins 2, 3 and 4, whilst the fan worker is joined to the starting loop at pin 1. The last white passive can be just tied in a reef knot beside pin 1. Remove the pins and once the lace is off the pillow trim off the surplus thread close to the reef knots.

Use a touch of glue behind each of the cloth stitch areas and around the edge of each fan to glue the motif into place on a gift tag. If you like you can add an embroidered motif to the centre to add a touch of Christmas colour.

Left: Gift tag with star and open fan.

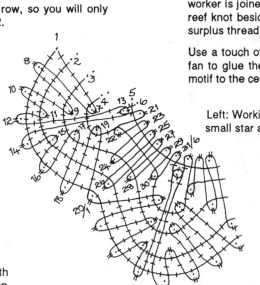

Left: Working diagram for the small star and open fan motif.

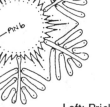

Left: Pricking for the small star and open fan motif.

FAN AND GROUND GIFT TAG.

This simple circle is made up of twelve small fans using a metallic thread as the workers. The passives in the trail which forms the inner edge are the same glittery thread. It's not a difficult project to work, particularly as you'll notice that the whole of the last repeat (and therefore the join) is completely hidden under the embroidered motif which gives the ring the appearance of a garland!

1 pair of DMC Clair Or or Argent as the fan workers. Cut 1 x 3yd (2.75m) length.
1 pair of the same thread for the outside fan passive. Cut 1 x 1 1/4yd (110cm) length.
2 pairs of the same thread for the inner trail passives. Cut 2 x 3/4yd (70cm) lengths.
1 pair of DMC 30 Brilliante for the trail worker. Cut 1 x 1 1/2yd (135cm) length.
3 pairs of DMC 30 Brilliante for the ordinary passives. Cut 3 x 1 1/2yd (135cm) lengths.

I used a gold metallic thread which contrasted most effectively with the red DMC 30. Against the background of a dark green card the finished project was most pleasing.

WORKING INSTRUCTIONS.

Hang the three ordinary passive pairs on pins 2, 3 and 4. The outside fan passive is the first pair to be hung on pin 1, push this to the left and then hang the fan worker on the same pin but put the bobbins down to the right of the previous pair. Twist the centre threads twice and you will find that the pairs are neatly interlinked. Twist both pairs once. You can now work the fan in the usual way remembering to twist the workers once between the outside passive and the rest of the fan passives on every row. The worker is twisted twice at the end of every row. The outside fan passive is twisted once each time the worker cloth stitches through it.

The DMC Clair is a beautifully glittery thread, but it is just a little more difficult to pull up at the end of the row, so take great care with your tensioning throughout the fan. I found it helped to tension the worker and outer passive threads immediately after working the cloth stitch with those two pairs at the start of each left to right row. It was much harder to tension the row well if I left the tensioning until the worker had reached the pin at the righthand end of the row.

Twist each passive pair coming out of the fan (after pins 11, 13 and 15) twice. Now you are ready to start the inner trail, so hang the trail worker on pin 6, and the two metallic passive pairs 'in order' on pin 5. Cloth stitch the worker through the two trail passives and through the passive pair lying immediately to their left (this passive pair left the fan after pin 11). Twist the worker twice and put up pin 17, cloth stitch back through all three passive pairs, twist the worker twice and put up pin 18. Do always get into the habit of working two trail rows at a time, bringing it from the inner edge through both permanent trail passives and the 'visiting' pair which always makes up the third pair of passives in the trail, before taking it back through all three pairs and leaving it once more parked safely around the pin at the inner edge of the trail.

The passive pair which has just entered the trail at pin 17, leaves immediately after, so twist it twice and it is then ready to become part of the ground. Make a Torchon ground stitch with the pair from pin 13 (half stitch, pin, half stitch and twist), putting up pin 19 between the two half stitches. You can now work the next ground stitch at pin 20 using the lefthand pair from pin 19 and the pair which left the fan after pin 15. Now you must go back to the pair which remains at pin 19. This pair now 'visits' the trail, so bring the trail workers across through all three passives and put up pin 21, after twisting it twice it

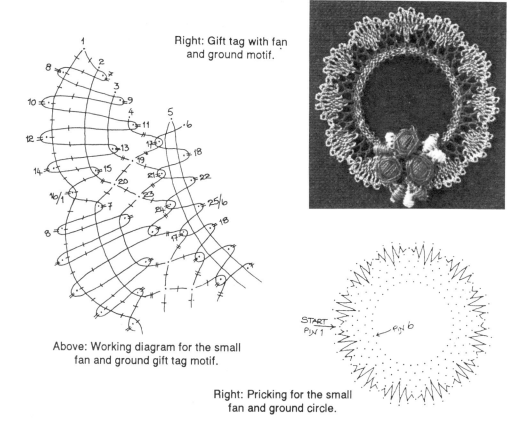

Right: Gift tag with fan and ground motif.

Above: Working diagram for the small fan and ground gift tag motif.

Right: Pricking for the small fan and ground circle.

goes back to pin 22 where it waits until you have completed the ground stitch at pin 23 with the righthand pair from pin 20 and the 'visiting' pair from pin 21. The righthand pair from pin 23 now 'visits' the trail at pin 24, then the workers return to pin 25 at the inner edge.

The area of ground is now complete and you are ready to work the next fan. Continue around the circle working fan and ground sections alternately. Join the trail worker to its starting loop at pin 6 and secure it with a reef knot. Do the same with the fan worker which must be joined into the starting loop at pin 1. If you are planning to use one of the embroidered motifs to decorate your circle, there is no need to join any of the other pairs into their starting loops, they can just be tied off with a reef knot and later trimmed close to the knot. If you plan to add a decoration to the centre of the circle then the join will be more visible, so you must join each pair to its corresponding starting loop in the usual way.

The lace circle is glued into place on a small gift card using a small amount of glue behind the densest part of each fan. As you can see from the illustrations you can add various decorations to the basic lace circle, so experiment with different coloured card backgrounds, leaves, flowers etc. until you reach an attractive combination.

CONCAVE FAN AND GROUND GIFT TAG.

This simple circle has an unusual fan which is concave rather than the more normal convex. This gives it an interesting pointed outline which I have emphasised with a metallic passive pair.

1 pair of DMC 30 Brilliant as the fan worker. Cut 1 x 2 1/2yd (225cm) length.
1 pair of the same thread for the trail worker. Cut 1 x 1 1/2yd (135cm) length.
3 pairs of the same thread for the ordinary passives. Cut 3 x 1 1/2yd (135cm) lengths.
1 pair of DMC Clair Or or Clair Argent for the outside fan passive. Cut 1 x 1 1/4yd (110cm) length.
2 pairs of the same thread for the trail passives. Cut 2 x 3/4yd (70cm) lengths.

For the sample I used red DMC 30 with gold passives in the inner trail and at the outside edge of the fan. A small triangle of gold holly leaves and a red ribbon rosebud give the finishing touch.

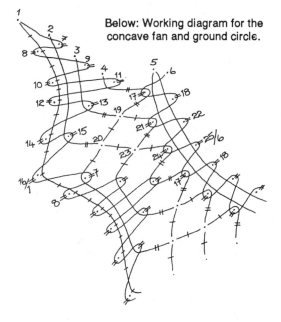

Below: Working diagram for the concave fan and ground circle.

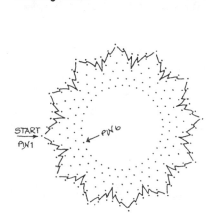

Above: Pricking for the concave fan and ground circle.

WORKING INSTRUCTIONS.

In actual fact this circular edging can be worked by following the instructions for the previous gift tag, as there are only three differences which do not greatly affect the working. Firstly you'll notice that the shape of the outside edge of the fan is concave rather than convex, but the number of pinholes is exactly the same. Secondly there is no twist on the workers between the edge passive and the other passives in the fan, and finally the fan workers are a different colour. The working diagram uses exactly the same numbers, so if you need to follow the detailed written instructions given for the previous project there is only one point which you need to ignore, and that is the instruction to twist the workers to form a space between the edge passive and the other fan passives.

Above: Gift tag with concave fan and ground circle.

To finish the circle you must first bring the trail workers through the starting loop at pin 6 and tie it off with a reef knot. The trail passives can just be tied off as the holly leaves will completely hide this part of your join. The fan worker must be joined to its starting loop at pin 1, but the outside fan passive can just be tied off with a reef knot. The three passives must be carefully joined to their corresponding starting loops at pins 2, 3 and 4. All can be tied off with a reef knot. Once the lace is off the pillow you can trim the surplus thread away close to the knots.

I chose to mount this piece on a white gift card putting a touch of glue behind each fan and at intervals on the inner trail. Position it on the card so that the join will be hidden behind one of the holly leaves which is also glued into position. A ribbon rose glued to the centre of the holly triangle completes your card.

FRENCH FAN GIFT TAG.

Once again the versatile French Fan provides a simple and quickly worked edging which makes a very effective decoration for a gift tag.

1 pair of DMC Clair Or or Argent for the fan workers. Cut 1 x 4yd (4m) length.
2 pairs of the same thread for the trail passives. Cut 2 x 3/4yd (70cm) lengths.
1 pair of DMC 30 Brilliant for the outside fan passive. Cut 1 x 1yd (1m) length.
2 pairs of the same thread for the ordinary passives. Cut 2 x 1yd (1m) lengths.
1 pair of the same thread for the trail workers. Cut 1 x 1 1/2yd (135cm) length.

I worked the sample in red and gold threads and mounted it on a red card which had the interesting effect of making the red threads disappear causing the gold threads to stand out most vividly.

WORKING INSTRUCTIONS.

Hang the two pairs of ordinary passives on pin 2 and interlink them in the usual way. Twist both pairs twice. Now set up the inner trail by hanging the trail workers on pin 5 and one pair of trail passives on each of pins 3 and 4. Cloth stitch the workers through both trail passives and the righthand pair from pin 2. Twist the workers twice and put up pin 6. Tension all the threads before cloth stitching back across the row. Put up pin 7 after twisting the workers twice as usual. Leave the workers here and take the pair of passives at the lefthand edge of the trail and twist them twice so that they are ready to enter the fan as the inner passive pair.

To start the fan hang the outside fan passive pair on pin 1 and push it to the left. Hang the fan worker on the same pin and put the bobbins down to the right of the previous pair. Twist the middle threads twice to interlink the two pairs. Now twist the outside passive once and the workers twice. Cloth stitch the workers through the passive pair hanging from pin 2, this will become the middle fan passive, twist the passive pair once and the worker twice. Cloth stitch the workers through the passive pair which has just left the trail making sure that it still has its two twists. After the cloth stitch twist the workers once and put up pin 8. Do not twist the inner passive at all. Pull the workers tight and tension each pair of passives, guiding them into the correct position so that the three passive pairs are evenly spread across the row with the inner and outer passive pair staying close to the pins.

Now work back to the outside edge cloth stitching through the inner passive without twisting it, but remembering to twist the workers twice before cloth stitching through the middle passive pair which is twisted once afterwards. Twist the worker twice and cloth stitch through the outside passive pair which is also twisted once. The worker is twisted twice at the end of the row as usual.

The next row of the fan is worked in exactly the same way as the first row, but at the righthand end of the row simply lift both of the worker bobbins and slip the threads behind pin 8. Twist the workers once and work back to the outside edge of the fan. You will use the pivot pin (pin 8) four times altogether without ever lifting it out of the pillow. Do take care with your tensioning at the end of every row, don't continue unless the workers are perfectly straight and each passive pair is following a nice smooth curve.

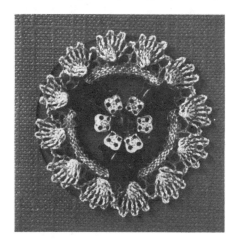

Left: Gift tag with a
French Fan circle.

The fan is complete when the worker reaches pin 12, it will stay here whilst you work the trail and the ground stitch between each fan. First you must add one extra twist to the middle passive to give it a total of two twists, the inner fan passive will need to be twisted twice at this point. If you like you can leave the pivot pin in this position and it will give your fan more depth as the four worker loops do tend to stack up quite high around this pin. If you prefer a flatter finish to each fan then now is the time to remove the pivot pin and gently pull on the inner passive pair. The passive threads will now take up each of the worker loops, which will sit comfortably side by side, rather than being piled one on top of the other. Both methods are quite acceptable, the choice is yours.

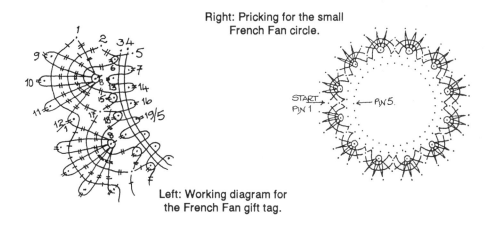

Right: Pricking for the small
French Fan circle.

Left: Working diagram for
the French Fan gift tag.

Now go back to pin 7 and pick up the trail worker. Cloth stitch across through the two trail passives, twist the workers twice and put up pin 13. Work back to pin 14 at the inner edge of the trail. The inner fan passive is now ready to visit the trail, so bring the trail worker through the two trail passives and work it straight through the inner fan pair, twist the workers twice and put up pin 15, cloth stitch it back through all three pairs and leave it at pin 16. Take the lefthand passive from the trail (the original inner fan pair) and twist it twice, now use it to make a Torchon ground stitch (half stitch, pin, half stitch and twist) with the middle fan passive at pin 17. The righthand pair from this pin now 'visits' the trail. Cloth stitch the trail worker across through all three pairs, twist it twice and put up pin 18, work it back to pin 19. Twist the lefthand trail passive twice as it leaves the trail and you are now ready to work the next fan.

On completion of your circle you must join the finishing pairs to the correct starting loop, but if you position the lace carefully on the gift tag you will find that the holly leaves added to the centre will completely cover the join in the inside trail! Join the fan worker into pin 1 and tie it off with a reef knot. The outside passive will be tied off without being joined to the starting loop. The trail worker must be joined at pin 5 and the two passives to pin 2. The trail passives can be tied off without being joined to their starting loops. Now position the lace circle in the centre of the card so that one of the holly leaves will cover as much of the join as possible. Fix it into place using a touch of glue behind the inner point of the fan where it is densest. Glue the holly triangle into place and then add a metal flower to the centre. For a little added sparkle I glued a 4mm faceted bead into the middle of the flower.

CAKE FRILL.

It's nice to have a festive cake frill, but before you embark on this project it's a good idea to measure the circumference of your usual size of Christmas cake as you'll be surprised at just how long a piece of lace you will need to make to go round even a small cake. It's a big project which definitely needs to be started well in advance, so be warned!

This design is worked with fine metallic passives and just four thicker worker pairs which give the fans and heart shapes a good solid colour.

2 pairs of DMC 8 Coton Perle in red as workers. Wind as much thread as you can onto both bobbins and be prepared to join on new lengths as required.

2 pairs of DMC 8 Coton Perle in green as workers. Again wind the bobbins with as much thread as you can. It's worth using unspangled Continental style bobbins to get the biggest possible thread capacity.

15 pairs of Mez Effektgarn in gold as the passives. Fill each bobbin to its limit to avoid as many joins as possible. (N.B. Although it is possible to substitute other fine metallic threads for many of these Christmas projects I strongly recommend that you use the Effektgarn for this particular piece.)

Obviously I used a red, green and gold colour scheme for this Christmas cake, but there is no reason why you shouldn't use an orange and yellow colour scheme for Easter, or white, blue and silver for a Wedding cake.

WORKING INSTRUCTIONS.

Hang one of the red worker pairs on pin 1 and push it to the left. Hang a gold passive pair to its right from the same pin, twist the centre two threads twice to interlink the two pairs. Twist the gold passive once and the red worker pair twice. Hang gold passive pairs from pins A, B and C and a green worker pair from pin D. You can now work the first fan in cloth stitch (pins 1-14) twisting the worker twice at the end of every row and twice between the outside passive pair and all the rest of the fan passives. The fan is completed by making a half stitch, pin, half stitch and twist with the red worker and the outside gold passive at pin 15. This will allow you to change the worker for the next fan.

Good tensioning is going to be vital throughout this piece as the threads in the cloth stitch areas are very densely packed and you must take very great care to ensure that

all the passive threads are pulled up really well at the end of every row. The gold passives will be rather overwhelmed by the thicker red and green workers, but despite the domination of the worker pairs the passives will add an attractive sparkle throughout the lace.

To start the first heart shape hang the red worker on pin 16, push it to the left and hang a gold passive from the same pin, but put the bobbins down to the right of the previous pair. Interlink the two just as you did at the start of the fan by twisting the centre two threads twice, but do not twist either pair afterwards. Hang 9 more gold passive pairs from pins E-M inclusive. Now you can work the first half of the heart shape in cloth stitch (pins 16-28). Leave the workers at pin 28 and twist the passives left out after pins 21, 23 and 25 twice. You are now ready to start the remaining fan.

Hang the last gold pair on pin 29, push it to the left and hang the green pair from the same pin, but put it down to the right, twist the two centre threads twice to interlink them, now twist both pairs once. The gold pairs will be the workers for the duration of this small fan. The main body of the fan is worked in half stitch, but you must make a cloth stitch and twist each time the worker comes to the green outside passive pair, this will ensure that the green pair stays at the edge of the fan. At the end of each row I added two additional twists to the 'worker' pair (making a total of three twists altogether as there is already one twist on that pair on the completion of the last half stitch), this will cause the thread which goes all the way across each row to change, so that the thread on one bobbin won't get used up more quickly than the others. Work pins 29-38 as described above, but for the final pinhole, pin 39, again you need to make a half stitch, pin, half stitch and twist so that the next fan is ready to be worked with different workers. Twist the pairs leaving the fan after pins 34, 36 and 38 twice and complete the remaining half of the red heart shape (pins 40-50).

Make sure that all the pairs coming into the next heart shape are twisted twice (these are the pairs which left the fan and the previous heart shape after pins 8, 10, 12 and 14, and 28, 41, 43, 45, 47, 49 and 50). To start the next heart shape with the green pair from pin 8 as your worker you will need to make a half stitch with this pair and the gold passive pair from pin 28, put up pin 51 and cover it with a second half stitch. The green pair will now lie to the right of the gold pair. Cloth stitch through the next gold pair to the right of the workers (from pin 41), twist the workers twice and put up pin 52. You can now work the first half of this heart shape in the usual way (pins 51-64). Leave the workers at pin 64, twist the pairs leaving the heart shape after pins 57, 59 and 61 twice and go to the lefthand edge of the piece to work the small gold fan.

Pricking for a Torchon lace cake frill.

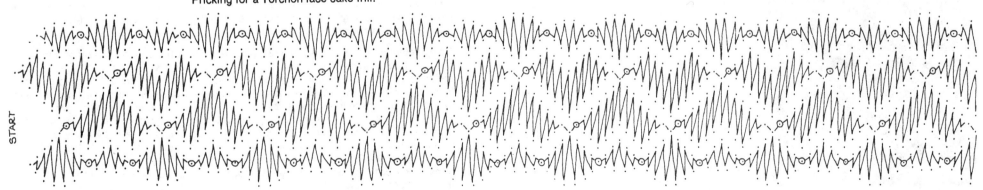

As with the small gold fan on the righthand side, this is worked in half stitch, with a cloth stitch and twist to keep the red pair as the outside fan passive. Like both of the previous fans the last pin (pin 74) is worked with a half stitch, pin, half stitch and twist.

Once the small fan is complete put two twists on the pairs leaving it after pins 69, 71 and 73. You can now return to the green heart shape and complete it in the usual way (pins 75-84). Twist all the pairs leaving the heart shape after pins 62, 64, 76, 78, 80, 82, 84 and 79, 81 and 83. You can now work the cloth stitch fan on the right of the work (pins 85-98) with the green pair as workers. Remember to twist the workers twice between the edge passive pair and the other gold fan passives and to work the last pin of the fan as a Torchon ground stitch in order to change the worker pair for the next fan. Twist the pairs leaving the fan after pins 91, 93, 95 and 97 twice so that they are ready to go into the next heart shape and don't forget to start the next heart shape with a Torchon ground stitch so that the red pair becomes the workers. To help you remember where to work these colour-changing Torchon ground stitches I have circled these pinholes on the pricking.

Continue in this way until your lace is long enough to go all the way around the cake. Tie off each pair with a reef knot and trim off the surplus thread. I chose a white paper frill with a clear plastic top layer as a backing for my lace to ensure that none of the fat from the cake would soak through and spoil it. As the depths of cakes may vary you will probably have to adjust the width of this commercial cake frill in order to make it fit your cake. I simply cut the paper frill along its length and overlapped the cut edges until the overall width was satisfactory. I then tacked the overlap into place using white sewing thread and small running stitches. I used the same white thread to stitch the lace onto the centre of the paper band taking small stitches over some of the twisted gold threads as they moved from heart shape to heart shape. To make a nice neat starting edge I then folded back one end of the frill and overlapped it onto the top of the finishing section. Pin it carefully into place and your cake is ready to take pride of place at any table!

A festive Torchon lace cake frill.

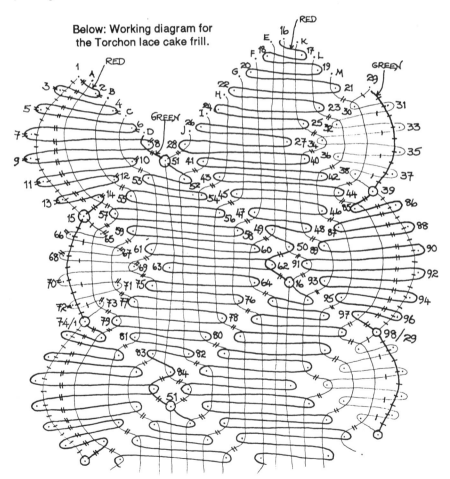

Below: Working diagram for the Torchon lace cake frill.

CHRISTMAS TREE DECORATIONS.
BRASS MEDALLION WITH BEADS AND TRAIL.

The brass medallion centre of this decoration was originally more curved and domed as it was intended as an egg decoration! However placing the piece between two blocks of wood and applying pressure, (either by hand or with a hammer!) easily flattens it out so that you can use it in this way. The lace itself is only a simple trail which is linked with the aid of beads to the brass centre. With the pierced and chased metal centre, the beads and glittery thread for the trail you can make a really stunning tree decoration very quickly indeed.

1 pair of DMC Metallise or DMC 80 Cordonnet Special as workers for the trail. Cut 1 x 3yd (3m) length.
2 pairs of DMC Clair Or or DMC 80 Cordonnet Special as passives. Cut 2 x 1yd (1m) lengths.
1 brass medallion centre which has been flattened.
8 oval beads approximately 7mm long in gold or pearly white.
16 tiny round beads 2mm in diameter to match the oval beads.
A length of thin gold thread (DMC Metallise) and a needle.

Christmas tree decorations with brass medallion centres.

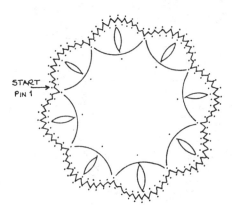

I worked one example all in gold, and the second I worked with white thread and white pearly beads. You'll notice that one has ordinary worker loops at the edge of the trail, whilst the other has a series of picots along the outer edge.

WORKING INSTRUCTIONS.

Thread a length of thin gold thread in a needle fine enough to go through the beads which you are using. Knot the ends of the thread together as you will be working with doubled thread. Attach the thread to the metal centre through one of the small outside round holes, now take the thread along the back of the medallion (the front is the side with the raised, rather than the impressed decoration) and up through the next hole. Thread on a small round bead and take the needle back down the same hole again. Run the thread along the back and out of the next hole and stitch on another bead. Do pull the thread taut between each bead as it is important that the beads should be firmly attached to the metal centre, if the thread is loose then the beads will wobble and you won't be able to attach the worker loops to them securely enough. So take your time as you stitch on the beads and make sure that there is no slack thread at any point. Continue all the way round and you will find that the medallion now has one bead at each of its eight points and one bead in the centre of each curve between the points. Tie off the thread really well, and if you are at all in doubt add a dab of glue to the ends to make sure that they cannot come undone.

Now pin your medallion down so that it fits inside the outline drawn on your pattern, there are plenty of holes in the decoration and four pins spread evenly around the inner circle should be enough to anchor the piece quite securely. Hang the workers on pin 1 and the passives on pins 2 and 3. Make a cloth stitch with the workers and the pair from pin 2, twist the worker once and cloth stitch through the passive from pin 3. Now add two twists to the worker and you are ready to join it to the metal centre. Just imagine that the bead is a pin and guide your worker threads around the bead making sure that the threads are positioned well underneath the curve of the bead's surface. Pull the workers straight and work across to pin 4 remembering to twist the workers once in the middle of the row between the two passives. Now make sure that your workers are pulled really tight so there is no danger of the worker loop slipping up and off the bead.

Below: Pricking for brass medallion with beads and trail.

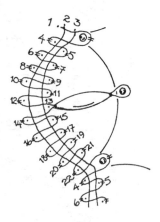

Above: Working diagram for brass medallion decoration.

Twist the workers twice and put up pin 4 and then work back to pin 5. At pin 6 you have a choice. You can either make a picot here, and at each one of the next seven pinholes along the outer edge, or you can continue with just the ordinary two twists around the pin at both ends of every row. I chose to add picots to the version made in the white Cordonnet Special, but the metallic worker pair of the gold version is much harder to use for picots, so I chose to give this a plainer edge.

Continue with the trail until you have put up pin 13, now it is time to add one of the oval beads and for this you will need a fine crochet hook or a Lazy Susan. If you are using a crochet hook simply thread the bead onto the hook and bring both worker threads through the bead. Loop both threads over the bead and tighten them carefully keeping one finger on top of the little round bead so that the threads cannot jump over the top of it. Pull the workers up well and continue across the next row to pin 14. Pin 22 is worked with just two twists around the pin even if you have chosen to edge your trail with picots, two plain pinholes here will emphasise the scalloped shape of the curve. After pin 22 you can follow the instructions from pin 1 once more.

When the circle is complete make a sewing with your workers into the starting loop at pin 1, replace the pin and work back across the row towards the bead. You can tie the workers off around that bead with a reef knot. The two passive pairs can each be tied in a reef knot (the trail is so narrow here that there is no real need to join them into their starting loops). Remove all the pins and trim off the ends. Use a small piece of the Clair gold thread, or Perle 8 for the white version, to make a hanging loop. As there is no pinhole at the centre of the scallop I used a crochet hook to bring the loop for the hanger through the gap where the worker is twisted between pinholes 12 and 14. Open the loop out and pass the ends through that loop, pull it tight and tie the ends in an overhand knot about 2" (5cm) from the trail.

CIRCLE OF WIRED TRAILS AND FLOWER BEADS.

This decoration holds its shape due to two thicknesses of fine paper covered florist's wire which form the centre 'passives' of each trail. The wire is soft enough to stay exactly where you want it, the only tricky bit is winding it onto a bobbin in the first place, indeed it is worth trying to work without bobbins on the wire at all! Starting and finishing the wire-stiffened trails neatly requires a little patience, but once underway there are no real problems, although you will need to take a little extra care when working pairs through the wires. When complete it makes a most attractive addition to any Christmas tree.

1 pair of DMC 80 Cordonnet Special or Fil a Dentelle as the workers for the outside trail. Cut 1 x 3yd (3m) length.
1 pair of the same thread as workers for the inner trail. Cut 1 x 2yd (2m) length.
1 pair of Twilley's Gold Dust as passives for the outer trail. Cut 1 x 1¼yd (110cm) length.
1 pair of the same thread as passives for the inner trail. Cut 1 x ½yd (50cm) length.
3 lengths of 26 gauge paper-covered florist's wire.
10 gold or silver plastic flower beads or similar beads 5mm in length.

I used white Cordonnet and white wires with gold coloured flower beads and Gold Dust thread for one version and as a varation I worked one entirely in green threads and wires with silver flower beads.

WORKING INSTRUCTIONS.

Hang the outside trail workers on pin 1. Now make a clove-hitch, or two loops at the end of each length of wire and tighten these around a long anchor pin (pin 2) a couple of inches (5cm) behind, but in line with, the starting point. Now put pins 3 and 4 into position so that the two wires lie between them. Hang the outer trail passive pair from pin 3, now lift the righthand of those two bobbins over the top of the wires and behind pin 4 and put it down to the right of both wires as shown in the working diagram.

You now have a rather unusual situation in that the two pairs of the trail are composed of unlike threads (one Gold Dust and one wire in each pair), but you completely ignore that fact as you cloth stitch the workers across the trail in the normal way. Twist the worker twice and put up pin 5, and leave the worker here. You'll notice that there is an extra pinhole in the deepest point of the V on the outer edge, this will not be used by the workers, but it does help the wires to make a sharper change of direction at this point. So put up pin A now to the left of all the trail passives.

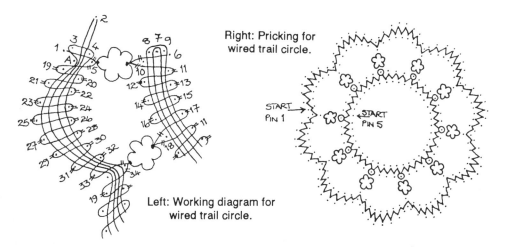

Right: Pricking for wired trail circle.

Left: Working diagram for wired trail circle.

To start the inner trail hang the worker on pin 6. Take the remaining piece of wire and fold it in half, now hang it from pin 7 in the middle of your trail. Put pins 8 and 9 into position and hang the Gold Dust passive pair around both just as you did for the outside trail. Cloth stitch the workers through to pin 10 where they will be twisted twice as usual. Now you can add the flower bead. As the beads have five petals, the hole passes through the centre of one petal and emerges between two petals on the opposite side, so you might like to decide which way you are going to thread the bead onto your crochet hook or Lazy Susan so that all your beads are positioned in the same way. If you think this is being too fussy, then of course there is no need to go to such lengths, as few admirers will go to the length of studying which way you put the beads on!

Use your crochet hook or Lazy Susan to bring one of the outside trail worker threads through the bead and make a loop, now pass one of the worker bobbins from the inner trail through that loop and pull both tight so that the bead slides up to rest between pins 5 and 10. Twist the workers twice more and resume work on the trails. The inner trail must pause on reaching pin 18 so that the outer trail can catch up, once the workers arrive at pin 34 you can add the next bead.

You will need to take care with your tensioning throughout as it is important to pull the wires straight as you go so that they follow the curves of the two trails nice and smoothly. When you have completed approximately half of the circle it is time to neaten the starting ends of the outside trail. Take out pin 2 and bring the ends of both wires towards you so that they now rest directly over the top of the wires in the first part of the trail. I used the head of a wooden bobbin to press the wires down against the trail to make a sharp 'fold' in both wires, so that the wires curl back over the first row of cloth stitch and give the trail a smooth starting edge. It is best to leave these wires at this length for the moment as they are less likely to tangle with the threads and wires as you approach the finishing join.

At the end of each trail I work a small overlap using the same pins in their original positions, just lifting them up to slip the workers behind them as required. On the inner trail use pins 6, 10 and 11 for a second time, then cloth stitch the workers through the passives and tie them off with a reef knot. On the outer trail use pins 1, 5 and 19 again, then work one more row without using the next pin and tie off the workers.

Unwind the bobbins, remove the pins and carefully lift your lace off the pillow. You must now trim off the starting ends of wire on the outer trail, an old pair of scissors should be able to cope with the wire without any problem. The ends should be short enough to be hidden behind the overlap, about 1/10" (3mm) away from the 'fold' in each wire. Now put a spot of glue on the trail over the top of the cut ends of wire, so that you can bring the overlap down and press it into place. Once the glue has set enough to hold the trails together you can carefully trim off the workers and the wires. Leave the wires just long enough to make sure that the last row of weaving cannot fall off the ends. If you are careful there is no need to trim off the Gold Dust threads as these can be brought to the edge of the trail and used to make the hanging loop. A touch of glue under the one from the inner side of the trail is enough to encourage it to go smoothly up to the outer edge. Now tie the two threads together in an overhand knot about 2" (5cm) away from the trail.

The inner trail is easier to finish off as the start of the wires was that much neater. The wires are only available in lengths of about 12" (30cm) which although when folded in half is just long enough to go round the inner circular trail, is insufficient for the longer, scalloped outer trail. So simply glue the overlap into place and trim off the surplus thread and wires.

FRENCH FAN BORDERS FOR FACETED STONES.

This very simple border is quick to work and when sandwiched between two faceted 'stones' they make a sparkling addition to any Christmas tree.

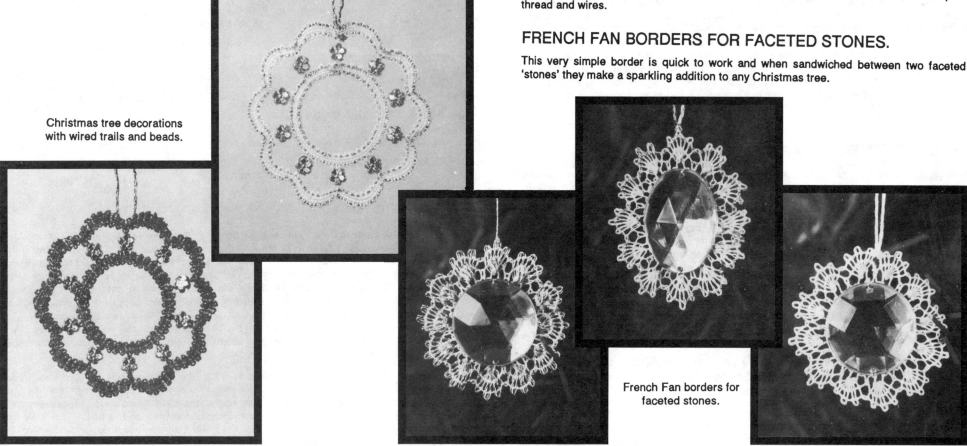

Christmas tree decorations with wired trails and beads.

French Fan borders for faceted stones.

The lengths required are the same for both round and oval trims.

1 pair of 36/2 Brok, DMC Fil Or Clair or Fil Argent Clair as the fan workers. Cut 1 x 3yd (3m) length. If you prefer you can use DMC Metallise which is available in a wide range of glittery colours, but you will need to use two thicknesses, so cut 1 x 6yd (5.5m) length and fold it in half before winding your bobbins.

1 pair of 36/2 Brok as workers for the inner trail. Cut 1 x 1yd (1m) length.

3 pairs of 36/2 Brok as passives (one of these will be the edge passive for the fan, so you could use a metallic thread such as DMC Clair or a doubled length of Metallise). Cut 3 x 1yd (1m) lengths.

2 pairs of 36/2 Brok as passives for the inner trail. Cut 2 x 1/2yd (50cm) lengths.

For one circular edging I used entirely 36/2 Brok. For the oval example I used the same thread but added a pair of DMC Argent Clair for the outside fan passive. For the other round edging I used DMC Argent Clair as the worker. I hope you will enjoy experimenting with your own thread combinations.

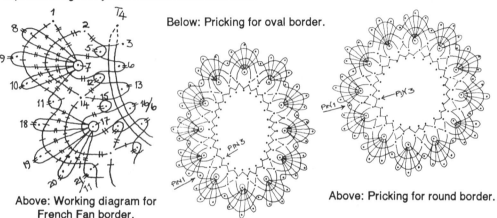

Above: Working diagram for French Fan border.

Below: Pricking for oval border.

Above: Pricking for round border.

WORKING INSTRUCTIONS.

Hang the edge fan passive on pin 1 and push it to the left, now hang the fan workers on the same pin and put them down to the right of the previous pair. Twist the middle two bobbins twice, now twist the passive pair once and the workers twice. Hang the two longer passive pairs from pin 2, interlink them in the same way as you have just interlinked the first two pairs, and twist both pairs twice.

Hang the trail worker on pin 3 and the two short passive pairs from a temporary pin (T4) placed a short distance behind pin 3 in the centre of the trail. The passives should be hung on 'in order'. Take the workers from pin 3 and cloth stitch across through the two pairs of passives from T4 and the righthand pair from pin 2. Twist the workers twice at the end of the row and put up pin 5, cloth stitch back to pin 6 through all three pairs of passives. Twist the workers twice and leave them at pin 6. Remove pin T4 and tension all the passives carefully. Take the lefthand pair of passives from the trail (originally the passive pair from pin 2) and twist them twice. You are now ready to start your fan.

Pick up the workers from pin 1 checking that they still have two twists, and cloth stitch them through the passive pair from pin 2. Twist the passive pair once and the workers twice before cloth stitching through the passive pair which left the trail after pin 5. Do

not twist this passive pair at all, and add only one twist to the worker pair before putting up pin 7 which will be the pivot pin for this fan. Tension all the threads carefully. Work back to the outside of the fan making a cloth stitch with the inner passive pair before twisting the workers twice, (the inner passives are not twisted at all). Cloth stitch through the middle passive pair and twist them once, the workers are twisted twice before cloth stitching through the outside passive pair which is also twisted once. Twist the workers twice before putting up pin 8 at the end of the row.

Work back across to the pivot pin following the same twist pattern, the workers always twist twice with one exception - they are only twisted once when they come to the pivot pin. The outside and middle passives are both twisted once, whilst the inner fan passive is not twisted at all. On reaching pin 7 for the second time the workers, with their single twist, are simply lifted and brought round the pivot pin without removing it from the pillow. They then work back across to the outside edge of the fan. Continue working the fan visiting the pivot pin four times in all and parking the workers around pin 11 which marks the completion of the fan.

Add one more twist to the middle passive pair as it leaves the fan and add two twists to the inner passive pair. It's easy to forget to add these twists at this point, so take care! The inner passive pair is now taken into the trail at pin 12, the worker from pin 6 simply cloth stitches through all three pairs of passives and returns to pin 13. If you prefer a flatter French fan you could at this point remove the pivot pin and gently pull on the passive which has just entered the trail. Twist the passive pair twice as it leaves the trail and make a Torchon Ground stitch - half stitch, pin, half stitch and twist, at pin 14. The righthand pair from this pin is now taken into the trail at pin 15. Return the worker to the inside edge of the trail and leave it at pin 16. Twist the passive twice as it leaves the trail and you are now ready to work the next fan.

Continue until all twelve fans are complete. Join the fan worker to its starting loop at pin 1 and tie it off with a reef knot. The outside passive can also be tied off, but without being joined to its starting loop. Bring one thread from the middle passive pair and one thread from the passives which have just left the trail, through their starting loop at pin 2. Tie off each pair in a neat reef knot. The trail worker must be joined to its starting loop at pin 3 before being tied off, but the two trail passives can be tied off without joining them to their starting loop as this trail will be completely covered when you glue the 'stones' into place. Remove all the pins and trim the ends close to the reef knots once the lace is off the pillow.

I used a white craft glue to fix the lace in place, but it is a good idea to test the glue you intend to use on one of the faceted stones first and let it dry as I did find that one glue adversely affected the backing which spoilt the clarity of the plastic stones. I found it easier to put a thin layer of glue on the back of one of the stones making sure that the glue went right up to the edge. I then placed the lace down onto the glue, positioning it so that the trail comes just up to the edge of the stone and that the two holes in the stone are positioned in line with the centre of the nearest fan. It is best to let this dry completely before attempting to add the second stone. To align the holes in the second stone with those of the first I pushed two pins up through the first stone so that the second, with a thin coating of glue on its backing, could be slipped onto the pins and pressed into place. The pins are removed once the glue is sufficiently set to hold the second stone in place.

I used a short length of DMC 8 Coton Perle to make a hanging loop which I hooked into the edge loop at the centre of the fan closest to one of the holes in the stones.

French Fan edging for a
brass ornament.

FRENCH FAN EDGING FOR A BRASS ORNAMENT.

This circular pattern makes an attractive edging for a finely pierced brass ornament for your Christmas tree. It could equally well be used as a frame for a photograph or a picture to make a card suitable for a variety of occasions.

1 pair of fan workers using a doubled length of DMC Metallise or Madeira's finest metallic thread. (I found that Madeira gold shade 8 matched the brass of the ornament perfectly.) Cut 1 x 9yd (8.25m) length and fold it in half to give you a working length of 4 1/2yds (4.12m). As it is difficult handling such a long piece of this rather springy thread, you may find it easier to cut 2 x 41/2yd (4.12m) lengths, then wind the two pieces onto the bobbins together.

4 pairs of DMC 30 Brilliant or equivalent as passives. Cut 4 x 11/4yd (110cm) lengths.

For my two examples I used a fan worker of gold Madeira and background threads of red and green DMC 30 Brilliant. However, there is no reason why this same pattern should not be worked all in white or entirely in a coloured thread. Alternatively you may like to use all one colour for the fan worker and three of the passive pairs and add a single metallic pair for the outside passive of the fan. (N.B. In this case there is no need to use a double thickness of thread for the fan worker, a single piece of DMC 30 is quite adequate.)

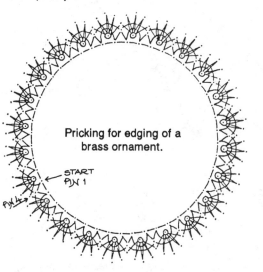

Pricking for edging of a
brass ornament.

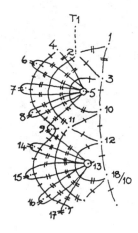

Above: Working diagram
for French Fan edging.

WORKING INSTRUCTIONS.

Hang two pairs of passives from pin 1 and interlink them in the usual way. Twist both pairs twice. Hang another passive pair from pin T1 and use it to make a half stitch with the lefthand passive pair from pin 1. Put up pin 2 and cover it with another half stitch, then twist both pairs once. Remove pin T1 and let the new pair slide down to rest snugly around the pin. Take the righthand pair from pin 2 and make a half stitch with the pair from pin 1, put up pin 3 at the inner edge and cover it with a half stitch and twist (i.e. twist both pairs once). This completes the triangle of three 'ground' pins which you will find between each fan. Now you are ready to start the fan.

38

Hang the remaining passive pair on pin 4 and push it to the left. Hang the fan worker pair around the same pin putting the bobbins down to the right of the previous pair. Twist the centre two bobbins twice to interlink the pairs. Twist the outside passive pair (the lefthand pair) once, and the fan worker (the righthand pair) twice. Now cloth stitch the worker pair through the pair from pin 2. Twist this middle passive pair once and the worker twice before cloth stitching through the inner passive pair (the lefthand pair from pin 3). Do not twist this passive pair at any point during the fan (but you must not forget to twist it twice as it leaves the fan to make the ground stitches). Twist the worker only once at this end of the row and put up the pivot pin 5 in the circled pinhole.

Return to the edge using the same twist pattern. The worker is twisted twice between each passive and at the outside end of the row, the outer and middle passives are twisted once and the inner passive is not twisted at all. Put up pin 6 at the outer edge. Now work back to the pivot pin and lift your workers (which you have only twisted once) around the back of the pivot pin without removing it from the pillow. Continue working the fan in this way until the workers reach pin 9, you will now have used the pivot pin 4 times in all. Leave the workers at pin 9 whilst you turn your attention to the passives and the triangle of ground at the inner edge.

First of all you can remove the pivot pin if you prefer a flatter fan. (Leaving the pivot pin in place keeps the worker loops stacked one on top of the other and this bunching gives the fan a more 3 dimensional effect.) Pulling on the inner passive pair causes those threads to slide down to fill the worker loops, removing the vertical stacking. Now add two twists to the inner passive pair and one additional twist to the middle passive pair to give it a total of two. Make three Torchon ground stitches (half stitch, pin, half stitch and twist) at pins 10, 11 and 12. Use the inner fan passive and the inner edge passive pairs to work pin 10, then the lefthand pair from pin 10 and the middle fan passive to work pin 11. Finally the righthand pair from pin 11 and the inner edge pair work pin 12. You are now ready to work the next fan (pins 13-17). Repeat from pin 10, not forgetting to add the extra twists to the middle and inner passives before working the three ground pins.

Continue in this way working alternately on the fan and then the ground. Don't make the mistake of trying to start one before you have finished the other. Make sure that your worker has reached the final pin at the outside edge before you turn to the three ground stitches, and then work all three before you start the next fan.

To join the circle when the lace is complete make sure that each passive pair has the usual number of twists on it and then tie off the inner fan passive and the inner edge passive into starting pin 1, the middle passive into pin 2 and the fan worker into pin 4. The edge passive can then be tied off without bringing it through any of the starting loops. Remove the pins and trim the ends close to the finishing reef knots.

You will need to use a glue like Bostik or Uhu to attach the lace to the brass ornament, but before you start gluing you must decide whether you prefer the lace to be positioned in front or behind the outside rim of the ornament. It is then easier to put the glue on the appropriate side of the rim with a pin and press the lace edging into position as you go. It is very difficult indeed to put the glue on the lace as the single twisted pair of the inner edge provides such a small gluing surface.

If you are planning to use this edging as a trim for a picture then glue it into place by putting a touch of glue behind the base of each fan where the threads are densest.

Right: Pleated paper circle with French Fan edging.

CONCERTINA FAN AND CIRCLE.

Both projects take advantage of the simple but effective French Fan edging which is remarkably quick to work. I have used it for a number of projects and make no apology for using it once again. Both projects are made out of pleated paper, the lace being glued to one edge before folding.

For the circle you must work 26 repeats with the following threads:-
1 pair of DMC Clair Or or Argent metallic thread for the outside fan passive. Cut 1 x 1 1/2yd (135cm) length.
1 pair of DMC 80 Cordonnet Special or DMC Fil a Dentelle as fan workers. Cut 1 x 5 1/2yd (5.10m) length.
1 pair of the same thread for the trail worker. Cut 1 x 2 1/4yd (210cm) length.
2 pairs of the same thread for fan passives. Cut 2 x 2yd (2m) lengths.
2 pairs of DMC 8 Coton Perle or Twilley's Gold Dust as trail passives. Cut 2 x 1yd (1m) lengths.

For the fan you must work 20 repeats with the following threads:-
1 pair of DMC Clair Or or Argent metallic thread for the outside fan passive. Cut 1 x 1 1/4yd (110cm) length.
1 pair of DMC 80 Cordonnet Special or DMC Fil a Dentelle as fan workers. Cut 1 x 4 1/2yd (4.25m) length.
1 pair of the same thread for the trail worker. Cut 1 x 2yd (2m) length.
2 pairs of the same thread for fan passives. Cut 2 x 1 1/2yd (135cm) lengths.
2 pairs of DMC 8 Coton Perle or Twilley's Gold Dust as trail passives. Cut 2 x 3/4yd (70cm) lengths.

I used red Fil a Dentelle with gold trail passives and outside fan passive for one of the pleated circles, and for the other I used all white threads with a single pair of gold passives at the outside edge of the fan. For the fan I used all white threads with just one pair of gold as the outside fan passive. However you can have fun arranging your own colour combinations to complement the paper you are using.

WORKING INSTRUCTIONS.

Hang the two ordinary fan passives on pin 1 and interlink them in the usual way. Twist both pairs twice. Now hang the trail worker on pin 2, the trail passives 'in order' from pin T3 and cloth stitch the worker across, twist it twice at the end of this and every row, and put up pin 4. After tensioning the threads cloth stitch back to pin 5 taking in the righthand passive from pin 1, don't forget to twist the workers twice before putting up the pin. Work back through all three passive pairs, twist the workers twice, and put up pin 6. Now remove pin T3 and tension the passives so that they rest comfortably around the workers to make a nice straight start to your trail. (Don't pull the trail passives too hard or they will pull the first worker row out of position resulting in a 'hammock' shaped curve at the start of your trail.) Add two twists to the passive pair at the lefthand edge (originally from pin 1) which now leaves the trail.

Hang the outside fan passive on pin 7 and push it to the left. Hang the fan worker from the same pin and put the bobbins down to the right of the previous pair. Twist the centre two threads twice to interlink the two pairs. Twist the outside passive once and the worker twice. Cloth stitch through the middle fan passive pair (the lefthand pair from pin 1) and again twist the worker twice but this time do not twist the passive pair. Cloth stitch through the inner fan pair (from pin 5), twist the worker twice and put up pin 8, but again the passive pair is not twisted at all. Work back to the outside edge of the fan following the same stitch and twist sequence. Continue using pin 8 as the pivot pin of your fan, simply lifting the workers around that pin at the righthand end of every row. You will have used it four times by the time the workers reach pin 12 at the end of the fan. Add two extra twists to the middle fan passive and the inner fan passive as they leave the fan. Work the trail worker across to pin 13 taking in the inner fan passive before putting up the pin. You can now remove pivot pin 8 and gently pull on the inner fan passive to remove the worker loops which had stacked up around it. Cloth stitch back to pin 14 and leave the workers there. Twist the lefthand passive pair twice as it now leaves the trail to make a Torchon ground stitch (half stitch, pin, half stitch and twist) at pin 15. You can now repeat the instructions from pin 4.

When you have worked the required number of fans the fan worker and the outside fan passive will finish at pin W, tie them off using double threads to make a single reef knot. Do make sure this knot is really secure, if you are in any doubt then tie the ends once more. The two fan passive pairs will be tied off at pin X. The trail worker must be brought through the trail to a new inside pin in line with pins W, X and Y. Tie the workers off around pin Z before tying each of the trail passives off with a reef knot.

To make the paper part of each project I used wrapping paper or the bright and shiny gold and silver paper used to cover cake boards which is available from cake-decorating shops. Wrapping paper varies widely in quality and having experimented with several I found some easier to work with than others. The worst wrapping paper was the plain metallic paper-backed foil so I would definitely advise you to avoid that. The easiest to use was the cake board foil, it was strong even when wet with glue and it scored and folded quite readily.

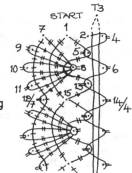

Right: Working diagram showing the start of the French Fan border.

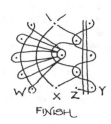

Above: Diagram showing the finish of the border.

MAKING UP THE FAN.

For the fan you need to cut a piece of paper 15cm x 20cm. Score it across the centre of the 15cm sides and glue the wrong side of one half. I found that the cake board foil was not affected by either Bostik or Copydex glues, but with other papers it would be best to test a small piece first. Fold the paper in half along the score line to make a piece 20cm long and 7.5cm wide. You now need to score a series of lines across the width of the strip. These lines are 1cm apart. As it is difficult to see pencil markings against the shine of the foil I found that the easiest way of doing this accurately was to cut a rectangular aperture 20cm x 7.5cm in a piece of card and mark the lines on the 6-8cm border which remains. You can then slip your double thickness piece of foil into the aperture which will hold it steady whilst you use a ruler to score the lines across the width. It is best to let the double thickness of foil dry completely before you try to score these lines, as if you attempt it whilst the paper is still soft and damp from the gluing there is a danger that your scoring will damage the surface of the paper. I used a blunt divider pin held at a very low angle to the surface of the paper so that the point would not dig in and tear the paper.

Once the scoring is complete, glue the lace to the folded edge of the paper. If you are using gold paper then do remember that if you get glue on the right side of the paper then it will remove the gold finish and leave you with areas of silver, so take care! The glue is applied to the back of the cloth stitch trail, the whole of which should overlap and be glued down onto the paper. As you glue down your lace you should keep checking that your piece of lace is going to fit from one end to the other, you can also try and arrange for the 12, 15 and 14 pin line to coincide with each score line as each repeat of the lace is 1cm long as is the distance between each scored line. Again let the glue dry before starting the folding process.

Looking at the picture of the finished fan you will see that the first fold of the fan comes forward - therefore the knots of the finishing edge will be going back away from you and will be less conspicuous. Once the first fold is going in the right direction you can continue folding the fan in the usual concertina fashion. Pinch all of the pleats together at the bottom edge and glue a narrow piece of ribbon around the fan about 1cm up from the lower edge. This should be glued on nice and tightly, so let the first part dry before winding the ribbon firmly round the pleats and gluing down the end. Holding the ribbon firmly in place ease the upper part of the fan open and encourage the side sections to fold just above the holding ribbon. You can now add a ribbon bow, a ribbon rose or an embroidered motif to give the finishing touch.

The hanging loop is made from a piece of surplus silver or gold thread. Take a short piece about 4" (10cm) long and fold it in half, push your fine crochet hook through the gap between the edge fan passive and the two ordinary fan passives, at the half way point of your lace (between fans 10 and 11), bring the loop of the metallic thread through the lace and open it out so that you can pass the ends through the loop. Pull it tight and tie the ends together in a simple overhand knot. Your fan is now complete.

MAKING UP THE CIRCLE.

For the pleated circle you will need to cut a piece of your chosen paper 27cm x 5cm. Score it along its length and glue the two halves together to form a finished strip 27cm x 2.5cm. You must now score it across the width at 1cm intervals. Glue your lace on to the folded edge, taking care to keep all the glue well hidden behind the cloth stitch trail. The start of your lace should be level with the lefthand edge of the paper strip. This leaves the righthand section of the strip free of lace as you have worked only 26 repeats.

Start the folding sequence in the same way as the fan so that the first fold from the lefthand end comes forward towards you. Continue in the usual concertina fashion. Now use a small amount of glue to cover the righthand half of the last, lace-free section. This is now tucked behind the first folded section to make a complete circle. Let the glue dry before attempting the next stage.

Thread your needle with a length of DMC Clair in gold or silver to match your paper circle. Use a needle with quite a large eye as it will help in the next stage if this thread can run smoothly and easily through a slightly larger hole. Don't tie a knot at the end of the thread, just leave a good 6" (15cm) of thread which you don't pull through after the first stitch. Working on the wrong side of the folded circle pinch the first pleat together and push your needle straight through the mid point of the two adjacent folded sections about 1/4" (5mm) in from the lower edge. Stitch through each pleat in this way being as accurate as you possibly can in the placing of your needle. When you are back at the start you can unthread your needle and take hold of both ends of thread. Tighten each end gently and as it gathers the pleats in, push the whole circle flat on the working surface, this will enable you to pull up the remaining slack thread. It is important to get the circle flat before completing this tensioning. To keep the gathering thread tight you need now to tie it in a special reef knot, adding the extra twist to the first part of the knot so that it will not slip whilst you get ready to tie the second half. I added a third 'half' just to make sure! These ends are then trimmed off - not too close to the knot which is after all on the wrong side.

Use some of the surplus thread to make the hanging loop. I used this to link the start and finishing edges of the lace by bringing the ends of the thread through pinholes 7 and W before opening out the loop and passing the ends through, then tie the ends together in an overhand knot. You can then add a small holly leaf triangle and a ribbon rose, or an embroidered motif to the centre, which conveniently hides any shortcomings in your gathering stitches!

If you are planning to do several of these extremely eye-catching decorations then I do advise you to plan the scoring in the most time-saving way. For instance if you are making six circles cut one piece of paper 15cm x 27cm and one piece 17cm x 29cm, and glue them together so that one piece projects 1cm beyond all the edges of the other. You can then make your pencil markings on the wrong side of these borders which will be trimmed off once the scoring is complete. (Don't forget to use the edges of the smaller piece of paper as your reference points just in case you haven't been able to glue the pieces together with a perfectly even border.) You will then need to slice the piece into 2.5cm wide strips. There will be a cut edge at the top and bottom of each piece, but as this will be hidden behind the lace anyway, there's no need to worry, and in this way you can score enough for six decorations in almost the same time as you can score the piece required for one, so it's well worth thinking in terms of 'mass-production'!

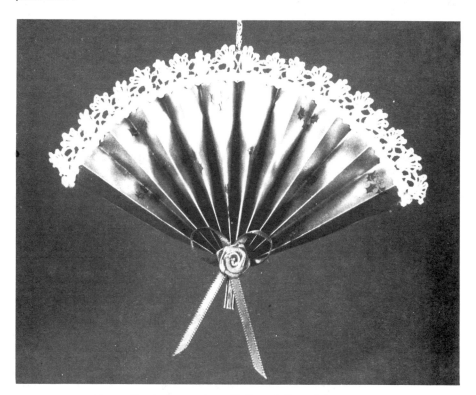

Above: Pleated paper fan with French Fan edging.

GATHERED LACE CIRCLES.

These Torchon edgings can be gathered up to make a most impressive circle of lace. The thread required is the same for both designs.

1 pair of DMC Clair (gold or silver) or a doubled length of DMC Metallise as the fan workers. Cut 1 x 4½yd (4.25m) length in Clair, or 1 x 9yd (8.5m) length in Metallise and fold it in half before winding your bobbins with doubled thread.

1 pair of the same thread for the outside fan passive. Cut 1 x 1½yd (135cm) length of DMC Clair or double that length in DMC Metallise.

2 pairs of DMC Metallise used double as the workers for the zigzag trails. Cut 2 x 8½yds (8m) lengths and fold them in half, winding your bobbins with doubled thread.

1 pair of 36/2 Brok cotton as footside edge passives. Cut 1 x 1yd (1m) length.

17 pairs of 36/2 Brok as ordinary passives. Cut 17 x 1½yds (135cm) lengths.

For the gimp required for the first design:-

2 gimp bobbins each wound with a 1yd (1m) length of Twilley's Gold Dust.

There are some very interesting combinations of threads and colours which are suitable for these two pieces. I worked one with a gold fan worker and outside passive which I matched with a gold gimp. To add a special subtle sparkle to the zigzag trails of the spider edging I used a double thickness of the pearly opalescent Metallise thread. I used a doubled length of the same pearly thread as workers for the fan, the zigzag trails and the outside fan passive, but there is no reason why you shouldn't try mixing the Metallise threads which would give you a shaded effect similar to that described in the section on lace fans.

For both of these designs I would recommend the Brok thread rather than alternative threads of a 30 thickness. I found that the Brok gave a fuller and crisper effect.

DIAMOND AND GIMP EDGING.

WORKING INSTRUCTIONS

Start in the centre at the widest point of the half stitch diamond using ordinary passive pairs. Hang one pair on each of the five temporary pins above pins 1 and 2. Hang one pair on pin 1 and use this as the worker to half stitch across through all five pairs to pin 2. I like to give the worker an additional two twists at the end of every half stitch row as this changes the worker thread each time and allows the thread on the bobbins to be used more evenly than it would be if you kept the same worker bobbin for each row.

Remove the temporary pins and let each pair slide down to rest over the worker thread. Work back across through the first four pairs of passives and put up pin 3, then across to pin 4 working through only three passive pairs, and finally back to pin 5 through just two passives. Cover pin 5 with another half stitch and make sure that all the pairs have two twists on them as they leave this area of half stitch before you hang on the gimps.

The gimps are single bobbins rather than a pair and I suggest that you leave about 9" (20cm) of thread free so that you have a reasonable length to use when you darn the starting ends into the finishing section. So use two temporary pins set well back from the work and knot each gimp to the pin. Pass each gimp through the three pairs of passives leaving the half stitch area and cross them in the centre. (To work a gimp through a pair lift the lefthand bobbin of that pair and pass the gimp under this bobbin and over the righthand bobbin of the pair.) To lock the gimp in place you now need to add two more twists to each of those six passive pairs. (This completes the 'gimp sandwich' - two twists, gimp, two twists.) At the point at the end of each diamond you must remember to cross the gimps. (You can cross the gimp bobbins right over left or left over right, but whichever way you choose, make sure that you use that method throughout the project.)

Now start the cloth stitch zigzag trails by hanging the workers on pins 6 and 14. Hang four passive pairs on the temporary pins above each trail. Work across through four pairs of passives and back through three pairs, until you reach pins 21 and 13. Leave the workers here for the moment. Don't forget to remove the temporary pins two or three rows after the start of each trail and tension the passives so that the starting loops of these pairs rest snugly around the worker threads of the first row. The workers are twisted twice at the end of every row.

To start the fan hang the outside fan passive on pin 22, push it to the left and hang the fan worker from the same pin to its right. Twist the centre two threads twice and then twist the passive pair once and the worker twice. Work the fan in cloth stitch remembering to add two twists to the worker between the outside passive and the ordinary passives and at the end of every row. The outside passive is twisted once each time the worker cloth stitches through it. Leave the worker at pin 32 at the end of the fan and twist each of the three passives leaving the fan twice.

Hang two pairs of passives on pin 33, interlink them and twist each pair twice. Hang the footside passive pair on pin 34 and the last remaining pair on pin 35 as the footside edge pair. Cloth stitch the righthand pair from pin 33 through the footside passive pair.

Pricking for the diamond and gimp edging.

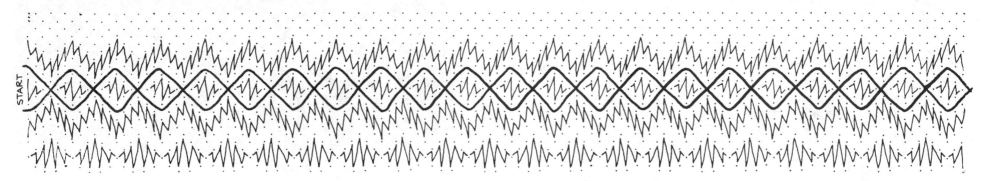

Now twist the footside passive pair once and the other pair twice before using it to make a cloth stitch with the footside edge pair from pin 35. Twist both pairs twice and put up pin 36 to the left of both of these pairs. Cloth stitch the lefthand pair from pin 36 through the footside passive pair and twist it twice. As always the footside passive pair is twisted only once. Work a row of torchon ground stitches (half stitch, pin, half stitch, twist) at pins 37, 38 and 39 using the lefthand pair from pin 33 and the pairs which left the zigzag trail at pins 6, 8 and 10. Use the pair from pin 37 together with the pair which has just worked through the footside passive pair to start the next row of ground stitches at pins 40, 41 and 42. Take the pair from pin 40, cloth stitch it through the footside passive pair and make up the footside at pin 43. Work back through the footside passive pair, twist it twice and work the next row of ground at pins 44 and 45. Go back and make up the footside at pin 46, work a ground stitch at pin 47 and return to make the final footside stitch at pin 48.

All your pairs are now in place. You can now work the next section of each zigzag trail - pins 49-54 and 55-60. Twist the passives twice as they leave the trail and work the gimps through the six pairs from pins 21, 50, 52 on the left and 13, 56 and 58 on the right. You can now work the half stitch diamond pins 61-68. Twist each pair leaving the diamond twice before working the gimps through all six. Don't forget to cross the gimps at the end so that they are ready to work the next diamond. Now work the next section of each trail pins 69-74 and 75-80. You can then work the next fan.

You will need 21 repeats and I suggest that you work two extra rows of pins at the end as I found that the neatest and easiest way of joining the start to the finish was simply to overlap the neater starting end on top of the finishing end. Each pair is finished off with a reef knot, trim off all the surplus thread except the gimps and one pair of long white threads from the inner edge. You can use one of these threads to stitch the overlap in place and the other will be used as a gathering thread. Once the overlap is secure then use a large-eyed needle to darn away all four ends of the gimp thread, the starting ends will join the gimp in the finishing section of lace and the finishing ends of gimp will be darned away in the opposite direction into the starting section. The gimp threads need only be darned in for about 1/2" (1.5cm).

Run your gathering thread through the holes along the footside and pull it up as tightly as you can (without breaking the thread!) Secure it with several backstitches. I added an 8" (20cm) length of narrow ribbon which I folded unequally and stitched into the centre so that the ribbon covered the overlap as it fell from the centre. I then glued three tiny holly leaves from a 'holly triangle' into place and topped them off with three ribbon roses. I used a short length of leftover gold thread to make a hanging loop in the centre of the eleventh fan which should be directly at the top of the finished circle.

Diamond and gimp edging gathered circle.

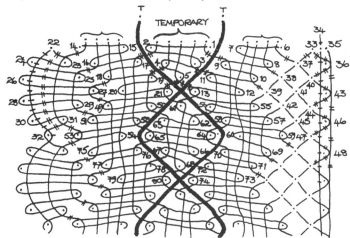

Above: Working diagram for the diamond and gimp edging.

Below: Photocopy of the finished lace.

Gathered lace circle with spiders.

GATHERED CIRCLE WITH SPIDERS.

WORKING INSTRUCTIONS

Hang one ordinary passive pair on each of the six pins just above the first spider (pins A-F). Put up pin 1 in the centre and make the second half of a 'haloed' spider. First of all cloth stitch the pair from pin C through the two pairs from pins D and E. Next cloth stitch the pair from pin B through the same two pairs. Now twist the centre four pairs twice to create the gap between the spider body and the 'halo'. Now cloth stitch the pair from A through the pair originally from D, twist both pairs twice and cloth stitch the pair from A through the next passive (originally from E) and again twist both pairs twice. The pair from F now cloth stitches through the pair originally from C, both pairs are twisted twice before cloth stitching the pair from F through the next passive which was originally from B. Again both pairs are twisted twice. The two pairs from A and F now work a half stitch, pin, half stitch and twist at pin 2. Tension all pairs and add one more twist to all six passives to make a total of 3 twists on each spider leg.

Hang the zigzag trail workers on pins 3 and 11 and four ordinary pairs of passives on the temporary pins above each trail. Cloth stitch the workers across and twist them twice at the end of each row. You will work across through four pairs of passives and then back through only three as the last passive leaves the trail at the outer edge of each row (after pins 3, 5, and 7, and 11, 13 and 15). Leave the workers at pins 10 and 18 and add two twists to the six pairs of passives leaving the trails.

Hang the outer fan passive on pin 19 then add the fan worker on the same pin with the bobbins to the right of the previous pair. Twist the centre two threads twice to interlink the two pairs. Twist the outer passive once and the worker twice. You can now work the rest of the fan taking in the pairs from 11, 13 and 15. Don't forget to twist the workers twice between the ordinary passives and the outside fan passive which is always twisted once. When the worker reaches pin 29 at the end of the fan twist the passives leaving the fan after pins 24, 26 and 28 twice.

Hang two pairs of passives on pin 30, interlink them and twist each pair twice. Use the lefthand pair to make a row of Torchon ground (half stitch, pin, half stitch and twist) at pins 31, 32 and 33. Hang the footside passive pair on pin G and the final pair on pin 34. Cloth stitch the remaining pair from pin 30 through the footside passive pair and twist it twice. The footside passive pair is only twisted once throughout. Make another cloth stitch with the pair from pin 30 and the footside edge pair from pin 34, twist both pairs twice and put up pin 35. Take the lefthand pair and cloth stitch it back through the footside passive pair and twist it twice. Twist the footside passive pair once as usual. Now make the next row of ground stitches at pins 36, 37 and 38. Go back and take the pair from pin 36 and make up the footside edge by cloth stitching through the footside passive and then the footside edge pair. Put up pin 39. Make the next row of ground at pins 40 and 41. Complete this triangle of ground by making the footside pin at pin 42, the last ground stitch at pin 43 and the final footside pin at pin 44.

All your pairs are now in place and you can continue by working the next section of each of the zigzag trails pins 45-50 and 51-56. Leave the workers here whilst you make your first complete spider. The six pairs from pins 18, 52 and 54, and 10, 46 and 48, will be the legs of your spider and must all be twisted three times. Make a ground stitch with the two pairs from pins 18 and 10 at pin 57 and twist both pairs twice. The pair on the left now works through the two passive pairs from pins 52 and 54 and the righthand pair works through the two passives from 46 and 48. Don't forget to add two twists to each pair between each cloth stitch. You can now work the first half of an ordinary spider with the four centre pairs. Put up pin 58 in the centre of the body. Now complete the second half of the body with the same four pairs, twist each of those pairs twice, then work each through the 'halo' pair on its way back to the trail. Again twist each pair twice after each cloth stitch. Bring the halo pairs together for a ground stitch at pin 59 then add one more twist to each of the six legs to bring the total up to three. If you are in any doubt about the working of this spider follow the enlarged working diagram.

Above: Photocopy of the finished spider edging.

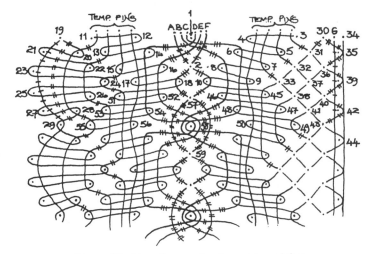

Above: Working diagram for the spider edging.

Continue working the next sections of trail, and then the edge fan followed by the next triangle of ground stitches at the footside edge. You will need 21 repeats in all plus two extra rows in order to give you the overlap required to join the ends together nice and neatly. Secure the threads by tying each pair off in a reef knot. Leave one pair of long white threads at the footside edge and trim off the surplus thread. Use one of these lengths to stitch the overlap in place and the other as the gathering thread. Pull up the gathering thread as firmly as you can and fasten it off securely. I added two ribbon bows in contrasting coloured ribbon, a length of tiny iridescent bead trim, three green leaves and three ribbon roses to the centre. A short length of white Coton Perle 8 provided the hanging loop.

Pricking for the spider edging.

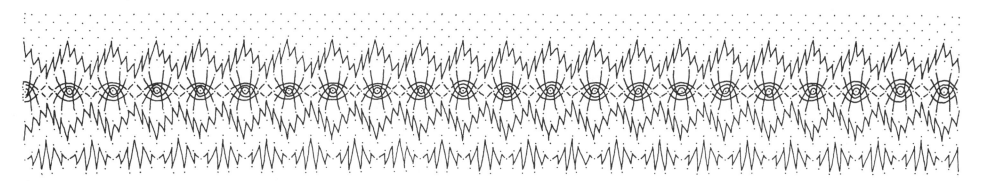

PLEATED LACE FANS.

I have designed several quite wide Torchon edgings which can be stiffened and pleated into a fan shape. There are two sizes to choose from. For one of the small fans I used gold Clair as the fan worker, the outside fan passive and one zigzag trail worker. The zigzag trail closest to the footside I worked with a Metallise worker pair wound with two thicknesses of the pearly white opalescent thread. The second small fan was worked with Metallise workers and outside fan passive, but I had fun combining two different shades of blue thread so that the colours became paler towards the centre. This was achieved by selecting a very pale blue and a mid blue Metallise. The fan worker and passive at the outside edge were worked with two strands of the darker blue. The inner zigzag trail was worked with two strands of the paler blue, but the worker pair for the zigzag trail inbetween was wound with one strand of the pale blue and one strand of the mid blue. So instead of cutting one long length of a single colour and folding it in half, cut two shorter lengths, one in each of the two colours and wind them onto the bobbin together. The gradual shading on the finished piece looks most effective. I used a similar principle for the third small fan which I worked using two strands of pink for the fan and outer fan passive, one shade of the same pink and one strand of pearly white for the worker of the first zigzag trail and two strands of the pearly white for the worker of the inner zigzag trail. Although there are several shades of pink and blue available there are fewer greens for example, so for the larger sized fan with the diamonds of Rose Ground I achieved a similar graded effect by using the pearly white thread as a second colour, the two combining to make a paler green for the two trails, which on this occasion were both worked in the same shade. The larger fan with zigzag bands of Rose Ground is worked with a combination of two different pinks. The one with blocks of small spiders I worked in two shades of pale blue. Using a mixture of these fine metallic threads in this way, together with the silver and gold Clair (which I find gives a purer colour than the gold and silver Metallise in this instance) I think you can find some really exciting combinations. So having planned your colour scheme cut the following thread lengths.

The pricking for the large lace fans has to be given in two halves. Simply photocopy both sections and stick the final row of pinholes on the first half over the first row of pinholes on the second half.

SMALL LACE FAN.

For the smaller edging you will need:-

1 pair of DMC Clair in gold or silver or a doubled length of DMC Metallise as the fan worker. Cut 1 x 4yd (3.75m) length of Clair or 1 x 8yd (7.5m) length of Metallise which must be folded in half and wound onto the bobbins double. As an 8 yard length is difficult to handle without tangling you may find it easier to cut two 4 yard lengths.

1 pair of the same thread for the outside fan passive. Cut 1 x 1yd (1m) length.

2 pairs of the same thread for the zigzag trail workers. Cut 2 x 4yd (3.75m) lengths of Clair or 2 x 8yd (7.5m) lengths of Metallise which is wound onto the bobbins double.

1 pair of the same thread for the footside passive pair. Cut 1 x 1yd (1m) of Clair or 1 x 2yd (2m) length of Metallise which again is used double.

22 pairs of 36/2 Brok for the ordinary passives. Cut 22 x 1¼yd (110cm) lengths.

WORKING INSTRUCTIONS

Place a support pin in each of the 15 pinholes marked along the starting edge. Whenever two pairs are hung around the same pin interlink them in the following way. Push the first pair to the left and put the second pair down on its right. Twist the centre two threads twice and twist each pair once.

Hang the pairs on in the following order starting at the left. On pin 1 hang the outside fan passive and then an ordinary white passive pair. On pin 2 first hang on the fan worker and then a white passive. Hang two ordinary white passives on pin 3. On pin 4 first hang one white passive pair and then the worker for the middle zigzag trail. Hang two pairs of white passives on pin 5. On pin 6 hang just one white passive pair. Hang two white passive pairs on pins 7, 8 and 9. On pin 10 hang a single white passive pair. Hang two ordinary passive pairs on pin 11. On pin 12 hang the worker for the inner zigzag trail and then an ordinary passive pair. Hang two ordinary passives on pin 13. The footside passive pair is hung on pin 14. On pin 15 hang the final two white passives and twist them both twice after interlinking them in the usual way. The lefthand of these two pairs now becomes the worker and cloth stitches all the way across to pin 16 and then back to pin 17 where the footside is made up by twisting the worker twice before and after cloth stitching through the footside edge pair (the pair remaining at pin 15). The old edge pair is twisted twice and the footside passive pair once. Again the lefthand pair will be the new worker.

Now you must work the row of pinholes which will provide the 'fold line' for the tiny hem which neatens the starting and finishing edges. Again start at the lefthand end of the row and bring the outside fan passive straight through the two cloth stitch rows and twist it once before and after pin 18 which is put up between the two threads of this pair. Next take the white passive pair from pin 1 and the fan worker from pin two and twist both pairs once, then work a half stitch, pin, half stitch at pin 19. You will use the same stitch sequence wherever two pairs come together to work a pin on this row. Where there is only a single pair at a pin twist that pair once before and after placing the pin between the two threads of the pair. You will use two pairs to work pins 20, 21, 22, 26, 27, 31 and 32. You will have single pairs at pins 23, 24, 25, 28, 29, 30 and 33. The footside passive pair remains untouched during this row.

Go back to pin 17 and pick up the new worker and cloth stitch it across to pin 34 where it is twisted twice. Work it back to the footside edge and twist it twice before making a cloth stitch with the footside edge pair. Twist both pairs twice and put up pin 35 to the left of both pairs. Bring the lefthand of these two pairs through the footside passive pair with a cloth stitch, twist the footside passive once and the old footside edge pair, which now comes into the area of ground, twice. Now twist the two pairs lying immediately to the left of this pair (one is originally from pin 33 and the other is the righthand pair from pin 32) and make a Torchon ground stitch (half stitch, pin, half stitch and twist) at pin 36. Take the righthand pair from pin 36 and make a ground stitch at pin 37 with the old edge pair which has now entered the ground. Now take the righthand pair out through the footside passive pair (twist the footside passive pair once and the 'worker' pair [from pin 37] twice) cloth stitch through the footside edge pair, twist both pairs twice and put up pin 38 to the left of both pairs. The lefthand pair now cloth stitches through the footside passive and is twisted twice so that it is ready to enter the ground at the end of the next diagonal row.

Start the next row by putting one twist on the righthand pair from pin 31 and the remaining pair from pin 32, and making ground stitches at pins 39-42 inclusive. Make up the footside in the same way as already described and put up pin 43. This section of ground is now complete.

To start the inner zigzag trail twist the trail worker twice and put up pin 44 to its left. You can now work the first row of the trail cloth stitching through the four white passive pairs to the left. Twist the workers twice and put up pin 45 at the end of the row. Work back through the same four pairs and then work a cloth stitch with the pair from pin 39, twist the workers twice and put up pin 46. Work back through just four pairs of passives, leaving out the last pair from the previous row which now leaves the trail between pins 45 and 47. Continue working the trail in this way taking in a new pair at the righthand end of each row and leaving a pair out at the lefthand end. When the workers reach pin 51 leave them here and add two twists to each of the passive pairs leaving the trail after pins 45, 47 and 49. Now start work on the spider at the lefthand side of the edging.

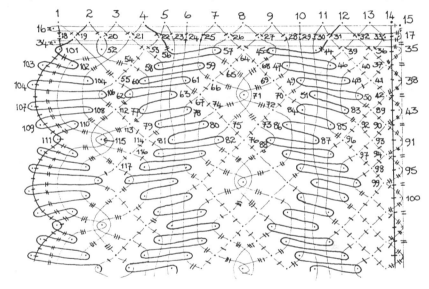

Above: Working diagram for the small lace fan edging.

Put up pin 52 between the two pairs from pin 20. These two pairs together with one passive pair on the right and the left of them make up the four pairs required for the spider. So cloth stitch the two pairs on the left of pin 52 through the two pairs lying to its right then twist all four pairs three times to make the spider legs. Twist the pair from pin 21 and the lefthand pair from pin 22 once and work a ground stitch at pin 53. Take the lefthand pair from this pin and work ground stitches with the two spider legs at pins 54 and 55. You can now start the second zigzag trail.

Take the worker from pin 22 and twist it twice. Put up pin 56 to its right and work the first row across to pin 57 through four pairs of passives. Work back across and take in a new pair from pin 53 before putting up pin 58. Work back through the first four pairs of passives, leaving one out at the righthand end of the row. Continue until the worker

reaches pin 63. Leave it here and twist each passive leaving the trail after pins 57, 59 and 61, twice. Now return to the two pairs remaining at pins 26 and 27. Twist them both once and make a ground stitch at pin 64. Now work two short diagonal rows of ground, one to the left - pins 65-67 and the other to the right - pins 68-70. Add one extra twist (to make a total of three twists) to each of the four spider legs (from pins 65, 66, 68 and 69) and work the spider putting up the centre pin at 71. Complete the second half of the spider and add three twists to each leg. Now work the surrounding ground pins at 72, 73, 74, 75 and 76.

Once this spider and ground is complete you can work the next two sections of the zigzag trails - pins 77-82 and 83-88, followed by the area of ground between the inner trail and the footside pins 89-100. Don't forget to add two twists to the passives as they leave the trail so that they are ready to go into the ground.

To start the fan take the fan worker and the outside fan passive (on its left) and make a cloth stitch. Put up pin 101 between the pairs. The fan worker is now lying to the left of the pin. Cloth stitch it through the outside fan passive and twist the passive once and the worker twice. Cloth stitch through the first spider leg, twist the worker twice because it is the end of the row and put up pin 102. Work back to pin 103 remembering to twist the worker twice between the ordinary passive and the outside fan passive, and to twist the outside passive once after the worker has cloth stitched through it. Continue the fan taking in a new pair at the righthand end of each row upto and including pin 106. After this one pair will be left out at the righthand end of each row until the worker arrives at pin 111 and the fan is complete.

Leaving the worker at pin 111 twist the pair coming out of the fan after pin 106 twice, and the pairs leaving the fan after pins 108 and 110 three times as these will be used as spider legs. Now work the row of ground through pins 112, 113 and 114, making sure that the pairs which have just left the trail (after pins 62, 77 and 79 and 81) have two twists on them before making the three ground stitches. Add an extra twist to the pairs from pins 112 and 113. You can now work the spider putting up pin 115 in the centre of its body. Complete the spider in the usual way and work the enclosing ground stitches at pins 116 and 117.

You have now worked a whole repeat of the pattern, so by following the previous instructions and the working diagram I hope you will be able to complete the length needed for this project.

Left: Enlarged photocopy of the start of the small fan edging.

Pricking for the small lace fan edging.

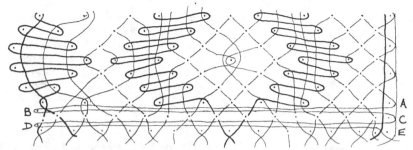

Above: Working diagram for the finish of the small fan edging.

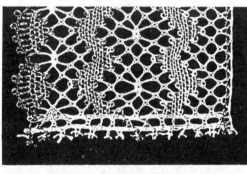

Above: Enlarged photocopy of the finish of the small fan edging.

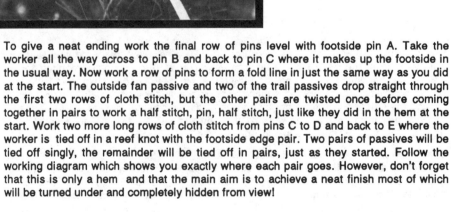

Small lace fans.

To give a neat ending work the final row of pins level with footside pin A. Take the worker all the way across to pin B and back to pin C where it makes up the footside in the usual way. Now work a row of pins to form a fold line in just the same way as you did at the start. The outside fan passive and two of the trail passives drop straight through the first two rows of cloth stitch, but the other pairs are twisted once before coming together in pairs to work a half stitch, pin, half stitch, just like they did in the hem at the start. Work two more long rows of cloth stitch from pins C to D and back to E where the worker is tied off in a reef knot with the footside edge pair. Two pairs of passives will be tied off singly, the remainder will be tied off in pairs, just as they started. Follow the working diagram which shows you exactly where each pair goes. However, don't forget that this is only a hem and that the main aim is to achieve a neat finish most of which will be turned under and completely hidden from view!

48

LARGE LACE FANS.

Although there are three pattern variations of suitable width all require identical lengths of thread.

1 pair of DMC Clair Argent or Or (silver or gold) or a doubled length of DMC Metallise as fan workers. Cut 1 x 6½yd (6m) length of Clair or 1 x 13yd (12m) length of Metallise to be halved and wound onto the bobbins double.

1 pair of the same thread as the outside fan passive. Cut 1 x 1¾yd (160cm) length of Clair or 1 x 3½yd (3.25m) length of Metallise to be used double.

2 pairs of the same thread for the trail workers. Cut 2 x 5yd (4.75m) lengths of Clair or 2 x 10yd (9.5m) of Metallise again to be used double.

1 pair of the same thread for the footside passive pair. Cut 1 x 1¼yd (110cm) length of Clair or 1 x 2½yd (220cm) length of Metallise used double.

28 pairs of 36/2 Brok as ordinary passives. Cut 28 x 1¾yd (160cm) lengths.

Pricking for the large lace fan with Rose Ground zigzag.

First section from start.   Second section to finish.

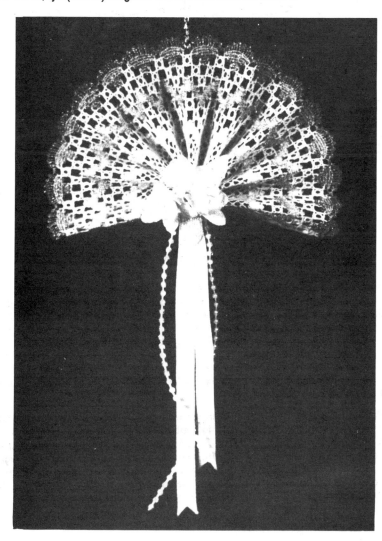

Large lace fan with Rose Ground zigzag.

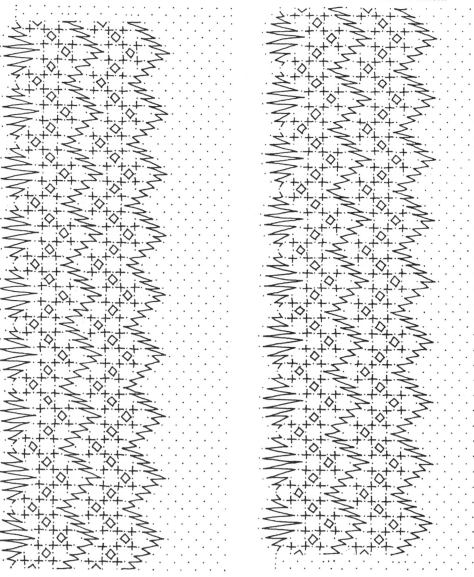

ROSE GROUND ZIGZAG DESIGN.

WORKING INSTRUCTIONS

Put up a pin in each of the 18 pinholes across the top of the pricking and hang on the pairs in this order starting at the lefthand edge. Wherever you hang two pairs on the same pin you must interlink them and then twist each pair once. On pin 1 hang the outside fan passive pair and push it to the left, hang one ordinary white passive pair from the same pin and interlink the two pairs by twisting the centre two threads twice before adding one twist to each pair. On pin 2 hang the fan worker and then an ordinary passive pair and interlink them in the same way. Hang two white passives on each of pins 3 and 4, but hang one pair only on pin 5, then two white pairs on pin 6. On pin 7 hang first the worker for the middle zigzag trail and then one white pair. Hang two white pairs on pins 8 and 9, but only one white pair on pin 10. Hang two white pairs on pin 11. On pin 12 first hang the worker for the inner zigzag trail and then one white pair. Hang two white pairs on each of pins 13, 14, 15 and 16. Hang the footside passive pair on pin 17 and the remaining two white pairs on pin 18. Interlink these last two pairs in the usual way and then add two twists to each pair as the righthand pair will be the footside edge pair and the lefthand will start off as the worker, cloth stitching all the way across towards pin 19 where it is twisted twice before working back to pin 20 where it cloth stitches through the footside passive pair (which is always twisted once) before being twisted twice and making a cloth stitch with the footside edge pair. Both pairs are twisted twice and pin 20 is put up to the left of both pairs. Cloth stitch the new worker (the lefthand pair at pin 20) through the footside passive pair and twist the worker twice and the passive once as usual. Leave the workers here for the moment.

Now starting at the lefthand edge work the row of pins which will form the 'fold line' for the tiny hem which will neaten both your starting and finishing edges. The outside fan passive pair will come straight down and be twisted once before and after pin 21 which will be placed between the two threads of this pair. The white passive from pin 1 will now come together with the fan workers from pin 2 to work pin 22. Where two pairs meet at one of these pinholes twist each pair once, then work a half stitch, pin, half stitch. You will use the same sequence at pins 23 and 24, but at pins 25, 26 and 27 a single pair is brought straight down through the two rows of cloth stitch and are twisted once before and after the pin which is simply put up between the two threads of the pair. Pins 28, 29 and 30 are worked in the twist, half stitch, pin, half stitch sequence. Pins 31, 32 and 33 are again put up between single pairs. Pins 34-38 are worked in the usual two pair way and pin 39 as a single pair. Now pick up the worker from just inside the footside passive pair and work two more rows of cloth stitch, bringing it back to pin 41 where the footside is made up by cloth stitching the worker straight through the footside passive pair. Twist the passive pair once and the worker twice. Now cloth stitch the worker and the footside edge pair together and twist both twice. Cloth stitch the new worker pair (the lefthand pair from pin 41) through the footside passive pair and twist it once, the footside passive pair is twisted once as usual. The pair immediately to the left of the footside passive pair is now ready to go into the ground.

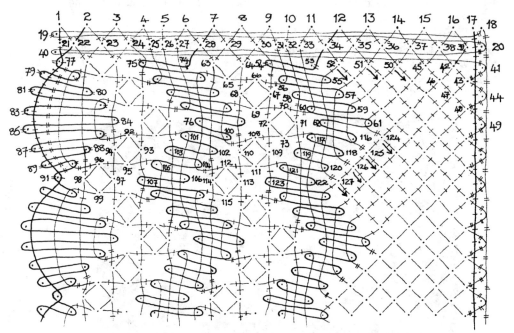

Above: Working diagram for the start of the Rose Ground zigzag design.

Start the area of ground at pin 42 by taking the two white passive pairs (one from pin 39 and one from 38), twist them once and make a Torchon ground stitch (half stitch, pin, half stitch and twist). The righthand pair from this pin now works diagonally down towards pin 44, making a second ground stitch at pin 43. Make up the footside as usual before putting up pin 44 and bring the old edge pair through the footside passive pair twisting it twice so that it is ready to be used in the ground. Now start the next row of ground at pin 45, working all the way down to pin 49. Start the next row at pin 50 and work it all the way down until it reaches the footside edge. Do exactly the same from pins 51 and 52.

To start the first zigzag trail twist the worker from pin 34 twice and put up pin 53 to its left. Now cloth stitch through the next four pairs of passives (from pins 30-33), twist twice at the end of the row and put up pin 54. Continue working to and fro across the trail following the markings on the pattern. You will take in one new pair at the righthand end of each row and leave out one pair at the lefthand end of each row. Leave the worker at pin 62 and twist each pair leaving the trail twice (after pins 54, 56, 58 and 60). You can now start the Rose Ground filling between the two trails.

Make a half stitch, pin, half stitch at pins 63, 64 and 65. (For pin 63 use the righthand pair from pin 28 and the lefthand pair from pin 29. For pin 64 use the lefthand pair from pin 30 and the righthand pair from pin 29. Pin 65 is worked with the righthand pair from pin 63 and the lefthand pair from pin 64. Now take the righthand pair from pin 65 and the pair left at pin 64 and make a cloth stitch and twist, but do not put up a pin. Do the same with the two pairs left at pins 63 and 65. These are the 'preparation' stitches required for Rose Ground which are indicated on the pattern with a cross. The little diamond shape indicates the four pins which are worked in a half stitch, pin, half stitch sequence. This is the version of Rose Ground which I have chosen to use, but of course there is no reason why you should not use one of the many other versions which will fit into this pattern just as well. Make preparation stitches with the two pairs leaving the trail at pins 54 and 56, and 58 and 60. Now work the four half stitch, pin, half stitch, sequences at pins 66, 67, 68 and 69. As soon as the 'diamond' is complete work the preparation stitches on the remaining two sides (using the righthand pair from pin 69 and the pair left at pin 67 on the right of the diamond, and the pairs from pins 68 and 69 on the left).You can now work the next diamond at pins 70, 71, 72 and 73. Again complete the 'preparation' stitches before moving on to the next section. Remembering to make the four 'preparation' stitches which surround each diamond is the hardest part about Rose Ground, so do check carefully as you go, and if you think your filling isn't looking quite as it should, then it is worth checking first to see if you have omitted some of these vital stitches.

Start the middle zigzag trail at pin 74 which is positioned to the left of the worker pair which has been twisted twice. Work through the four white passives immediately on the left of the workers before putting up pin 75. Continue in just the same way as you worked the previous trail until the workers arrive at pin 76. Leave them here and twist each of the four pairs leaving the trail along the lefthand edge, twice.

Work the first section of the Rose Ground filling between the middle zigzag trail and the headside fans in precisely the same way as you worked the previous area of Rose Ground (pins 63-73). You are now ready to work the first fan. Make a cloth stitch with the outside fan passive and the fan worker and put up pin 77, twist the passive once and the worker twice and follow this twist pattern at the outside edge at the beginning and end of every row throughout the fan. When the workers reach pin 91 the fan is complete, so leave the workers here and twist each passive leaving the lower edge of the fan (after pins 84, 86, 88 and 90) twice. Now use these four pairs to make the usual 'preparation' stitches. You can now work the next two diamonds of Rose Ground - pins 92-99. Once this section of Rose Ground is complete you can work the next section of the middle zigzag trail - pins 100-107. Twist the pairs coming out of the trail twice and then work the next section of Rose Ground - pins 108-115. This will allow you to then work on the second section of the inner zigzag trail - pins 116-123. Again remember to twist the pairs leaving the trail twice and they are then ready to be worked into the ground, so start the next series of diagonal ground rows at pin 124. Work similar rows starting from pins 125, 126 and 127. When this section of ground is complete you will have finished a whole repeat and should now be able to continue with the aid of the working diagram.

Below: Working diagram for the finish of the Rose Ground zigzag design.

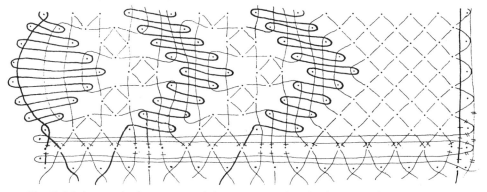

The finish is merely the reverse of the start, so after the last row of pattern pinholes, work two rows of cloth stitch before tackling the 'fold line' row of pins. Three of the trail passives will drop singly through the cloth stitch, but the other pairs will work through diagonally and meet up with a second pair to make a twist, half stitch, pin and half stitch. Work two more rows of cloth stitch and then tie each pair off with a reef knot at the row of finishing pins.

Above: Photocopy of the Rose Ground zigzag design.

DIAMONDS OF ROSE GROUND DESIGN.

WORKING INSTRUCTIONS

Whenever two pairs are hung from the same pin they must be interlinked by putting the bobbins of the second pair down to the right of the first pair and twisting the centre two threads twice. One twist is then added to both pairs. Starting at the lefthand side hang on the following bobbins. First hang the outside fan passive and then an ordinary white passive on pin 1. On pin 2 hang the fan worker and then a white passive pair. Hang a single white passive pair on pin 3, and two white passive pairs on pin 4. Hang the middle zigzag worker and then a white passive pair from pin 5. Hang two pairs of white passives on each of pins 6 and 7. Hang a white passive pair and then the inner zigzag trail worker on pin 8. Hang two pairs of white passives on pin 9 and a single pair of white passives from pin 10. Two pairs of white passives are hung on pins 11, 12, 13, 14, 15 and 16. The footside passive pair goes on pin 17 and the remaining two white passives on pin 18. Add an extra twist to both pairs on pin 18 and take the lefthand pair as the worker, the righthand pair remains at pin 18 as the footside edge pair. Work two rows of cloth stitch, taking the worker across to pin 19 and back to pin 20 where you must make up the footside by cloth stitching the worker pair through the footside passive and twisting it twice. The footside passive is always twisted once. Now make a cloth stitch with the worker and the footside edge pair. Twist both pairs twice and put up pin 20 inside both pairs on their left. Make a cloth stitch with the lefthand pair and the footside passive, as always this passive is twisted once but on this occasion the new worker is not twisted after this stitch.

Now work the row of pinholes which form the 'fold line' for the narrow hems which neaten both the starting and the finishing edges. Where there are two pairs arriving at one of these pinholes twist them both once and work a half stitch, pin, half stitch. Where there is only one pair twist it once and put up the pin between the two threads before twisting the pair once more. Again start at the lefthand side. The outside fan passive works straight through the two rows of cloth stitch to pin 21. The white pair from pin 1 and the fan worker from pin 2 now join at pin 22. The white pair from pin 2, the single pair from pin 3 and the lefthand white pair from pin 4 now work single pins 23, 24 and 25. The other pair from pin 4 and the middle zigzag worker come together at pin 26. Using the white pairs from pins 5 and 6, 6 and 7, and 7 and 8 work pins 27, 28 and 29. The inner zigzag trail worker from pin 8 and the lefthand white pair from pin 9 are used to work pin 30. The other pair at pin 9, the pair from pin 10 and the lefthand pair from pin 11 work single pins at 31, 32 and 33. Two white passives will come together to work each of pins 34-38 inclusive. The final white pair (originally from pin 16) is worked as a single pair at pin 39. The footside passive pair stays unused.

Pick up the worker from just inside the footside pair after pin 20, and work two rows of cloth stitch to pin 40 and back to the footside edge at pin 41. Take the worker through the footside passive pair and twist the worker twice and the passive once. Now make a cloth stitch with the footside edge pair. Twist both pairs twice and put up pin 41 to their left. Cloth stitch the lefthand pair through the footside passive pair, twist the passive once and the other pair, which now enters the ground, twice. You can now make a series of diagonal rows of ground starting from pin 42. Before making the first ground stitch in each row twist both pairs once, then make the usual Torchon ground stitch (half stitch, pin, half stitch and twist). The first row will start at pin 42 using the righthand pair from pin 38 and the single pair from 39. Pin 43 will be worked with the righthand pair from pin 42 and the pair which has just entered the ground after footside pin 41. Make

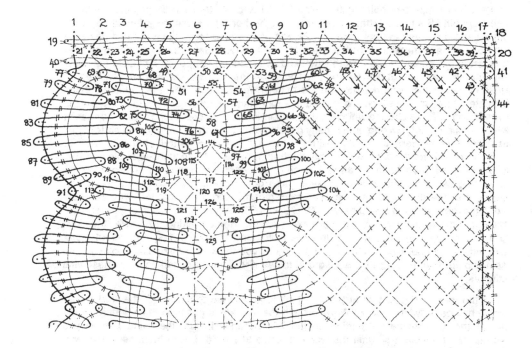

up the footside pin 44 in just the same way as you did at pin 41. You can then start the next row of ground working diagonally down from pin 45. Work three more complete rows of ground starting at pins 46, 47 and 48, each row will finish at the footside edge pin. You must now move across to the diamond shaped area of Rose Ground.

Take the righthand pair from pin 26 and the lefthand pair from pin 27 and make a half stitch, pin, half stitch at pin 49. Using the remaining pair from pin 27 and the lefthand pair from pin 28 do the same at pin 50. Now bring the centre two pairs (the righthand pair from pin 49 and the lefthand pair from pin 50) together and do the same at pin 51. This completes the part of the Rose Ground diamond which is normally indicated by a small diamond drawn in the centre of four pin holes. (This particular one has only three pinholes because the fourth hole was cut off by the rows of cloth stitch.) Do the same at pinholes 52, 53 and 54 using the righthand pair from pin 28, both pairs from pin 29 and the white passive pair from pin 30. To make Rose Ground filling it is essential to remember to work the 'preparation' stitches which surround each small diamond. There are normally four, one at each edge of the diamond, and they are indicated on the pattern by a small cross. In the version of Rose Ground which I chose for this project the preparation stitch consists of a cloth stitch and twist, so using the pair from pin 49 and the lefthand pair from pin 51 make the first of the preparation stitches. Similar stitches must be worked with the pairs from pins 50 and 51, 52 and 54, and 53 and 54. It's a good idea to get into the habit of working all the concluding preparation stitches before regarding the area of Rose Ground as complete. The pairs are now in the correct position to work the next four pinholes of half stitch, pin, half stitch. For this diamond you will use the four centre pairs (from the two central preparation stitches). The centre two pairs (one from the lefthand and one from the righthand preparation stitch originally from pins 51 and 54) will work pin 55, the remaining pair from the lefthand preparation stitch now joins with the lefthand pair from pin 55 to work pin 56. The other pair from pin 55 and the remaining pair from the righthand preparation stitch will work pin 57. The two central pairs (the righthand pair from pin 56 and the lefthand pair from pin 57) will work pin 58. This area of Rose Ground is not complete until you have worked the final two preparation stitches, the first is worked with the pair from pin 56 and the lefthand pair from pin 58. The pair from pin 57 and the other pair from pin 58 make the final cloth stitch and twist. The Rose Ground diamond is now complete.

To start the inner zigzag trail twist the worker (from pin 30) twice and put up pin 59 to its right. Cloth stitch the workers across through the four pairs of white passives lying to the right, twist them twice at the end of the row and put up pin 60. Work back across towards pin 61 and take in the righthand of the pairs from the preparation stitch which followed pins 53 and 54. Now put up pin 61 before cloth stitching back through only four pairs of passives and putting up pin 62. Continue in this way taking in a new pair at the lefthand end of every row and leaving one pair out at the righthand end of each row. When the worker reaches pin 67 leave it and twist each of the pairs which have left the trail (after pins 60, 62, 64 and 66) twice.

Now start the trail on the other side of the Rose Ground diamond. Twist the worker (from pin 26) twice and put up pin 68 to the left of it. Cloth stitch through the four pairs of white passives lying on the left, twist the worker twice here (and at the end of every row) and put up pin 69. Continue working taking in a new pair at the righthand end of each row and leaving one out at the lefthand end of every row. Leave the workers at pin 76 and twist each of those passives leaving the trail after pins 69, 71, 73 and 75, twice. You are now ready to start the fan.

Make a cloth stitch with the outside fan passive and the fan workers and put up pin 77 between the two pairs. Twist the passive once and the worker twice. Cloth stitch the worker through the outside fan passive and again twist the worker twice and the passive once, then cloth stitch through the pair of white passives which left the trail after pin 69. Twist the fan worker twice and put up pin 78. Continue to work the fan remembering to twist the workers twice between the outside fan passive and the ordinary white passives and at the end of every row. The outside fan passive is twisted once after each cloth stitch. The fan continues to get wider, and therefore takes in a new pair at the righthand end of each row upto and including pin 84, from then on one pair of passives is left out at the righthand end of each row. Twist these passives twice as they leave the fan. Leave the worker at pin 91 and go back to the area of Torchon ground at the opposite edge of the lace.

Check that the pairs from pins 60, 62, 64 and 66 have retained their two twists and start on the next complete rows of ground working diagonally down towards the footside edge. The first row will commence at pin 92, the next at 93, then 94 and finally 95. You can then continue with the next section of the inner zigzag trail, picking up the worker at pin 67 and working on until you reach pin 104. Leave the workers here and move over to the second section of the middle zigzag trail working pins 105-113. You can now work the diamond of Rose Ground between the two trails beginning with the all-important preparation stitches using the pairs leaving the trail after pins 76 and 106, 108 and 110 on the left and 67 and 97, 99 and 101 on the right. Work the first small diamond of half

Below: Large lace fan with diamonds of Rose Ground.

stitches at pins 114-117. Make two more preparation stitches and then work the half stitch pins 118-121 and 122-125. Make four preparation stitches after this before working the final diamond of half stitches at pins 126-129. Two more preparation stitches complete the larger Rose Ground diamond. You have now worked a whole repeat and with the aid of the working diagram should be able to continue, but if you need more detailed instructions you can go back to pin 60 which corresponds to pin 104.

Pricking for the diamonds of Rose Ground design.

Above: First section from the start.

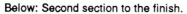
Below: Second section to the finish.

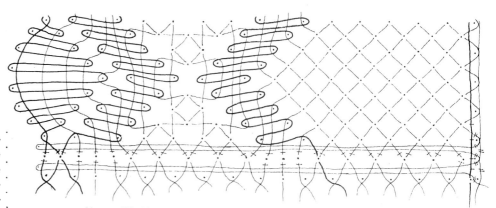

Above: Working diagram for the finish of the Rose Ground diamonds.

Continue working until the pattern pins of the pricking are complete. The two rows of finishing pins are worked in a similar manner to the starting rows, but in reverse. The working diagram will show you which pairs will come through the two rows of cloth stitch single and which will be worked as part of a pair. Work two more rows of cloth stitch and then tie off each pair around a pin in the final row.

Above: Photocopy of the Rose Ground diamonds design.

BLOCKS OF SPIDERS DESIGN.

Large fan with blocks of spiders.

Pricking for the large fan with blocks of spiders.

Above: First section from start.

Below: Second section to finish.

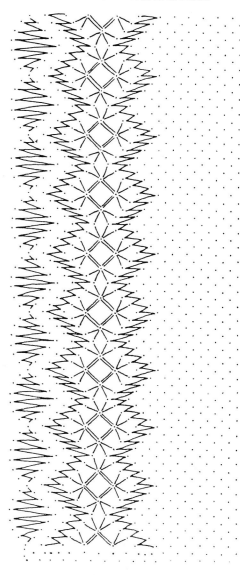

WORKING INSTRUCTIONS FOR THE FAN WITH BLOCKS OF FOUR SPIDERS.

Hang the pairs on the starting pins positioned along the top edge of the pricking. Wherever two pairs are hung on the same pin make sure that the first pair is pushed to the left so that the second pair lies to its right. Twist the centre two threads twice to interlink the pairs and then twist each pair once.

On pin 1 first hang the outside fan passive pair, and then an ordinary white passive pair. Hang the fan worker and then a white passive pair on pin 2. Hang a single white passive pair on pin 3, and two white passives on pin 4. Hang the middle trail worker followed by a white passive pair on pin 5. Hang two white passives on pins 6 and 7. Hang a white passive and then the inner trail worker on pin 8. Hang two pairs of white passives on pin 9, one on pin 10, and then two on each of pins 11-16 inclusive. Hang the footside passive pair on pin 17 and the last two pairs of white passives on pin 18, but add an extra twist to each pair once they are interlinked, to make a total of two twists on each pair.

Take the lefthand pair from pin 18 as your workers and cloth stitch them across to pin 19. Twist the workers twice before cloth stitching back across towards pin 20. Once you have worked through the footside passive pair twist the passive once and the workers twice before cloth stitching through the footside edge pair (the pair remaining at pin 18). Twist both pairs twice and put up pin 20 to the left of both pairs. Make a cloth stitch with the left hand pair and the footside passive pair. Twist the passive pair once but do not twist the new worker pair at all. Now work the row of pins which will form the 'fold-line' of this tiny hem which is used to neaten both the starting and finishing edges of the fan.

Whenever a single pair arrives at one of these 'fold-line' pinholes twist it once before and after placing the pin, which is positioned between the two threads of the pair. When two pairs meet at one of these pinholes then twist each pair once before making a half stitch, pin, half stitch. Starting at the left work the pins in the following manner. The outside fan passive is on its own at pin 21. The white passive pair from pin 1 and the fan worker from pin 2 are used to work pin 22. The white passive pair from pin 2 comes singly to pin 23, as does the single passive from pin 3 and the lefthand passive from pin 4 at pins 24 and 25 respectively. The other passive from pin 4 meets the middle trail worker at pin 26. At pin 27 the other pair from pin 5 joins the lefthand passive from pin 6. Pins 28 and 29 are worked in a similar way with the pairs from pins 6 and 7, and 7 and 8. The inner trail worker from pin 8 meets the lefthand passive from pin 9 at pin 30. The next three white pairs arrive singly at pins 31, 32 and 33. Pins 35-38 inclusive are each worked with two white passive pairs from adjacent starting pinholes. The righthand pair from pin 16 arrives at pin 39 on its own. The footside passive remains in its position without a pin.

Pick up the worker from just inside the footside passive pair after pin 20 and cloth stitch it across to pin 40 and back again. Cloth stitch through the footside passive pair, twist the passive once and the worker twice before making a cloth stitch with the worker and the footside edge pair. Put up pin 41 to the left of both pairs. Twist both pairs twice and cloth stitch the lefthand pair through the footside passive pair which is again twisted once. Put two twists on the other pair so that it is ready to go into the ground. This completes the footside which should be worked in this way throughout the piece.

Below: Working diagram to show the start of the spider edging.

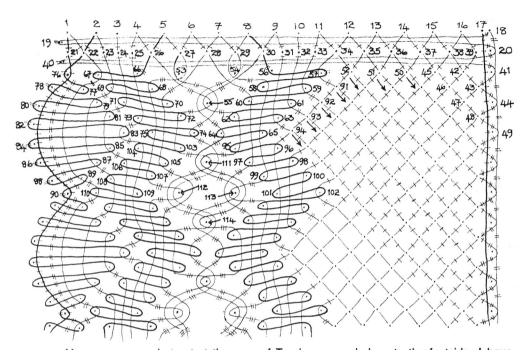

You are now ready to start the area of Torchon ground close to the footside. I have worked the ground throughout with a half stitch, pin, half stitch and twist. So starting at pin 42 make a ground stitch with the righthand pair from pin 38 and the pair from pin 39. The righthand pair from this pin now continues to do the same ground stitch at pin 43 with the pair which has just worked through the footside passive pair. The righthand pair now works through the footside passive pair and makes up the footside at pin 44. Don't forget that the footside is not complete until the new lefthand pair comes back through the footside passive and is twisted twice so that it is ready to go straight into the ground during the course of the next row. Start the next row at pin 45 and work diagonally down to the footside edge at pin 49. You will work three more whole rows starting at pins 50, 51 and 52 before switching your attention to the block of spiders between the two trails.

To start the spiders put up pins 53 with the righthand pair from pin 26 and the lefthand pair from pin 27 on the left of the pin and the righthand pair from pin 27 and the lefthand pair from pin 28 to the right. Now work the second half of the spider around pin 53, cloth stitching first one pair and then the other through the two pairs from the opposite side of the pin. Twist all four legs three times. Make a similar half spider around pin 54 using the four pairs from pins 28, 29 and the lefthand pair from pin 30. Once these two 'half spiders' are complete you can make a whole spider at pin 55 using the two righthand legs from spider 53 and the lefthand legs from 54. Don't forget to twist the spider legs three times once the cloth stitch body is complete. You can now start the zigzag trails.

The inner zigzag trail worker (from pin 30) is twisted twice and pin 56 is put up to its right. Now cloth stitch it through the four pairs of passives to its right. Twist it twice and put up pin 57. Work back across towards pin 58 but take in a new pair in the shape of the first spider leg from spider 54. Work back through only the first four pairs of passives and put up pin 59 at the end of the row. Continue in this way taking a new pair in at the lefthand end of every row and leaving one pair out at the righthand end of each row. Pause when the worker reaches pin 65 and twist the passive pairs which leave the trail after pins 57, 59, 61 and 63 twice so that they are ready to go into the ground. You are now ready to start the other trail.

Twist the middle zigzag trail worker (from pin 26) twice and put up pin 66 to its left. Work through the four pairs of passives immediately to its left and put up pin 67 after twisting the workers twice. Work to and fro following the zigzag markings on the pattern very carefully. This time new pairs will be added at the righthand end of each row and pairs will be left out at the lefthand end of each row. Leave the worker at pin 75 whilst you turn your attention to the outside fan, but don't forget to add two twists to the passives leaving the trail after pins 67, 69, 71 and 73 so that they are ready to go into the fan.

Make a cloth stitch with the outside fan passive and the fan worker and put up pin 76. Twist the worker twice and the passive once, you will follow this twist pattern throughout the piece. Now cloth stitch the two pairs together once more and again add two twists to the worker and one to the passive, cloth stitch through the incoming passive which left the trail after pin 67. Twist the worker twice and put up pin 77. Work back across to the outside of the fan remembering to twist the worker twice between the white passive and the outside fan passive. Again twist the outside passive once and the worker twice before putting up pin 78. Continue in this way taking in one new pair at the righthand end of each row until the worker reaches pin 83. After that one pair will leave the fan at the righthand end of every row until you arrive at pin 90 where you leave the worker. Put two twists on each of the passive pairs which leave the fan after pins 83, 85, 87 and 89. Now go back to the ground between the inner zigzag trail and the footside and work diagonally down to the footside edge starting a new row at pinholes 91, 92, 93 and 94.

Now work the next sections of each of the zigzag trails pins 95-102 and 103-110. Then you can work the block of four spiders centred around pins 111, 112, 113 and 114. The spiders are all worked with four pairs and each leg is twisted three times.

You have now finished the whole of one repeat so with the aid of the working diagram I hope you will be able to complete the length required for the fan. If you need more detailed instructions go back to pin 57 which corresponds to pin 102 at the point of the inner trail. At the end you will work four rows of cloth stitch across the whole width of the edging, in a very similar manner to the rows you worked at the start. Again you will need to work a row of 'fold-line' pinholes and you can see on the working diagram exactly which pairs drop singly through these cloth stitch rows and which meet up at the 'fold-line' pinholes in pairs. After the final two rows of cloth stitch the pairs are tied off with a reef knot.

Below: Photocopy of the finished spider edging.

Below: Working diagram for the finish of the spider edging.

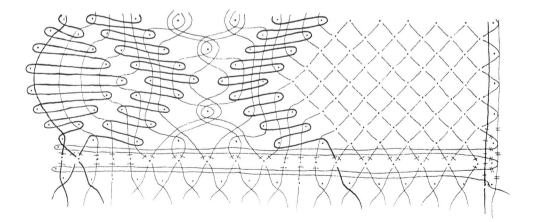

59

MAKING YOUR EDGING INTO A FAN.

Once the lace is off the pillow you can use some of the surplus thread lengths to stitch the tiny hem into place at both the starting and finishing edges. Fold the lace along the row of pinholes in the middle of the four long rows of cloth stitch. Use a fine needle and small running stitches to catch the underlap in place. Now you must decide how you are going to stiffen the lace. For two of the small sample fans I used a commercial spray starch . This stiffened the lace just sufficiently to give it a crispness which allowed me to make the necessary folds. I made no attempt to 'iron in' each fold, the pleats are far too small to do this accurately. Simply take the lace in your hands and make the first upwards fold along the row of pinholes which run level with the end of each fan and through the points of both trails. As you can see from the photographs folding it forwards along the first pleat line takes the two little hems to the back of the work, which makes them very inconspicuous. Continue folding to and fro until you have three or four pleats in your fingers, then stab stitch through the whole thickness just inside the footside passive pair. Several stitches will anchor all the pleats securely whilst you fold in the remaining ones. At the end stitch all firmly together and fasten off your thread.

As you can see from the photographs there is no visible difference between the small fans which were stiffened with spray starch and the one which was stiffened in a completely different way because the lightly stiffened finish of the spray starch was quite sufficient to hold the pleats in place. However spray starch on the larger fans was not so effective. You can see from the photographs that the one I stiffened in this way has not kept its shape so well and the ends have dropped quite considerably. I therefore experimented with a different method of stiffening which I have found to be very much more effective as it soaks into the lace and, when dry, leaves the lace as stiff as a piece of stiff paper. To make this stiffening solution I used one teaspoonful of the white woodworking glue 'Resin W' which I diluted with two teaspoonfuls of water. Mix it well on an old saucer and apply it to your lace with a fine sponge. I found the triangular make-up sponges ideal. As you are applying a liquid to the lace I do recommend that the lace is pinned out right side up on a block of polystyrene, putting a polythene bag between the polystyrene and the lace. I used fine, stainless steel pins pushed right down into the block and positioned every two or three repeats along both edges. This will prevent the lace from shrinking or losing its shape.

Dip the flat surface of your sponge into the diluted glue and gently press it on to the surface of your lace. There is no need to be over-generous, just make sure that all the threads have been covered before moving on to the next section. Leave the lace to dry overnight, but wash your saucer, mixing spoon and sponge immediately. Obviously this process is not reversible, so if you are at all unhappy about coating your lace with this solution, stick to the spray starch, but as you can see from the photographs, the two fans I stiffened in this way hold their shape beautifully and will have the strength to stand up to years of service on the Christmas tree! You might like to experiement on a length of machine made lace or an odd piece of hand made lace, before going ahead on the real thing. Alternatively you can purchase one of the commercial fabric stiffening preparations made in America.

Once your lace is completely dry remove the pins and lift the lace from the polystyrene. If you have been a little heavy handed with your stiffening solution you may have some extra flakes of dried glue between the diamonds of ground, I removed these by brushing it over with a clean, dry nailbrush. You can now fold the lace in the same way as the small fans, following the lines of pinholes at the end of each fan and through the point of the zigzag trail. I found it easiest to make all the folds in one direction, turn the lace over and then make all the folds in the opposite direction. Don't forget to make the first fold come towards you so that the hems finish towards the back of the fan. Once I had made all the folds I ran in two 'gathering' threads, one through the points of the front of each pleat, and one through the point at the back of each pleat, positioning the needle to go just behind the two twisted bars of the footside edge pin and between the footside edge pair and the coloured footside passive pair. When these two threads are pulled up tight and securely fastened off you'll see your fan beginning to take shape. I used one of these threads to ladder stitch the straight edges of the first and last pleat section together along their two footsides. When pulled tight this row of stitching forces the fan to remain in a beautifully open position. You can now add a variety of ribbons, roses, flowers, leaves and glittery thread with beads on the end. Attach a hanging loop between the two middle fans.

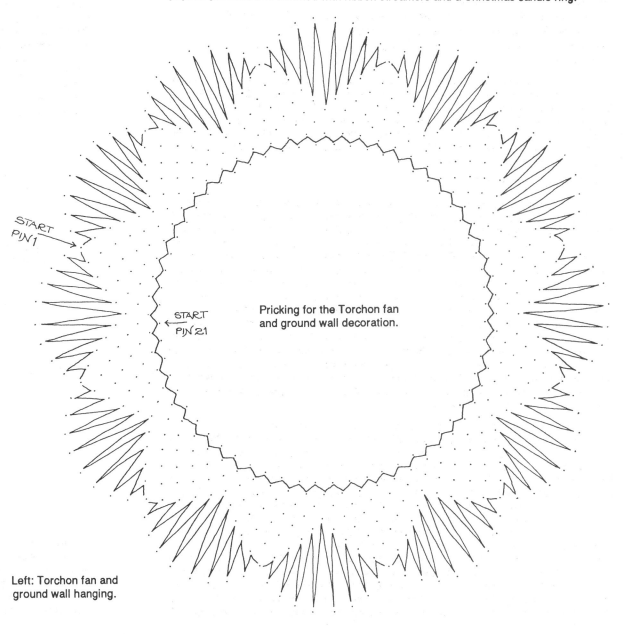

WALL DECORATION WITH TORCHON FAN AND GROUND EDGING.

This large scale Torchon circle worked entirely in silver and gold thread is mounted on a circular cork mat and trimmed with ribbon streamers and a Christmas candle ring.

START PIN 1

START PIN 21

Pricking for the Torchon fan and ground wall decoration.

Left: Torchon fan and ground wall hanging.

1 pair of Twilley's Gold Fingering as the fan worker pair. Cut 1 x 9½yd (9m) length wound onto Continental style bobbins to enable you to cope with such a long length of thick thread.

1 pair of Twilley's Gold Fingering in the same colour as the fan worker for the outside fan passive pair. Cut 1 x 2yd (2m) length

2 pairs of the same thread for the inner trail passives. Cut 2 x 1yd (1m) lengths.

1 pair of the same thread as the inner trail worker pair. Cut 1 x 2yd (2m) length.

6 pairs of Twilley's Gold Dust perhaps in a contrasting colour, for the passives. Cut 6 x 2yd (2m) lengths.

For the sample I used a gold and silver colour scheme. The fan worker and outside passive and both the passives and worker for the inner trail were in gold, and the six ordinary passive pairs were in silver. The heavier gold thread of the fan worker overwhelms the silver passives of the fan giving a predominantly gold effect, but the simple Torchon ground worked entirely in silver provided an interesting contrast. I used red, gold and silver ribbons which when combined with the Christmas colours of the candle ring gave a very festive effect.

WORKING INSTRUCTIONS.

Hang the outside fan passive pair on pin 1 and push it to the left. Hang the outside fan worker pair on the same pin and put these bobbins down to the right of the previous pair. Interlink the two pairs by twisting the centre two threads twice, the worker pair is now twisted twice, but the outside fan passive pair is not twisted at all. Hang the six ordinary passive pairs on pins A, B, C, D, E and T1. Now work the fan taking in one of the new passive pairs at the righthand end of each row, remembering to twist the worker twice between the outside passive and all the other fan passives. Do not remove pins A-E as you work the fan as these will preserve the starting loops of these five passive pairs which will make it much easier for you to finish the piece at the end. As the worker thread is so thick one twist at the end of each row will be sufficient. When the worker reaches pin 10 there will be a total of six passive pairs in the cloth stitch, five ordinary pairs plus the outside fan passive. After pin 10 once the worker has reached the pinhole at the outer edge, the passive pair at the righthand of each row will be pushed aside to leave the fan, so that by the time the worker reaches pin 19 at the end of the fan, only the outside fan passive will remain. Twist the five passive pairs leaving the fan twice so that they are ready to go into the ground.

Take the passive which left the fan after pin 10 and use it to make a Torchon ground stitch (half stitch, pin, half stitch and twist) with the pair from T1 at pin 20. When the stitch is complete you can remove the temporary pin (T1) and tension the lefthand pair to remove the starting loop. Now hang the trail worker pair on pin 21 and the two trail passives on pins F and G, again do not remove these pins as they'll make your finishing that much easier. Cloth stitch the worker pair through the two trail passives and straight through the righthand passive pair from pin 20. Twist the worker twice at the end of this row and put up pin 22. Now cloth stitch the worker back to pin 23. Leave it here whilst you twist the passive pair at the lefthand edge of the trail (which is only just 'visiting' the trail) twice so that as it leaves the trail it is immediately ready to join the ground. Now start the next row of ground at pin 24 using the pair which leaves the fan after pin 12 and the pair left at pin 20. For pin 25 use the righthand pair from pin 24 and the pair which has just left the trail after pin 22. Now pick up the trail workers from pin 23 and cloth stitch across through the three pairs lying to its left, two are the ordinary trail passives and the third will be the new incoming or 'visiting' pair of passives from the ground.

Twist the trail worker twice as usual and put up pin 26 before working back across the trail and leaving the worker at pin 27. Start the next row of ground at pin 28, the next at 33 and the final row of ground at pin 39. The triangle of ground is now complete and you are ready to start your next fan.

Continue round the circle in this way working alternate areas of fan and then ground. To join the edging bring each pair back to its own starting loop, so one of two trail worker threads will be brought through the starting loop at pin 21 and then both will be tied off with a reef knot. The inner of the two trail passives will be joined to the starting loop at G, and the outer to F. Five of the passive pairs will be joined into their own starting loops at pins A-E, and the sixth (which has just left the trail) will be tied into pin 20. The outside fan passive and the fan worker will be joined into pin 1. Tie off each pair securely with a reef knot and when the pins are removed and the lace is off the pillow you can trim off the surplus thread close to the knots.

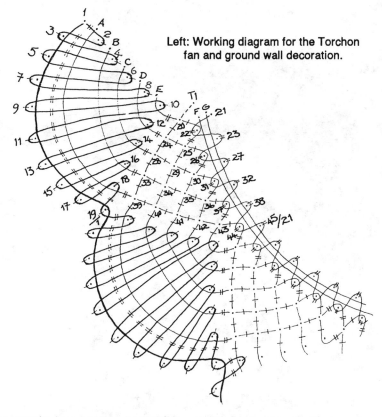

Left: Working diagram for the Torchon fan and ground wall decoration.

To mount the lace I used a cork 'drinks mat' approximately 4" (8cm) in diameter. Glue the wrong side of the trail and smooth the lace down so that it lies flat with the inner edge of the trail about 1/4" (5mm) in from the edge of the mat. Prepare the ribbon trim so that when it is pinned into place (lining it up with the centre point of the first fan it covers most of the join! You'll find that you now have a fan exactly opposite at the top of the circle so add a ribbon hanging loop so that it too sits at the centre of a fan. The hanging loop is a 6½" (16cm) piece of ribbon folded in half and simply glued onto the cork circle with a ¾" (2cm) overlap. I added a tiny loop of Gold Dust thread through this ribbon loop so that the whole decoration can lie flat against the wall from a pin or hook (hanging it up directly from the ribbon loop makes it want to turn sideways!) I put an old lace pin into the centre of the ribbon streamers 1/4" in from the edge of the mat, positioning it vertically so that it came away from the cork just enough to allow me to hook the plastic base of the candle ring over the pin. This way you can change the candle ring, ribbons and your colour scheme!

WINDOW OR WALL DECORATION WITH TORCHON FAN AND GROUND EDGING.

This decoration is made in much the same way as the previous one, but in place of the cork circle, it is worked around a 4" (10cm) metal ring. The lace itself is very simple consisting of the basic Torchon fan and ground, with the ground being joined to the ring at the inner edge of each row as you go along.

Below: Window or wall decoration with Torchon fan and ground edging.

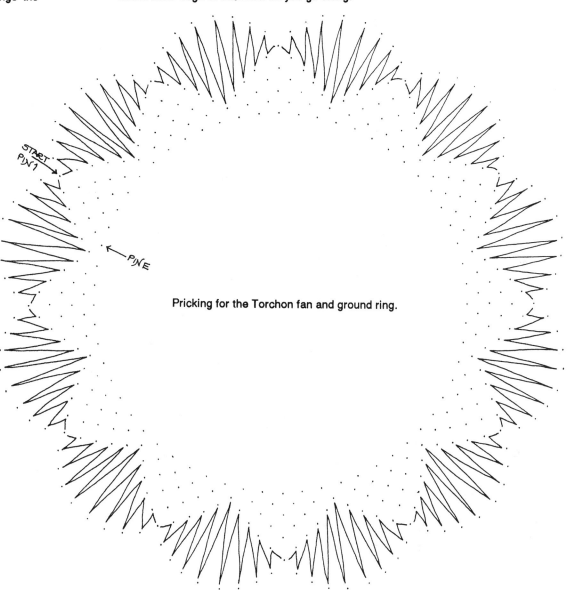

Pricking for the Torchon fan and ground ring.

1 pair of Twilley's Gold Fingering as the fan worker. Cut 1 x 9½yd (9m) length and wind it onto a pair of Continental style bobbins.
1 pair of Twilley's Gold Dust as the outside fan passive. Cut 1 x 2½yd (225cm) length.
5 pairs of Twilley's Gold Dust as ordinary passive pairs. Cut 5 x 2½yd (225cm) lengths.

I used silver thread for the fan worker pair and gold for all the other pairs. This gives the finished effect of a silver fan (as the thicker thread of the workers dominates the passives in the fan) with a gold triangle of ground. I sprayed the ring with gold paint so that the linking stitches going over the ring were less conspicuous. I bought a ready-made arrangement of bells and ribbon to hang from the top of the circle.

WORKING INSTRUCTIONS.

As the fan worker needs to be so long and the thread is extremely thick it's very important to use bobbins which are capable of accommodating such a quantity. None of my ordinary spangled East Midland type of bobbins would have coped with this sort of yardage, so I used a pair of Belgian style 'Continental' bobbins which proved quite satisfactory even if they do have a tendency to roll about on our domed pillows!

Wind the outside fan passive and 4 of the ordinary passive pairs in the normal way, but the fifth passive pair needs to be joined to the ring and it is easier to do this before winding the thread onto the bobbins. Take the length of thread and fold it in half to find the mid point, bring this loop up through the centre of the ring and open it out so that you can pass the two ends through the loop and pull it tight. Now position the pattern in the centre of your pillow and pin it down well. The ring is placed on the pricking so that you can just see the inner row of pinholes outside the ring. Don't worry if your ring does not appear to be perfectly circular when you place it on the pattern, in my experience metal rings rarely are, so be prepared to move ALL your pins forward as you work the lace (with the obvious exception of those in the most recently worked fan and area of ground) so that you can re-position the ring every two repeats or so. In this way the lace will shape itself to fit the ring. Pin the ring down in its starting position so that the thread you have just joined to it is at starting pinhole E and the inner row of pinholes on the pattern is correctly positioned for the first two repeats or so. Placing three or four pins close to the inner edge of the ring at roughly equal intervals around it should keep it steady. Push these pins well down so that they don't catch on the threads as you work. Place pin E in its correct position through the loop attaching the thread to the ring and wind on the last pair of bobbins. Twist this pair twice before you leave it to start the outside fan.

Hang the outside fan passive on pin 1 and push it to the left. Now hang the fan worker from the same pin and put the bobbins down to the right of the previous pair. Twist the centre two threads twice to interlink the two pairs. Now add one twist to the passive pair and two twists to the workers. Hang one of the four ordinary passive pairs on each of pins A, B, C and D. You can now work the fan in cloth stitch taking in one of the new pairs at the righthand end of each row as far as pin 8. At pin 10 you will take in the passive pair which was attached to the ring. From that pin on you will leave one pair out at the righthand end of each row until the worker reaches pin 19 at the end of the fan. Throughout the fan you must remember to twist the worker once at the end of every row, and twice between the outside fan passive and all the other fan passives. The outside fan passive is twisted once each time the worker cloth stitches through it. Take care with the tensioning of the fan as the workers are much thicker than usual.

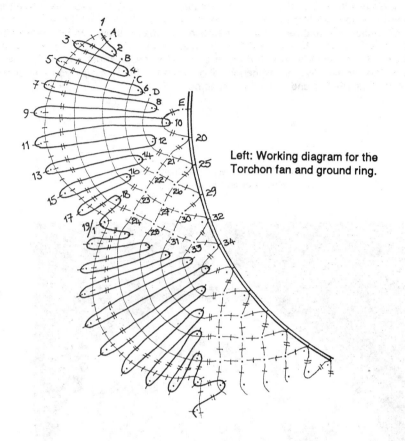

Left: Working diagram for the Torchon fan and ground ring.

Twist the five passives which leave the fan after pins 10, 12, 14, 16 and 18, twice so that they are ready to go into the ground. Take the pair from pin 10 first and link it to the inside ring by pushing the nearer of the two threads under the ring (with a pin, your finger nail or a pin-lifter). Catch that loop on the inside of the ring and enlarge it so that you can pass the other bobbin of this pair through it, pull both threads tight and put up pin 20. I found it best to place the pin in front of both lots of threads, rather than having the pin between the threads as they go towards and then away from the ring. Twist the pair twice and then work a row of Torchon ground (half stitch, pin, half stitch, twist) starting at pin 21 and finishing at pin 24. Start the next row by taking the innermost pair and using them to make the link with the ring at pin 25. Once they are attached to the ring twist them twice and continue along the row of ground pins 26-28. Do the same for two more rows of ground starting at pins 29 and 32. The triangle of ground is only complete once you have linked the inner pair to the ring at pin 34 so don't forget that all important last step. All the pairs are now in position to allow you to work the next fan.

Continue in this way working alternate areas of ground and fans. Having worked the second fan check the position of the ring and if necessary remove the centre anchoring pins and adjust its placing so that the inner row of pinholes can just be seen outside the ring. As you work further it may be necessary to remove the pins from earlier repeats to allow the ring to move more freely. Once the edging is complete pin down the first fan and join your lace by bringing one of the threads from each passive pair through their own starting loop at pins A, B, C and D and tying a reef knot. The fifth passive is joined into the loop which attached it to the ring at pin E. The worker pair is joined to pin 1 as is the outside fan passive. You can now remove all the bobbins and pins, then lift your lace off the pillow and trim away the surplus passive threads. Tie an overhand knot in the two worker threads 2-3" (5-7cm) away from the lace to make the hanging loop. The commercial arrangement of bells and ribbon which I used also had a hanging loop and I just slipped this loop over the hanging loop on my lace.

DIAMOND SHAPED WINDOW DECORATION WITH SNOWFLAKE AND MAGIC CHAIN TRAIL.

This project is made up of a single trail forming a series of loops which are linked to an adjacent trail and at crossing points by sewings. The trail is decorated with a magic chain stitch effect in a thick glittery thread. The snowflake is stitched into position on completion of the lace.

1 pair of DMC No 8 Coton Perle as the workers. Cut 1 x 14yd (13m) length and wind it on to Continental style bobbins.

2 pairs of trail passives in the same thread. Cut 2 x 3¾yd (3.5m) lengths.

2 pairs of Twilley's Gold Dust as magic chain passives. Cut 2 x 3¾yd (3.5m) lengths.

I used green Perle for both the workers and outer trail passives. The magic chain was worked with two pairs of gold, but could equally well be worked with two different colours which would show up the 'chain stitch' effect even more noticeably.

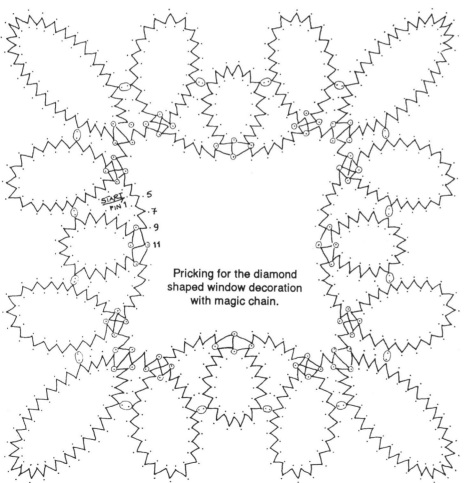

Pricking for the diamond shaped window decoration with magic chain.

Key to the working diagrams of this and the following two projects.

⊙----- = Make a sewing into this pinhole the second time you use it.

⊙----- = Lift the pin and use it a second time without removing it from the pillow.

——→ = Direction of work.

----- = Pathway of workers when these pins are used a second time.

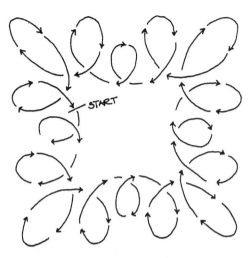

Above: Diagram to show the direction of working for the trails in the diamond shaped window decoration.

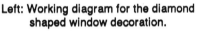

Left: Working diagram for the diamond shaped window decoration.

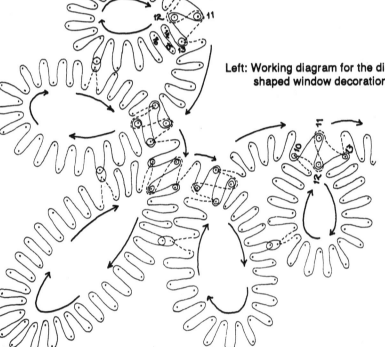

WORKING INSTRUCTIONS.

Hang the worker pair on pin 1, a Perle passive pair on each of pins 2 and 4, and the Gold Dust passives pairs 'open' around pin 3. Cloth stitch the worker through the first pair of passives, now lift the first gold thread and pass the worker bobbins (held together as if they were one bobbin) underneath it, they are then passed over the next two gold threads and underneath the fourth. To finish the row work a cloth stitch with the workers and the outside Perle passive pair. Twist the workers twice because it is the end of the row and put up pin 5. Work back across the row in a similar way, making one cloth stitch with the outside passive pair, going under the first gold thread, over the centre two and under the final 'magic chain' passive with both workers working together as one thread. A final cloth stitch completes the row at pin 6. Having worked two rows in this way the worker has returned to the lefthand edge of the trail and it is now time to change the order of the magic chain passives to form the actual 'chain' stitches. So pick up the two outer gold passives (leaving the two centre gold threads slightly apart on the pillow) and bring them together above the work, they are now put down between the other two gold threads. In fact the original righthand two bobbins have now been twisted once (right over left), and the lefthand two threads have made a cross (left over right). You now resume the same stitch sequence as before, cloth stitch, under one, over two, under one, cloth stitch for the next two rows. Every time the worker arrives at the lefthand edge of the trail you know it is time to 'flip' the magic threads. If you forget to do this you will find that you will suddenly have a very long chain stitch which stretches over four rows instead of the usual two, so you must go back and put it right.

Keep going round the trail, carefully following the zigzag pathway of the workers marked on the pattern. As you approach the end of the first loop you will see that there are four circled pinholes on the pricking. These four are 'shared' pinholes. You have already used them once for an earlier part of the trail (shown on the working diagram as a solid line), now you need to use them a second time (shown on the working diagram as a dotted line), and in order to link the two sections of trail firmly together at this crossing point you will need to make two sewings. I chose to make those two sewings at the first shared pinhole and at the last of the four. I feel there is no need to make sewings at all four as once you have made two, the worker loops in between are unable to move anyway. So in this particular instance I would make sewings at pinholes 10 and 13. To make a sewing I like to twist the worker pair once before removing the previously used pin and bringing the outside worker thread through the worker loop revealed by the removal of the pin. I usually find that I can manage this with the aid of a .6mm crochet hook, but you can use a Lazy Susan or similar tool if you prefer. Once you have that worker thread making a nice loop above the trail enlarge it so that you can pass the other worker bobbin through that loop. Replace the pin taking care not to split any of the threads, then pull both threads tight. You may twist them once before starting the next row. At pinholes 11 and 12 where you do not need to make sewings simply raise the pin already in those pinholes and use it again by lifting the worker threads around the back of the pin without removing it from the pillow.

With so many loops and crossings you will need to be continually turning your pillow in order to give yourself the most comfortable working position. You will also need to remove surplus pins and press remaining ones well down into the pillow so that they don't interfere with later work.

Three quarters of the way around the second loop you will come to a pair of circled pinholes. This indicates that you need to make a sewing in order to link the two adjacent trails together. This is done in just the same way as the sewing at the 'shared' pinholes. Remove the pin from the worker loop which you need to sew into (ie the pin in the circled position in the previously worked trail), bring the outer worker thread through that worker loop to form a loop of its own, pass the other worker bobbin through that loop, replace that pin and continue the trail.

No matter what else might be going on in the way of sewings, you must continue to remember to flip the gold threads after every two rows.

When your diamond is complete bring the workers back to the pin they started from, unwind one bobbin and bring that thread through the starting loop at pin 1. Tie the two worker threads off securely with a reef knot. The two Perle passive pairs are joined into their respective starting loops at pins 2 and 4 and knotted off in a similar way. I made no attempt to join the magic chain threads whilst the piece was still on the pillow, so remove the pins and lift the lace off the pillow. Then using a large-eyed needle I sewed the gold threads through the starting loops, doing my best to keep up the continuity of the 'chain stitch' effect before fastening off each thread in turn with a small back stitch.

Below: Pricking for the loop and star window decoration.

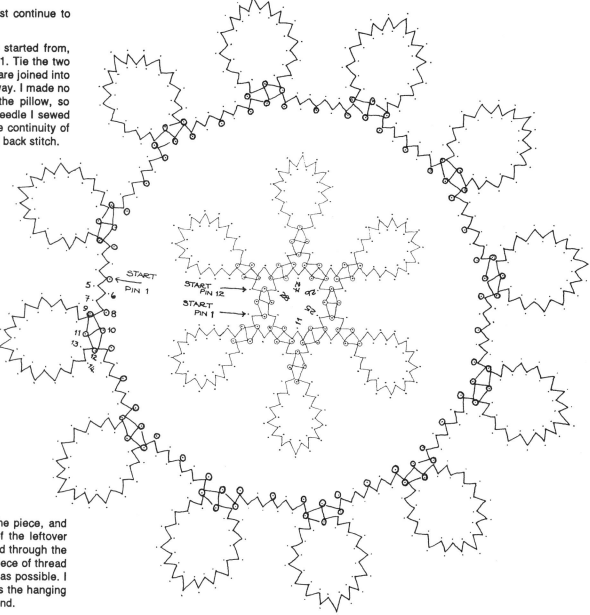

I used a three-dimensional gold snowflake decoration for the centre of the piece, and this was stitched in place with a doubled thickness made up of some of the leftover Perle threads. I started from the top point of the diamond, came down and through the loop at the top of the snowflake, then I buttonhole stitched over the first piece of thread on the way back up to the lace where I fastened off the thread as invisibly as possible. I did exactly the same at the bottom. A piece of leftover Perle thread makes the hanging loop which is attached to the tip of the largest loop at the point of the diamond.

LOOP AND STAR WINDOW DECORATION.

This project uses the same magic chain stitch effect to add interest and sparkle to a simple tape lace edging which is attached to the ring as the work progresses. The centre motif is a little more complicated although it is worked in the same stitch. The centre 'star' could be worked on its own to make a Christmas tree decoration.

For the border of the 4" (10cm) ring :-

1 pair of DMC No 8 Coton Perle as workers for the trail. Cut 1 x 10yd (9m) length and wind it on to Continental style bobbins.

2 pairs of the same thread as edge passives for the trail. Cut 2 x 4yd (3.75m) lengths.

2 pairs of Twilley's Gold Dust for the magic chain passives. Cut 2 x 4yd (3.75m) lengths.

For the centre 'star' :-

2 pairs of DMC No 8 Coton Perle for the workers. Cut 2 x 3yd (2.75m) lengths.

4 pairs of the same thread for the edge passives of each trail. Cut 4 x 1yd (1m) lengths.

4 pairs of Twilley's Gold Dust for the magic chain passives in each trail. Cut 4 x 1yd (1m) lengths.

I worked the sample entirely in white and gold, but because the centre motif is made up of two trails it is possible to use a different colour scheme for each trail. You can work the border in one of those colours. I suggest that you keep the magic chain passives the same colour throughout so that the differently coloured trails have one common element. If you prefer you can use the same coloured Perle throughout and then use two different colours of Gold Dust in each trail to emphasise the magic chain which will then appear to be made up of chain stitch loops in alternate colours.

WORKING INSTRUCTIONS FOR THE BORDER.

Take the mid-point of the trail worker pair and bring the loop up inside the ring. Pass the two bobbins tail-first through that loop and pull them tight to attach the worker pair to the ring. Pin the pattern down in the middle of the pillow, and then centre the ring inside the border pinholes so that the worker bobbins are by pin 1. Anchor the ring in place using three or four pins at roughly equal distances inside the ring and close up against it. Put in pin 1 through the loop which has attached the thread to the ring with the bobbins outside the ring. Hang the two Perle edge pairs on pins 2 and 4, and the two Gold Dust pairs 'open' on pin 3.

Cloth stitch the workers through the edge passives and then pass the two worker bobbins together under the first Gold Dust passive, over the middle two, and under the final glittery thread. Finish the row with a cloth stitch, twist the worker twice and put up pin 5. Work back across to pin 6 starting the row with a cloth stitch, then going under one, over two, under one, through the magic chain passives, and completing the row with a cloth stitch through the Perle pair. Twist the workers twice and put up pin 6. You have now worked two rows and it is time to change the order of the four glittery passive threads in order to form the chain stitch effect. To do this simply lift the two outside Gold Dust threads into the centre positions. In this way the righthand pair of threads have actually been twisted once (right over left), and the lefthand pair have made a cross (left over right). It is essential to remember to 'flip' the threads in this way at the end of every two rows. If you forget then you'll find that suddenly you have a chain stitch which is twice as long as it should have been. So wherever you are and whatever else is going on at the time (e.g. sewings, crossings or linking the trail to the ring) as soon as the worker arrives at the righthand end of the row 'flip' your Gold Dust passives.

Work two more rows and once you have put up pin 8 and 'flipped' your magic chain threads, you can link the workers to the ring. To do this twist the workers once (instead of the usual twice at the end of the row) and push the nearest worker thread under the ring with a pin, your finger nail or a pinlifter. Catch the loop which that thread makes on the inside of the ring and enlarge it so that you can pass the other worker bobbin through that loop. Pull both threads tight and add one more twist, now bring both worker threads behind pin 8 and work back across the trail. I find that keeping all of the threads BEHIND the edge pin at the link with the ring stops the loops from sliding forwards along the ring and makes a tidier join.

Continue working round the loop, moving the pillow as you go so that you are always working with your trail coming directly towards you. As you near the end of this first loop you will find that your trail crosses the earlier part of the loop, and to link these trails together to secure the loop it is necessary to use four of the earlier pins again - these are circled on the pricking. Once the worker has reached pin 16, make one more row (and don't forget to 'flip' the Gold Dust threads at the end of it) and twist the workers once. Now use a crochet hook (or a Lazy Susan) to bring the edge worker thread through the worker loop at pin 9, pass the other worker bobbin through this loop and replace the pin taking care not to split any of the threads in the process. Pull the workers tight and tension the passives in the usual way. Make the next two rows (to pins 11 and then 10) without sewings, simply lift those two pins sufficiently to slip the worker pair around the back and then work the next row. You must make a sewing at the fourth shared pinhole (pin 12). Immediately after the final sewing of the crossing you will join the trail to the ring at pin 17. Continue the trail linking the workers to the ring whenever they arrive at one of the circled inner pinholes.

To join the border at the end bring the workers back to pin 1, twist them once and remove the bobbin from the thread nearest the ring. Using a crochet hook bring that thread up through the loop which joined the worker pair to the ring at the start. Tie a reef knot with the two worker threads. The two edge passive pairs are each joined into their own starting loops at pins 2 and 4. Tie both pairs off with a reef knot. Now remove all the bobbins and pins and once the lace is off the pillow use a large-eyed needle to join the magic chain threads stitching them down through the trail to catch their starting loops doing your best to maintain the chain stitch pattern of the threads. Darn the ends away and trim off all the surplus threads. Use some of the left over Perle to make a hanging loop which should be attached at the tip of one of the border loops.

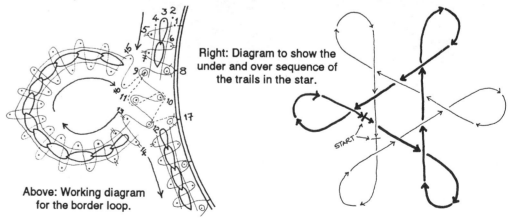

Above: Working diagram for the border loop.

Right: Diagram to show the under and over sequence of the trails in the star.

WORKING INSTRUCTIONS FOR THE 'STAR' MOTIF.

Start the first of the two trails by hanging the worker pair on pin 1, the two edge passives on pins 2 and 4, and the two glittery magic chain pairs 'open' on pin 3. Cloth stitch the worker pair through the first Perle passive pair and then holding the two worker bobbins together lift the first Gold Dust thread and pass the workers under it. Lift the two worker bobbins over the next two Gold Dust threads and then under the fourth. Finish the row with a cloth stitch through the final Perle passive. Twist the workers twice and put up pin 5. Work back in the same way starting off with a cloth stitch, going under one, over two and under one of the magic chain threads, and finishing with a cloth stitch before twisting the workers twice and putting up pin 6. Because you have now worked two rows it is time to change the order of the magic chain threads in order to form the first 'chain' loop. To do this bring the two outer Gold Dust threads into the centre so that the righthand pair is twisted once (right over left) and the lefthand pair forms a 'cross' (left over right). Continue the trail remembering to change the order of the Gold Dust threads in this way every time the worker pair reaches the lefthand edge of the trail.

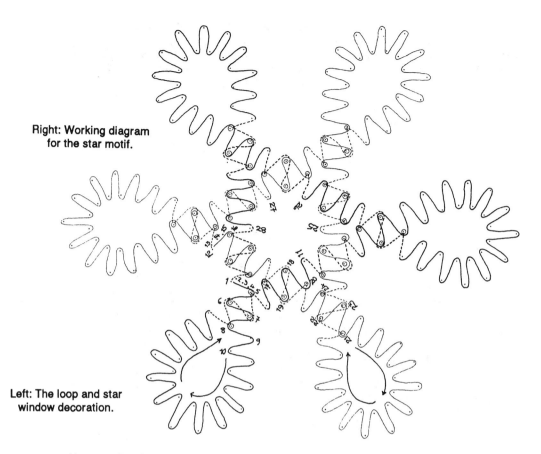

Right: Working diagram
for the star motif.

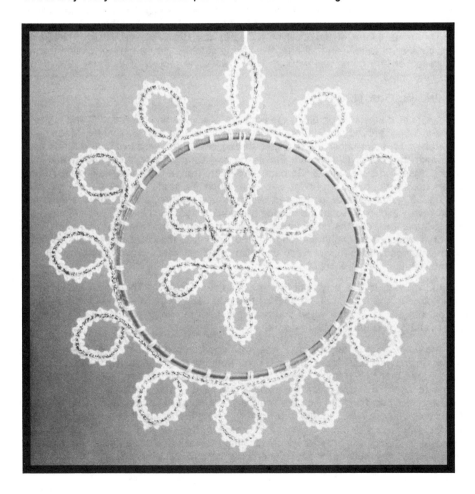

Left: The loop and star
window decoration.

Keep turning the pillow as you go round the curve making up the first loop. You'll need to press most of the pins down into the pillow so that as you work back towards the starting line they don't get in the way. You will need to use four of the pins again as the trail crosses over the start. I made a sewing at all four pinholes (8, 6, 7 and 5 in that order), but you can manage with just two - one into the first and one into the last of the 'shared' pinholes (8 and 5). The two pins between can be used again by simply lifting them high enough to wind the worker pair behind them without removing it from the pillow. Don't forget that despite the interruption caused by the sewings you must still change the order of the magic chain threads every two rows. Continue with this trail until the worker reaches pin 11. Leave it here whilst you start the second trail.

Hang the worker on pin 12, the outside trail passives on pins 13 and 15, and the two pairs of Gold Dust threads 'open' on pin 14. This trail is worked in just the same way as the first, with the order of the magic chain threads also being altered every time the worker pair reaches the lefthand edge of the trail. This trail will go over the top of the first trail at pins 17, 18, 19 and 20, so make your usual sequence of sewings here. This trail then works the second 'loop' crossing back over itself at pins 21-24. Continue with this trail until the weaver reaches pin 25. Leave it here and go back to work the next section of the first trail picking up the worker at pin 11.

From pin 11 the first trail crosses over the other trail and then works the third 'loop', crossing over itself in the process. Leave the worker at pin 26 and go back to pin 25 to restart work on the second trail. Again this trail goes over the other trail at the first crossing, then makes the fourth 'loop' crossing over itself before being left at pin 27.

The second working diagram will tell you which trail has 'priority' and which trail has to pause whilst the other works across the crossing point first. Your aim is to weave the two trails together in an under, over, under sequence, using sewings to link the trails securely together whenever they cross.

To join the trails and maintain the correct under and over sequence, you must complete the second trail first. So having finished the fifth 'loop' leave the workers at pin 28 and go back to pick up the second trail's workers at pin 27 and work the final 'loop'. After the last sewing at the crossing point work one more row to bring the workers back to pin 12 where they started. Bring one worker thread through that starting loop and tie off the pair with a reef knot. The two edge Perle passive pairs are tied off into their starting pinholes at pins 13 and 15. Remove all the bobbins from this trail and take all the threads to one side so that you can work the last few pinholes of the first trail which is complete when the worker reaches pin 1. The edge passives are joined into pins 2 and 4. Again remove the bobbins, then the pins and lift the lace off the pillow. You can now use a large-eyed sewing needle to fasten off the magic chain threads making sure that you catch the starting loops and that you maintain the chain stitch pattern of these threads. You can darn the ends away behind the nearest trail crossing. Trim away all the surplus threads, and use a small length of the Perle to make a hanging loop into the topmost pinhole of one of the 'loops' of the star. If you are using this motif as a centre piece for the ring this hanging loop is then attached to the ring at the base of the loop where the main hanging loop has been attached. Bring the two ends from the 'star' up through the space between the border and the ring between the two groups of threads linking the edging to the ring. Bring one thread down to the right of the hanging loop and the other to the left, turn the ring over and tie the ends of this hanging loop in a small reef knot behind the loop threads. A spot of glue will secure the ends and also prevent this loop from slipping along the metal ring.

CIRCULAR WINDOW DECORATION WITH DOUBLE MAGIC CHAIN TRAILS.

This project uses many of the techniques required for the previous window decoration, so it may be a good idea to work that one first as it is a good bit simpler than this one which has two trails running parallel throughout and which form rather more awkward crossings. Once you have mastered the magic chain sequence and have thoroughly conquered the process of making sewings you'll be better prepared for this one!

For the outer of the two trails you will need :-

1 pair of DMC No 8 Coton Perle as the trail workers. Cut 1 x 12yd (11m) length and wind it onto large capacity Continental bobbins.

2 pairs of the same thread for the edge passives of the trail. Cut 2 x 4yd (3.75m) lengths.

2 pairs of Twilley's Gold Dust for passives to make the magic chain. Cut 2 x 4yd (3.75m) lengths.

For the inner trail you will need :-

1 pair of DMC No 8 Coton Perle as the trail workers. Cut 1 x 10yd (9.25m) length and wind it onto Continental bobbins.

2 pairs of the same thread for the edge passives of this trail. Cut 2 x 3yd (2.75m) lengths.

2 pairs of Twilley's Gold Dust for passives to make the magic chain. Cut 2 x 3yd (2.75m) lengths.

I used red Perle throughout which I felt made a good background for the gold threads of the magic chain. Although I would recommend that you use the same colour Perle throughout (because the workers will change trails during the kisses which link the trails) there is no reason why you can't be more adventurous with your choice of glittery threads for the magic chains. You can use two different colours in each trail which will emphasise the chain stitch effect even more, or you could use one colour for the magic chain in one trail and a different colour in the other trail. So I hope you'll enjoy making up your own colour schemes. (If you have your heart set on using different colours for the Perle part of the two trails, then instead of the kisses which link the two trails you could use a cloth stitch, pin, cloth stitch sequence creating a new pinhole between the two trails in the centre of the X which indicates the kiss. This will ensure that each worker goes back to its own trail after the linking stitches. You will need to allow some extra thread on the outer trail workers if you work the project in this way, 2yd (2m) should be plenty.)

WORKING INSTRUCTIONS.

Hang the inner trail worker on pin 1, the edge trail passives on pins A and C and the two gold pairs 'open' around pin B. Cloth stitch through the first trail passive pair, then take both workers together under the first gold thread, over the centre two gold threads and underneath the fourth gold thread. Finish the row with another cloth stitch, twist the workers twice and put up pin 2. Go back across the trail in the same way, cloth stitch, workers under one, over two, under one, cloth stitch. Twist the workers twice more and put up pin 3. You have now completed two rows and the magic chain threads must be 'flipped' every two rows, so lift the outside two gold threads, one in each hand, and bring them together between the other two gold threads. You must remember that each time the worker reaches the righthand edge of the inner trail the order of the gold threads must be changed. If you forget to do this then the chain stitch loop at this point will be very much longer than it should be.

Continue working in this way until your workers reach pin 11. They must pause here whilst you start the other trail, but just so that you don't forget, I suggest that you 'flip' the gold threads now, then when you return to this trail you'll be able to pick up the workers and go straight on with the work.

Hang the outer trail worker on pin 12, the two edge trail passives on pins D and F, and the two magic chain pairs 'open' on pin E. You work the rows in exactly the same way as those of the other trail starting with a cloth stitch, then taking the workers under one of the magic chain threads, over the centre two, and under the last. A cloth stitch completes the row. Twist the workers twice and put up pin 13. Work back across to pin 14 and now you are ready to 'flip' the workers, lifting the two gold outside threads into the middle. So every time the worker reaches the lefthand edge of the trail you need to remember to change the order of the magic chain threads. You may find it best to put a pencil note on the outside of your pattern reminding you to change the order of the magic chain threads whenever the workers reach the inner edge of either trail.

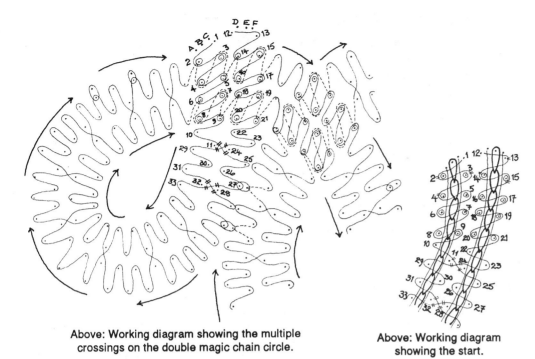

Above: Working diagram showing the multiple crossings on the double magic chain circle.

Above: Working diagram showing the start.

immediately after completing the last block of crossings. However, before you can join the worker pairs into their starting loops you will see on the pattern that they need to make the final kiss, so cloth stitch them together and then join the worker pair from the righthand trail into the starting worker pinhole of the lefthand trail and vice versa. The Perle passives will also be joined into their respective starting loops. Tie each of these pairs off with a reef knot, and remove all the bobbins, before taking out the pins and lifting the lace off the pillow. I used a needle to finish off the magic chain threads, stitching the ends down through the trail to catch the starting loops and making any extra stitches required to maintain the continuity of the chain stitch sequence. Fasten each thread off securely and trim away the surplus thread. Use one length of Perle to attach a hanging loop to the centre pinhole at the tip of the outside trail. Your window decoration is now complete.

When the workers on the outer trail reach pin 24 check that the workers from both trails have been twisted twice and that both pins 11 and 24 are in position. You are now ready to make the 'kiss' which is the stitch which links the two trails at intervals throughout the piece. Make a cloth stitch with the two pairs of workers and twist both pairs twice more. They will then continue as the workers on the opposite trail. At pins 28 and 32 the workers will make a similar kiss as indicated by the X drawn on the pricking between the two trails. One word of warning - don't forget to 'flip' the magic chain threads in both trails before starting the rows immediately following the kiss!

Keep turning the pillow as you work your way round the first loop, remove surplus pins and press down remaining pins to keep them out of the way. Don't remove any of the starting pins, or any of the pins from circled pinholes. As you near the end of the first loop you will see that the worker zigzag leads you to circled pinholes which have already been used at an earlier point in the trail. You will need to make sewings into pinholes 2 and 5, and 14 and 17 for the outer trail and at pinholes 6 and 9, and 18 and 21 for the inner trail. At the pinholes between you will simply raise the pin already in that pinhole and use it again by lifting the worker threads around the back of the pin. Once again, throughout these multiple crossings you must continually check that you have not omitted any of the changes in the order of the magic chain threads which must be made after every two rows if a regular pattern is to be maintained.

Three quarters of the way round the second loop you will see that there are two more circled pinholes between the two adjacent outer trails. You need to make a sewing between these two pinholes to link the trails together. Continue in this way until the eight loops have been completed. The two trails will be joined to their starting pinholes

Below: Pricking for the double magic chain circle.

START
PIN 1 ←

← START
PIN 12

SCENTED SACHETS.

A small sachet of lavender or pot pourri is a sweetly scented addition to your Christmas tree decorations, or makes a welcome small gift at any time of year. I have used a variety of edgings, all of which children are quite capable of working. The first edging is particularly easy and being very quick to work could be a useful project for Christmas Fairs.

LAVENDER BAG.

2 pairs of Twilley's Gold Dust for the glittery passives. Cut 2 x 1¼yds (110cm) lengths.
4 pairs of DMC No 8 Coton Perle as the ordinary passives. Cut 4 x 1½yds (135cm) lengths.

I used purple nylon net lined with a thin knitted nylon fabric of a similar colour to make the sachet which I filled with lavender. Continuing the purple and mauve theme I used purple Gold Dust and a mauve Perle for the threads. I used the same two threads to make a small gathered flower, which together with two green fabric leaves added the finishing touch.

WORKING INSTRUCTIONS FOR THE LACE EDGING.

Two basic stitch sequences are used throughout this edging. One is half stitch, pin, half stitch, and the other is cloth stitch, pin, cloth stitch and twist. To help you remember which to use where, you need to understand the effect that each of these two types of stitches has on the coloured threads. When making a half stitch, pin, half stitch you'll find that both pairs continue smoothly along their diagonal pathways without deviation, but with a cloth stitch, pin, cloth stitch and twist, each pair will change direction and take up a new diagonal pathway. So the centre pinholes of the edging are all worked with half stitches so that the pairs can work through each other without interruption, forming the diamond shapes which make up the pattern. At the sides however, you need to change the direction of the pairs so that they can turn around the edge pins and come back in towards the centre following a new diagonal line. There are just two exceptions to this rule and these occur in the corner of the design, instead of the normal half stitches, you must use a cloth stitch, pin, cloth stitch and twist so that the glittery pair stops short of the corner and turns through 90 degrees at both of these pins before taking up its new pathway. I have circled these two pinholes on the pricking to remind you. When working this pattern with children I found that it helped if I used a coloured highlighter on all of the pinholes along both straight sides and to emphasise the two circled pinholes in the corner. These are the pinholes which must be worked in a cloth stitch, pin, cloth stitch and twist sequence. Every other pinhole of this project is worked with a half stitch, pin, half stitch sequence. I then used a different colour to mark in the diamond pathway of the glittery threads enabling them to check that the Gold Dust pairs were in the correct position. On the pricking the glittery threads are marked with a heavier black line, these would be the ones to highlight if you choose to use this system.

Hang one glittery passive pair on pin 2 and push it to the left, hang an ordinary Perle passive from the same pin and put the bobbins down to the right of the previous pair. Twist the centre two threads twice to interlink the two pairs. Now twist each pair once. Hang a Perle pair on each of pins T1 and T3, and a Gold Dust pair on T2. Take the Perle pair from T1 and the glittery pair from pin 2 and make a half stitch, pin, half stitch at pin 3. Take out the temporary pin (T1) and tension the Perle pair so that its starting loop drops down to rest around pin 3. Leaving this Perle pair behind continue working with the glittery pair following the heavier line on the pricking working the next half stitch, pin, half stitch at pin 4 with the Gold Dust pair from T2. Remove the temporary pin and tension both pairs. The original glittery pair continues working along this diagonal and makes a similar stitch at pin 5 using the Perle pair from T3. Don't forget to remove the temporary pin before you tension both pairs. Hang the final Perle pair on pin 1 and use it with the glittery pair to work pin 6. Because this pinhole is on the edge of the lace you must work it with a cloth stitch, pin, cloth stitch and twist. After this pin check that the Perle pair is still at the edge and the glittery pair is lying to its right, ready to start a new diagonal pathway.

Once you have worked a row finishing at the edge pinhole you must return to the opposite edge to start the next row. Take the Perle pairs from pins 2 and 3 and work the edge stitch at pin 7 using the cloth stitch sequence. The lefthand of these two pairs now works the length of the next diagonal row starting at pin 7 and finishing at pin 11. The first and last pins, being the edge pins, will be worked with cloth stitches and the three pins between will all be worked with the half stitch, pin, half stitch sequence. Again return to the highest empty pinhole, which is on the righthand edge and start a new row working the usual cloth stitch sequence with the two pairs at the right of the work. This will complete pin 12. Pins 13 and 14 are both worked with half stitches as the glittery pair continues its diagonal pathway, but at pin 15, the first of the circled pins, you must make a cloth stitch, pin, cloth stitch and twist, which will mean that the glittery thread is left behind at this pin whilst the Perle pair continues to work the edge stitch at pin 16. This is worked in the usual way with a cloth stitch, pin, cloth stitch and twist, then make another cloth stitch, pin, cloth stitch and twist immediately afterwards, putting up pin 17. Now turn the pillow and for the first few rows you will start at the outside edge. The righthand pair from pin 17 starts the next row making a cloth stitch, pin, cloth stitch and twist at the next circled pin (pin 18) the glittery pair now continues along this new diagonal working half stitch pins at 19 and 20. Work the usual cloth stitch edge sequence at pin 21. Go back to the outside edge and start the next row at pin 22 using the two lefthand pairs to make the first stitch. Work three more half stitch pins at 23, 24 and 25 and leave the Perle pair here, returning to the outside edge to start the next row at pin 26. Work only two half stitch pins after the cloth stitch edge pin, leaving the glittery pair at pin 28. Start the next row at pin 29, but only work one half stitch pin at 30 before leaving the Perle pair and making the edge stitch at pin 31. You can now start the next row at the inner edge at pin 32 and continue working whole rows until you arrive at the next corner.

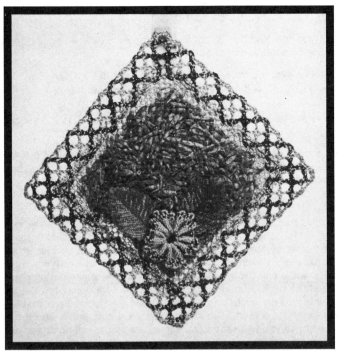

Left: Lavender bag with simple edging and lace flower trim.

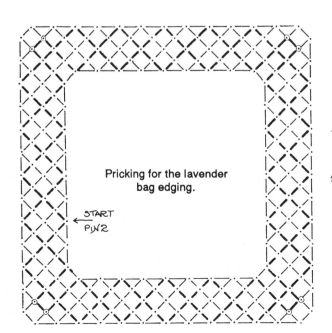

Pricking for the lavender bag edging.

START
← PIN 2

Left: Working diagram for the lavender bag edging.

Once you have completed your square you'll find that each pair has returned to its starting pinhole. The Perle pair and the glittery pair at the righthand edge will be joined into pin 2, so bring one thread from each pair through the interlinked starting loop and tie off each pair with a reef knot. Working towards the left, the next Perle pair will be joined into pin 3 and the glittery pair to its left will go into pin 4. The righthand Perle pair from the last edge pin will be tied off at pin 5 and the lefthand pair from the same pin will join its own starting loop at pin 1. Remove the bobbins and lift the lace from the pillow. Trim off the surplus thread.

MAKING THE FABRIC SACHET.

To make the fabric square to hold the lavender or pot pourri I used two layers of very fine knitted nylon with a layer of net above and below it, but you can use four layers of net instead if you prefer. Cut a piece of paper 2" (52mm) square and pin it on to the fabric layers. Stitch around the edge of the paper pattern leaving a 1" (25mm) opening in the centre of one side. Unpin your pattern and trim the turnings about 1/4" (5mm) from the stitching. (It is much easier to do the stitching first and then cut it out, than to try and stitch narrow turnings on such a small piece with so many layers - particularly if you are using a sewing machine.)

To fill your sachet I suggest you use a small piece of paper loosely rolled to form a funnel, you can use a knitting needle to encourage the filling to drop into your sachet. You won't need very much filling as it is important to keep the sachet fairly flat so that the lace lies comfortably round the edge. Stitch along the opening once your sachet is full, then place your lace on the top of the fabric square and stitch it into place along its inner edge. Cut a 4" (10cm) length of 1/4" (5mm or 6mm) ribbon, fold it in half and stitch it onto one corner between the lace and the fabric of the sachet. You can then add a flower and some leaves, which I glued into place, to give the finishing touch.

LACE FLOWER.

For the shorter lengths required for this very simple flower you may be able to use some of the longer threads left over from the sachet edging.

1 pair of DMC No 8 Coton Perle as the workers. Cut 1 x 11/2yd (135cm) length.
3 pairs of the same thread for the inner passives. Cut 3 x 14" (35cm) lengths.
1 pair of Twilley's Gold Dust for the outer passive pair. Cut 1 x 14" (35cm) length.

WORKING INSTRUCTIONS.

Hang the glittery passive pair on pin T1 and push it to the left, hang one Perle pair from the same pin and put it down to the right. Hang two Perle pairs 'in order' from pin T2 and the worker on pin 1. Cloth stitch the worker through the three Perle pairs and twist them once before cloth stitching through the glittery edge pair. Twist the workers twice at the end of the row and put up pin 2. Work back across towards pin 3 remembering to twist the workers once between the glittery passive and the three Perle passives. When the worker reaches pin 3 remove pins T1 and T2 and tension the passives gently so that your starting edge is a smooth straight line rather than a hammock-shaped curve! Continue working until your workers reach the last pinhole at the bottom of the straight edge. Tie a reef knot with the workers around this pin. Tie off each of the passive pairs with a reef knot, remove the bobbins and take the lace off the pillow. Trim the passive threads quite close to the finishing knots, but do not trim off either of the worker threads. Thread one of these into a needle and run in a gathering thread through the worker loops along the straight edge bringing the needle up through the first loop and down through the next. Pull up the gathering thread as tightly as you can and secure it with a double backstitch. Now overlap the neater starting edge so that it hides the knots of the finishing edge and stab stitch it into place. Finish it off with a back stitch and then both remaining threads can be trimmed off, and your flower is ready to be glued into place.

Left: Pricking for the lace flower.

FAN AND SPIDER TORCHON EDGING.

Here is the first of two very simple Torchon designs which makes a delicate edging for a sachet which can be filled with lavender or pot pourri.

1 pair of DMC No 8 Coton Perle for the fan workers. Cut 1 x 51/2yd (5.25m) lengths.
1 pair of DMC No 8 Coton Perle in a different colour for the outside fan passive. Cut 1 x 11/2yd (135cm) length.
5 pairs of DMC 80 Cordonnet Special for the ordinary passives. Cut 5 x 13/4yd (160cm) lengths.

For the sample I used a pale pink Perle as the workers with a darker pink outside passive for the fan. I made the fabric sachet in white , trimming it with a pink ribbon bow topped with a small embroidered motif.

WORKING INSTRUCTIONS.

Hang the outside fan passive pair from pin 1 and push it to the left. Hang the fan worker pair on the same pin and put it down to the right. Twist the centre two threads twice to interlink the pairs. Twist the worker pair once, but do not twist the passive pair at all. Hang one ordinary white passive on each of pins T1, T2, T3, T4 and T5. Cloth stitch the fan worker through the first white pair (from T1), twist the worker twice and put up pin 2. Work back to the outside of the fan remembering to twist the workers once between the outside fan passive and the ordinary white passive pair. Twist the workers twice at the end of the row as usual. Once pin 3 is in position work back towards pin 4. The fan is still getting wider at this point so you will need to take in a new pair at the righthand end of the row (from T2). Work back to the outside edge and put up pin 5, and then back towards pin 6. Again the fan is still getting wider, so you will need to bring another passive pair into the fan (from T3) at the end of this row. Work back to the outside edge once more and consider the length of the next row. This row will be shorter than the last row you worked, therefore you must leave out the righthand passive pair before you twist the workers and put up pin 8. Work back to the outer edge of the fan once more and again consider the length of the next row. The fan is still getting narrower, so push the righthand passive pair to one side as it will not be needed in this row. Put up pin 10 at the end of the row and work back to the outside edge once more. This brings you to pin 11 which marks the end of this fan. The three passive pairs which leave the fan after pins 6, 8 and 10 must all be twisted twice. This is very important - but it is all too easy to forget, so make sure that you don't make that mistake.

Take the passive pair which left the fan after pin 6 and the new pair from T4 and make a Torchon ground stitch (half stitch, pin, half stitch and twist) at pin 12. Continue by making a similar stitch at pin 13 with the righthand pair from pin 12 and the new pair from T5. Remove pins T4 and T5 (but not pins T1, T2 or T3 as these will be needed to preserve your starting loops and make joining that much easier at the end of your project) and tension the threads so that they slip down to rest around the permanent pins. These pairs are already twisted twice as part of the covering stitch, so there is no need to add any extra twists for the spider legs. Make the spider with the two pairs from pins 8 and 10 on the left and the lefthand pair from pin 13 together with the pair from pin 12 on the right. Make a cloth stitch with the centre two pairs, then the righthand two pairs, then the lefthand two pairs and then the centre two pairs again before putting up pin 14 in the middle with two pairs on either side. You'll find that if you have done this correctly the pairs which entered the spider from the left are now on your right and vice versa. You must now make four more cloth stitches in the same order, the first with the centre two pairs, the next with the righthand pairs, the next with the lefthand pairs and finally with the centre two pairs once more. Add two twists to each of these four pairs of 'legs' and your spider is complete.

The righthand leg now goes to the edge of the lace to work a Torchon ground stitch at pin 15 with the pair from pin 13. The lefthand pair from pin 15 now works a ground stitch at pin 16 with the second spider leg. The righthand pair from this pin now works the edge pin at pin 17 with the pair which remains at pin 15. Once these three ground pins are worked you can start on the next fan picking up the worker from pin 11 and working through pins 18-27. Again don't forget to put two twists on the three pairs of white passives as they leave the fan after pins 22, 24 and 26. There are two more ground pins to be worked before you can make the next spider. The pair which left the fan after pin 22 works diagonally out to the edge making ground stitches at pins 28 (with the lefthand pair from pin 17) and then 29 (with the other pair from pin 17). You are now ready to start the next spider.

Continue working alternate fans and spiders with the linking areas of ground until you reach the next corner. The last spider on this side is worked around pin 30, and after the spider you must work two ground pins at 31 and 32, then you go straight into your next fan (pins 33-43). Once pin 43 is in position cover it with a cloth stitch and twist and then work another cloth stitch before putting up pin 44, once again you'll find that the worker is on the left of the pin ready to start the next fan. First turn your pillow through 90 degrees and twist each of the three passive pairs leaving the fan twice as usual. You can now work the first fan of the new side (pins 44-54). Leave the worker at the outside pin and twist the white passive pairs twice as they leave the fan. The pair from pin 49 now makes a ground stitch with the pair from pin 32 at pin 55, and the same pair works on to make another ground stitch at pin 56 with the pair from pin 31. You are now ready to work the next spider around pin 57.

When you have completed the edging, fasten the worker into its own starting loop at pin 1. Once the worker has been secured with a reef knot you can tie off the outside passive without actually bringing it through its starting loop. The three white passive pairs from the last fan are twisted twice before being joined to their respective starting loops at pins T1, T2 and T3. The remaining two white passives are joined to their starting loops at pins 12 and 13. Remove the lace from the pillow and trim the ends off close to the reef knots.

To make a fabric sachet follow the instructions given above, but use a paper square 2¼" (57mm) as your template for the stitching. Some silk flowers, a spray of embroidered flowers or a ribbon bow completes the project.

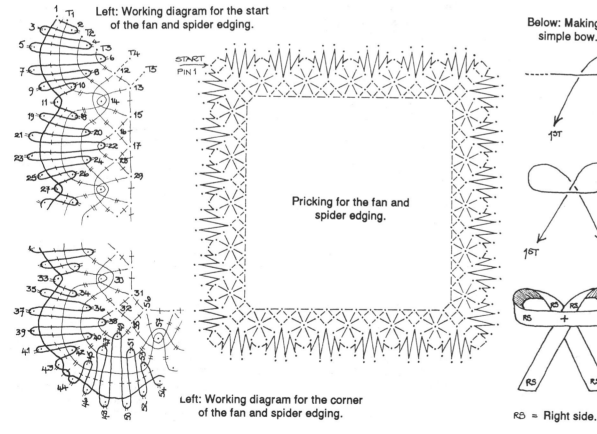

Left: Working diagram for the start of the fan and spider edging.

Pricking for the fan and spider edging.

Left: Working diagram for the corner of the fan and spider edging.

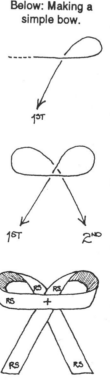

Below: Making a simple bow.

RS = Right side.

FAN AND ROSE GROUND TORCHON EDGING.

This edging requires a little more concentration than the previous design, but the diamond of Rose Ground between each fan makes it an attractive and interesting piece to work.

.1 pair of DMC No 8 Coton Perle as the fan workers. Cut 1 x 51/2yd (5.25m) lengths.

1 pair of DMC No 8 Coton Perle as the outside fan passive. Cut 1 x 11/2yds (135cm) length.

5 pairs of DMC 80 Cordonnet Special as the ordinary passives. Cut 5 x 13/4yd (160cm) lengths.

I used an embroidered motif to decorate the centre of one sachet which I made in pale blue fabric and net. The second sachet was also made in pale blue fabric and trimmed with a pale blue silk flower spray. Both edgings were made with a blue worker, one had the outside fan passive in the same colour and the other has a darker blue passive pair along the edge of the fan.

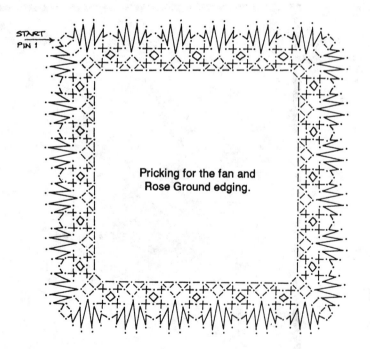

Pricking for the fan and Rose Ground edging.

WORKING INSTRUCTIONS.

I started this edging along the corner line as it makes the joining a little bit more straight forward. Hang the outside fan passive on pin 1 and push it to the left. Hang the fan worker pair from the same pin and put the bobbins down to the right of the previous pair. Twist the centre two threads twice to interlink them. Twist the worker pair once, but do not twist the passive pair at all. Hang one white passive pair from each of pins T1, T2, T3, T4 and T5. Cloth stitch the fan worker pair through the first white passive pair (from T1), twist the workers twice and put up pin 2. Cloth stitch back through the same white pair and twist the workers once before making a cloth stitch with the outside passive pair at the end of this row. Twist the workers twice as usual and put up pin 3. Because the fan is getting wider at this point you will need to bring in a new white passive pair (from T2) at the righthand end of this row, so cloth stitch across, remembering to twist the workers once between the edge passive and the white passives as usual. After cloth stitching through the two white passives, twist the workers twice and put up pin 4. Work back across the row to pin 5. The next row will be longer than the previous one, so again you must bring in a new pair (from T3). Put up pin 6 at the end of this row and then work back to pin 7 at the outer edge. The next row is shorter than the previous row, so this time you need to leave out a pair from the righthand end of the row, so push that pair to the right and work only through the outer passive pair and two white pairs. Put up pin 8 at the end of this row and then work back across to pin 9. Do the same for the next two rows as the fan is getting narrower all the time now. Work back to pin 11 which brings you to the end of the first fan.

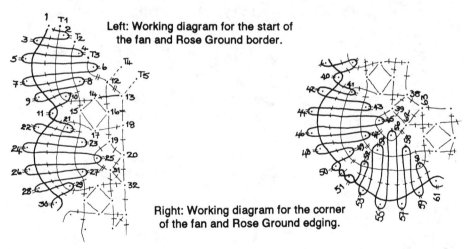

Left: Working diagram for the start of the fan and Rose Ground border.

Right: Working diagram for the corner of the fan and Rose Ground edging.

Leave the worker at the edge and twist the two white pairs which leave the fan after pins 8 and 10 once and make a cloth stitch and twist with them. The white pair which left the fan at its point (after pin 6) is twisted twice and then makes a half stitch, pin, half stitch at pin 12 with the pair from T4. Add an extra twist to the righthand pair from pin 12 and make the same half stitch, pin, half stitch with the pair from T5 at pin 13. Again add an extra twist to the righthand pair. Now remove pins T4 and T5 and tension the threads so that they rest snugly round pins 12 and 13. Take the lefthand pair from pin 13 and the pair from pin 12 and make a cloth stitch and twist. You are now ready to work the four pinholes which make up the Rose Ground filling. First check that the two preparation stitches (the cloth stitch and twist) have been made correctly with the four pairs from pins 8 and 10, and 12 and 13. Then using only these four pairs take the two centre pairs and work a half stitch, pin, half stitch at pin 14. Take the two lefthand pairs and work a similar half stitch, pin, half stitch at pin 15, then do the same with the two righthand pairs at pin 16. Finally make a half stitch, pin, half stitch with the two centre pairs at pin 17. To complete the Rose Ground make a cloth stitch and twist with the two lefthand pairs, and then do the same with the two righthand pairs. Take the righthand pair from this group and use it to make a half stitch, pin, half stitch and twist at pin 18 with the pair from pin 13. The lefthand pair from this pin then works diagonally to make the same stitch at pin 19. Take the righthand pair from this pin and make the same half stitch, pin, half stitch and twist with the pair from pin 18, putting up pin 20 in the middle. You are now ready to work the next fan in the same way as before (pins 21-30).

When the fan is complete don't forget to add two twists to the white passive pair which leaves the fan at the point, the other two passives leaving the fan are only twisted once. Take the pair from the point and work two half stitch, pin, half stitch sequences at pins 31 and 32 remembering to add an extra twist to the righthand pair only after the two half stitches at each pin. Now make the two 'preparation' stitches which must be done before you start the four pinholes at the centre of the Rose Ground. For this version of Rose Ground I chose to use a cloth stitch and twist before making a half stitch, pin, half stitch at each of the four centre pins, but there is no reason why you shouldn't choose a different version if you wish. To complete the Rose Ground you make two more 'preparation' stitches with the four pairs as they leave the diamond-shaped centre. These cloth stitch and twist sequences should perhaps more correctly be referred to as 'conclusion' stitches here. If you forget this cloth stitch and twist either before or after the centre four pinholes, you'll be very disappointed in the appearance of your Rose Ground, so watch out for the cross shapes on the pattern which indicate this 'preparation' or 'conclusion' stitch.

After the two 'conclusion' stitches of the last area of Rose Ground on this first side you will make ordinary Torchon ground stitches (half stitch, pin, half stitch and twist) at pins 38 and 39. You must then work the next fan (pins 40-50). At pin 50 twist the worker twice as usual, then cover the pin with a cloth stitch and twist, then immediately make another cloth stitch and put up pin 51, twist the worker pair (which is now on the left of the pin) twice, turn your pillow and you are now ready to start the next fan. This time all three passive pairs are twisted twice as they leave the fan after pins 45, 47 and 49, these pairs will go straight into the next fan (pins 51-61). Leaving the worker at pin 61 add the usual twists to the white passives as they leave the fan and take the pair from the fan point diagonally through the pairs from pins 39 and 38, to make pins 62 and 63. You are now ready to make the 'preparation' stitches for the next area of Rose Ground.

When you have completed all four edges of your square you will find that the pairs automatically return to their starting points. The fan worker will be joined into pin 1 and tied off with a reef knot. The outside passive can be tied off without joining it to its starting loop, as once the worker is secured, the passive is also quite safe. The three white passives from the fan must be twisted twice before being joined to their respective starting loops at T1, T2 and T3. The other two white passives are joined into pinholes 12 and 13. Make sure that all your reef knots are secure and then, once the lace is off the pillow, you can trim those ends close to the knots.

Your lace can then be mounted on a small fabric sachet and trimmed in the same way as described for the previous edging.

Sachets of pot pourri or lavender trimmed with a fan and spider or fan and Rose Ground edging.

SIMPLE BOOKMARKS.

The following bookmarks are quite straight forward. Two are very easy consisting of a cloth stitch fan and either a small spider or a single diamond of Rose Ground. The three which are based on a fan, honeycomb and half stitch variation are a little more challenging and they can be worked with a gimp. The basic designs may be simple, but when worked with colourful and glittery threads they make attractive gifts which are well within the capabilities of even a young lacemaker. Older lacemakers may find them useful fund-raisers at Christmas Bazaars as they are extremely quick to make.

The colour schemes for all the bookmarks can be varied according to the occasion. You might like to use white with gold or silver for a Confirmation, wedding or anniversary; pinks, blues or mauves for a birthday; yellows, oranges and gold for Easter, or red, green and gold for Christmas.

FAN AND SPIDER BOOKMARK.

This little bookmark couldn't be simpler, consisting only of a fan and a spider.

2 pairs of DMC No 8 Coton Perle as workers for the fans. Cut 2 x 3yd (2.75m) lengths.
2 pairs of Twilley's Gold Dust as outside passives for the fans. Cut 2 x 1yd (1m) lengths.
4 pairs of DMC 80 Cordonnet Special for the ordinary passives. Cut 4 x 1yd (1m) lengths.

For the sample I used red Perle workers for both fans and gold for the outside fan passive pairs.

WORKING INSTRUCTIONS.

Hang one worker pair on pin 1 and push it to the left. Now hang the second worker pair from the same pin putting it down to the right of the first pair. Twist the centre two threads twice right over left to interlink the two pairs. Twist each pair twice. Hang one ordinary white passive pair from each of pins T1 and T2. Using the righthand pair from pin 1 work a Torchon ground stitch (half stitch, pin, half stitch and twist) with the pair from T1, putting up pin 2 after the first half stitch. The coloured worker pair now continues on its diagonal pathway and makes a second ground stitch with the white pair from pin T2 at pin 3. Push the worker pair well out to the right now and hang the Gold Dust outside fan passive on pin 4 between the white passives on its left and the coloured workers on the right. Now make a half stitch with the worker pair and the outside fan passive pair. Lift pin 4 and put it up again in the middle of the two pairs, cover the pin by crossing the two centre threads left over right. The coloured worker threads will now be on the left and the outside fan passive will be on the right. Twist the worker pair once, but do not twist the outside fan passive pair at all. Leave the worker here whilst you hang on the pairs for the other side of the bookmark, but first remove the temporary pins at T1 and T2 and tension the white passives so that they sit snugly around pins 2 and 3.

The remaining worker from pin 1 is used to make two ground stitches with the white passive pairs from T3 and T4. Push the coloured worker pair well to the left and hang the outside fan passive on pin 7 between the worker and all the white passive pairs. Make a half stitch with the worker and the glittery pair lifting and then replacing pin 7 in the centre of these four threads. Cross the centre two threads left over right to cover the pin, and twist the worker pair once, but not the passive pair. Remove pins T3 and T4 and tension the white passive threads.

Make the first spider using the four white passive pairs in the middle of the work. First twist each pair once more to give each leg a total of three twists. Make a cloth stitch with the two centre pairs, then with the two righthand pairs followed by a cloth stitch with the two lefthand pairs, finally make a cloth stitch with the centre two pairs once more. The two pairs which started on the left of the spider (from pins 5 and 6) are now on the right and vice versa. Put up pin 8 in the centre of these four pairs, then repeat the same cloth stitch sequence, starting with the two centre pairs, then the righthand pairs, the lefthand pairs and finally the two centre pairs again. The spider's body is now complete and it just remains for each leg to be twisted three times, then you can turn your attention to the fans at the edge of the bookmark.

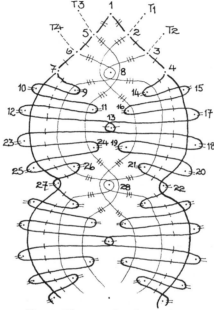

Above: Diagram showing the start of the fan and spider bookmark.

Below: Diagram showing the finish of the spider bookmark.

It doesn't matter which fan you start with. I worked the lefthand edge first so pick up the worker which lies to the right of pin 7 and check that it still retains the single twist which you put on it earlier. Now cloth stitch it through the first spider leg lying immediately to its right. This will be the end of the first row, so twist the workers twice and put up pin 9. Tension the threads and work back to the outside of the fan cloth stitching through the white passive pair, and twisting the worker once before cloth stitching through the outside fan passive pair when the workers will be twisted twice around pin 10. Work back across the row cloth stitching through the next incoming spider leg before putting up pin 11. Don't forget to twist the workers twice at the end of every row and once between the glittery outside passive pair and the white passive pairs on every row. Work back to the outside edge and put up pin 12. Then work back towards the centre, but once you have cloth stitched through the two white passive pairs put up pin 13 and 'park' the workers temporarily around this pin, but leave them untwisted. Now you must go back to the fan on the opposite side of the bookmark.

Take the worker from the left of pin 4 and cloth stitch it through the first spider leg, twist the worker twice and put up pin 14. Work back to the outside edge and pin 15. At the lefthand end of the next row you will work through the second spider leg before putting up pin 16. Work two more rows, but again do not twist the workers as you come towards pin 13. Leaving that pin in place for a moment make a cloth stitch with the two worker pairs, remove pin 13 and put it up in the same pinhole between the two pairs. Twist both pairs once and then cover the pin with a second cloth stitch, but do not twist either of the pairs before they return to continue their fans. The righthand worker now cloth stitches back to the edge of the fan at pin 18. Work the next row through the edge passive and both of the white passives. Put up pin 19 and then work back to pin 20 at the outer edge. The white passive pair closest to the centre (at the lefthand end of the last row) is now pushed to the left as it leaves the fan here and will not be worked into the next row. Work across through the outside glittery pair and just one pair of white passives, put up pin 21 and then once the workers arrive at pin 22, the fan is complete, so leave the workers here whilst you work on the second half of the lefthand fan in exactly the same way, bringing the worker to pin 27 at the end of the fan. Both fans are now complete and you are ready to tackle your next spider.

First you must twist the spider legs, you need to put three twists on each of the four pairs of white passives which will make up the spider. These have left the fans after pins 26, 24, 19 and 21. Make the four cloth stitches which make up the first half of the spider and put up pin 28 in the centre of its body, then make four more cloth stitches to bring the pairs back to the sides which they started from. Add the three twists to each leg and you are ready to start the next pair of fans.

Continue in this way working fans and spiders alternately until you come to the bottom of the pricking. Finish the last spider, then cloth stitch the righthand worker from pin 30 through the outside passive pair twist it once and make a half stitch with the first spider leg at pin 31, cover the pin with a second half stitch, and add one extra twist to the coloured worker pair only. Do the same with the next spider leg at pin 32. With the worker from the lefthand fan make similar stitches at pins 34 and 35. Now bring the workers together and make a half stitch, pin, half stitch at pin 36. Before you start the next row remove the twist from the white passive pairs at pins 31, 32, 33 and 34. Now take the outside fan passive pair from the righthand edge and after twisting it once, cloth stitch through both white pairs from pins 31 and 32 and then through the righthand worker pair from pin 36. Leave the glittery pair here without adding any further twists. Go back to the outside white pair (from pin 31) and twist it once before cloth stitching it through the next white passive and the worker pair only. Leave it here and go back to the white pair from pin 32, twist it once and cloth stitch it through the worker pair only. Do the same on the other side so that the glittery fan passive pairs are now lying together at the centre and the coloured workers are at the outside edges. Remove the bobbins from the worker threads and using the threads of each pair together tie the first half of a reef knot with an extra 'over and under' on top of all the other threads. Now pick those threads up as a bundle and pass the righthand worker pair underneath to lie on the left and vice versa. Put the bundle of bobbins down and pulling the worker threads tight, tie a full reef knot on the top to secure the workers and to create a nice tassel. Tension each passive pair carefully before trimming the ends off 2-3" (5-8cm) below the knots.

You can then slip your finished bookmark into a plastic sleeve or stitch it onto a length of ribbon or petersham.

Above: Fan and spider bookmark pricking.

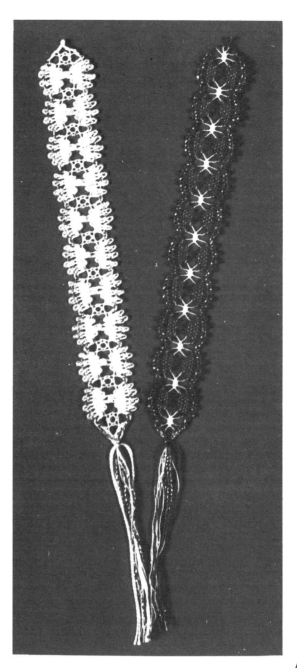

Above: Right - Fan and spider bookmark.
Left - Fan and Rose Ground bookmark.

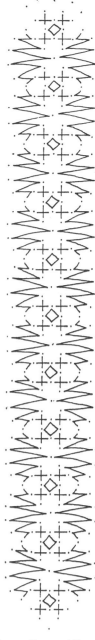

Above: Fan and Rose Ground bookmark pricking.

FAN AND ROSE GROUND BOOKMARK.

This version is a little more challenging than the previous design as the Rose Ground filling does require more concentration!

2 pairs of DMC No 8 Coton Perle as workers for the fans. Cut 2 x 3yd (2.75m) lengths.
2 pairs of Twilley's Gold Dust as outside passives for the fans. Cut 2 x 1yd (1m) lengths.
4 pairs of DMC 80 Cordonnet Special for the ordinary passives. Cut 4 x 1yd (1m) lengths.

I worked the sample with white Perle workers for the fans and outer passives in gold.

WORKING INSTRUCTIONS.

Hang one fan worker pair on pin 1 and then hang the second worker pair from the same pin putting the bobbins down to the right of the first pair. Twist the centre two threads twice to interlink the pairs. Twist both pairs twice. Hang the four ordinary white passive pairs from pins T1, T2, T3 and T4. At pin 2 make a Torchon ground stitch (half stitch, pin, half stitch and twist) with the righthand worker pair and the white pair from pin T1. Do the same at pin 3 with the same worker pair and the next white passive (from pin T2). Push the worker pair to the side and put up pin 4 between the worker and the white passives. Hang the outside fan passive from this pin. Use this pair and the fan worker to make a half stitch, remove pin 4 and put it up again in the centre of these four threads. Now make a cross (left over right) with the two centre threads to cover the pin. Twist the worker pair once, but do not twist the passive pair. Remove the temporary pins at T1 and T2 and tension the white passive pairs so that they slip down to rest around pins 2 and 3. Repeat this sequence of stitches at pins 5, 6 and 7 on the opposite side of the starting point. You are now ready to start the Rose Ground filling.

The four crosses on each side of the diamond indicate the 'preparation' stitch which has to be worked without a pin, before you can go on to work the four pinholes at the points of the diamond. There are many different variations of Rose Ground, but the one I have chosen for most of my projects requires a cloth stitch and twist preparation stitch and a half stitch, pin, half stitch sequence at the diamond points. So take the two white passive pairs from pins 5 and 6 and make a cloth stitch and twist. Do the same with the two passive pairs from pins 2 and 3, then you can work the first half stitch with the two centre pairs of passives (the righthand passive from the lefthand group and vice versa). Put up pin 8 and cover it with a second half stitch. Now use the two lefthand white passive pairs to make a half stitch, pin, half stitch at pin 9. The two righthand passives make a similar stitch at pin 10. The two centre pairs (the righthand pair from pin 9 and the lefthand pair from pin 10) make the final half stitch, pin, half stitch at pin 11. The four diamond pins are now complete, but you must remember to conclude this filling in the same way as you started it - and that is to make two 'preparation' stitches (although perhaps it would be more appropriate to call them 'conclusion' stitches here) with the passive pairs as they come out of the diamond. The two lefthand passives are worked together to make a cloth stitch and twist, and then the two righthand pairs do the same. The Rose Ground filling is then complete and you can return to the edge to make the fan.

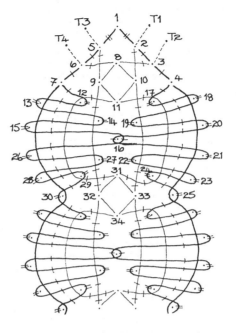

Above: Working diagram for the start of the Rose Ground bookmark.

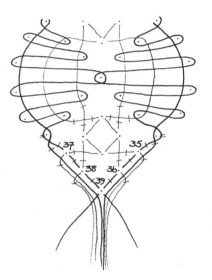

Below: Working diagram for the finish of the Rose Ground bookmark.

The fans are worked in the same way as those of the previous bookmark.

It doesn't matter which of the two edge fans you choose to work first. I worked the lefthand one first, so pick up the worker which lies inside the outer passive at pin 7, check that it is still twisted once and then cloth stitch it through the white passive pair lying on its immediate right (the lefthand pair from pin 11). Twist the worker twice and put up pin 12. Cloth stitch back through the first passive and twist the worker once before cloth stitching through the outside fan passive, twist the worker twice because it is the end of the row and put up pin 13. The worker then cloth stitches through the glittery passive pair and is twisted once before cloth stitching through the first white passive and then through the next white passive (from pin 9). Twist the worker twice and put up pin 14. Work back to the outside edge remembering to twist the workers once to divide the glittery outside pair from the ordinary white passives. Put up pin 15 at the end of the row. Work back towards the centre cloth stitching through both of the white passive pairs. Do not twist the workers at this point, simply 'park' them at pin 16 whilst you start the fan on the opposite side.

Take the worker pair from pin 4 and cloth stitch through the first white passive pair (the righthand pair from pin 11) to complete the first row, twist the worker twice and put up pin 17. Work back to the outside twisting the worker once between the white and the glittery passive pairs. Put up pin 18 at the end of the row and work the next taking in a new white passive (from pin 10) before putting up pin 19. Work back to the outside of the fan at pin 20, and then back to the centre and work a cloth stitch with the other worker pair waiting at pin 16, twist both pairs once and remove pin 16 and put it up again so that it lies in the centre of the two worker pairs. Cover the pin with a second cloth stitch. The righthand worker now goes back to the edge at pin 21, before returning to the centre through both white passive pairs, twist it twice and put up pin 22. Work back to the outside edge once more and push the lefthand white passive to the left as it will not be part of the next row. Work back through the outer passive and only one white pair before putting up pin 24. Work back to pin 25 at the end of this fan.

You can now go back to pin 16 and resume work on the lefthand fan. The first three rows (to pins 26, 27 and 28) will include both of the white passive pairs, you will then push the righthand white pair to one side and work the final two rows of the fan through only the glittery outer passive and the other white passive pair. Both fans are now complete and it is time to work the next diamond of Rose Ground, but first make sure that you put one twist on each of the white passive pairs as they leave the fans so that they are ready to make the 'preparation' stitches.

The two pairs which left the righthand fan after pins 22 and 24, and the two from pins 27 and 29 on the left, make a cloth stitch and twist. Then the two centre pairs make a half stitch, pin, half stitch at pin 31. The two lefthand pairs do the same at pin 32 and the two pairs on the right make a similar stitch at pin 33. The two centre pairs complete the diamond with the same stitch sequence at pin 34. Now make a cloth stitch and twist with the two righthand pairs and then the two lefthand pairs. The Rose Ground diamond is now complete. Do take care whilst making this filling that you keep a close eye on your lace. It really will spoil the appearance of your bookmark if you omit any of the 'preparation' or 'conclusion' cloth stitch and twists, so beware!

Continue down the bookmark until you reach the last row of pins. Make sure that the final area of Rose Ground is completed correctly, then take the worker pair from the right and cloth stitch it through the glittery passive pair, twist it once and make a half stitch, pin, half stitch with the first white pair at pin 35. Put an extra twist on the worker pair only and make a similar stitch with the worker and the next white passive at pin 36. Do the same with the worker from the opposite side at pins 37 and 38. The workers make a half stitch, pin, half stitch at pin 39. Remove the single twist from each of the white passive pairs, then twist the glittery edge passive once and cloth stitch it down through both of the white passives and the first worker pair it meets. Abandon it at this point, you will not work through it again. Take the new edge pair (the first white passive), twist it once and cloth stitch it down to the point, leaving it after it has worked through the first worker pair. Do the same with the next white pair and you will find that once more the worker pair is at the outside edge. Leave it here and do the same on the opposite side of the finishing point. Now remove all the bobbins from the worker threads so that you can use them to tie the finishing 'collecting' knot. This is tied with double threads, so take the worker pair from each side and tie the first half of a reef knot, with an extra 'over and under' so that the threads don't slip whilst you lift all the other bobbins up so that you can take the righthand worker underneath and across to the left and vice versa. Put the bobbins down and tie an ordinary reef knot on the top of all the threads. Tension each individual bobbin carefully, smooth out all the threads and then trim them off approximately 3" (7-8cm) from the knot to make a tassel.

Prickings for the bookmarks with fans, half stitch and honeycomb.

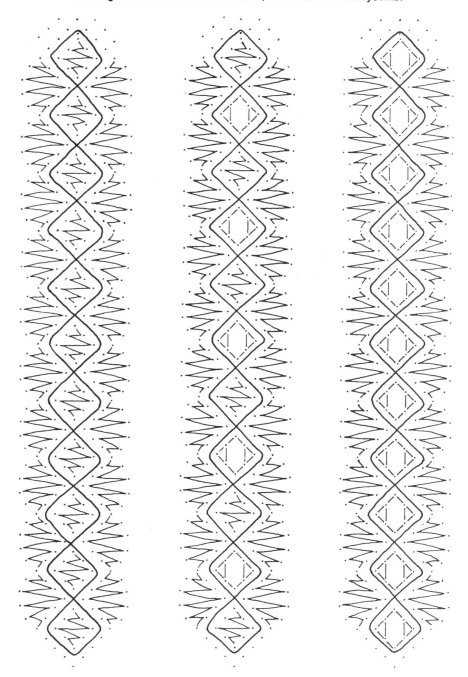

BOOKMARK WITH FANS, HALF STITCH AND HONEYCOMB.

This pattern is a little more complicated than the previous designs, providing the opportunity to master honeycomb stitch. You can also work in a gimp.

2 pairs of DMC No 8 Coton Perle as the fan workers. Cut 2 x 3yd (2.75m) lengths.
2 pairs of Twilley's Gold Dust as the outside fan passives. Cut 2 x 1yd (1m) lengths.
6 pairs of DMC 80 Cordonnet Special as ordinary passives. Cut 6 x 1 1/2yd (135cm) lengths.
1 pair of Twilley's Gold Dust as a gimp. Cut 1 x 1 1/2yd (135cm) length.

This piece can be worked in a variety of colour schemes. For the outside fan passive you can choose a glittery thread to tone or contrast with the fan workers, but for the gimp thread I do suggest that you choose a contrasting colour, so that it stands out quite clearly.

WORKING INSTRUCTIONS.

Hang one fan worker pair on pin 1 and push it to the left so that there is room to hang the second fan worker from the same pin and put the bobbins down to the right. Twist the centre two threads twice to interlink them, then twist each pair twice. Hang one white passive pair on each of the temporary pins (T1-T6). Take the righthand pair from pin 1 and work a Torchon ground stitch (half stitch, pin, half stitch and twist) at pin 2 using the first white passive pair from pin T1. Do the same at each of the next two pins on this side so that the coloured worker pair follows the diagonal line of pins 2, 3 and 4, and the white passives come to rest on the left of this line. Push the coloured workers to the side of the pillow and put up pin 5 between the worker and the white passives. Hang the glittery outside fan passive on this pin and use this pair and the workers to make a half stitch. Take out pin 5 and put it up again in the centre of these four threads. Cover the pin by crossing the centre two threads left over right. The outside fan passive is now at the edge of the work and the worker lies to its left. Twist the worker pair once. Remove pins T1, T2 and T3 and tension the white passives so that they lie close around pins 2, 3 and 4.

Do exactly the same for the lefthand side of the starting point. Don't forget to remove the three temporary pins before hanging on the gimp by placing an extra pin half way between pin 10 and pin 1. Hang the gimp pair on this pin and work the righthand bobbin through the three white passives from pins 2, 3 and 4 by lifting up the lefthand bobbin of each pair and passing the gimp thread through between the two passive threads. Put the passive bobbin down in its starting position and twist the pair twice. The gimp is then sandwiched firmly in position by two twists on the passive both above and below it. Take the other gimp thread through the three passive pairs to its left (again always lift the lefthand bobbin of the passive pair and twist that pair twice once the gimp has gone through). You are now ready to start the first half stitch diamond.

Take the centre two pairs of passives (from pin 6 and pin 2) and work a half stitch. Put up pin 10 in the centre of these four threads. The lefthand pair will start as your 'worker pair' half stitching through the other passive at pin 10 and then the next passive (from pin 3). This is the end of the row so twist the edge pair twice more (giving a total of three twists) and put up pin 11. Work back across through the first two pairs of passives and take in the next passive from pin 7 to bring the total in the diamond up to three. Twist the edge pair twice more and put up pin 12. Bring in the next pair from pin 4 and half stitch across through four pairs of passives. Put up pin 13 at the end of the row. Work

back to pin 14 bringing in the last of the white passives from pin 8. Before you start the next row push aside the pair at the righthand end of the row, this pair will leave the diamond after pin 13 so will not be included in this row. Work across and put up pin 15. Because the diamond is getting narrower, one pair is left out at the end of each row, so the next pair to leave will be the pair at the lefthand end of the row, so that as you work to pin 16 you will work through only three pairs of passives. After pin 16 you will work through only the first two pairs of passives before putting up pin 17. Cover this pin with a half stitch to complete the half stitch diamond.

Each pair coming out of the diamond must have two twists. You'll find that every pair already has one twist on it as part of the half stitch sequence, so just add one more twist to each. The gimp is then passed through the six white passive pairs. The righthand gimp will go through the three pairs from pins 13, 15 and the righthand pair from pin 17; and the lefthand gimp through the pairs from pins 14, 16 and the lefthand pair from pin 17. When the two gimps come together in the centre they must cross over each other. It doesn't matter whether you do this right over left or left over right, but which ever way you choose you must make sure that you cross them in the same way throughout the piece. The centre diamond area is now finished, so you can work the two side fans next.

The fan worker on the right has already worked through the outside fan passive, but check that it still retains the twist which you put on that worker at the start of the piece. Now cloth stitch through the first white passive pair lying to its left, twist the worker twice (as you will do at the end of every row) and put up pin 18. Cloth stitch back through that same passive pair and twist the workers once before cloth stitching through the glittery outside pair. Twist the workers twice at the end of the row, but do not twist any of the passive pairs during the fan. Put up pin 19 and then work back, remembering to twist the workers once between the outside passive and the white passives. Take in the next white passive pair (from pin 15) before twisting the workers and putting up pin 20. Work back to pin 21 before returning to pin 22. Again you will take in a new white passive pair before putting up the pin. The fan is now at its widest and at this point contains all three white passives from this half of the bookmark. From now on you must remember to leave one pair out at the inner edge of each row because the fan will now get progressively narrower. Work back to pin 23 at the outer edge and push aside the white passive pair at the extreme left of that row, it will leave the fan after pin 22. Cloth stitch across to pin 24 and back to pin 25. Again push aside the lefthand passive pair before starting the next row which will contain only one white passive pair and the outside glittery pair. Put up pin 26 and work back to pin 27 which is the end of the fan, so leave the worker here whilst you work a similar sequence of stitches on the opposite side of the bookmark (pins 28-37).

The six white passive pairs coming out of the fans must now be twisted twice before and then twice after the gimp has passed through them all. You can now work the diamond of honeycomb. Start with the two centre pairs (one from pin 32 and one from pin 22) and make a honeycomb stitch (half stitch, twist, pin, half stitch and twist) at pin 38. Make a similar stitch with the lefthand of these two pairs and the passive from pin 34 at pin 39. Again take the lefthand pair and work the same stitch at pin 40 with the pair from pin 36. The righthand pair from pin 40 and the remaining pair from pin 39 make a similar stitch at pin 41. Take the remaining pair from pin 38 and the next passive pair from pin 24 and work a honeycomb stitch at pin 42. Again take the righthand pair together with the pair from pin 26 and work a similar stitch at pin 43. With the lefthand pair from pin 43 and the pair remaining at pin 42, work the same stitch at pin 44. The two centre pairs (the righthand pair from pin 41 and the lefthand pair from pin 44) now come together and work a honeycomb stitch at pin 45. The honeycomb diamond is now complete and as each pair already has two twists upon it you can pass the gimp through the three pairs on each side immediately. Twist the passive pairs twice after the gimp has passed through them and then cross the gimps in the centre. You can now work the next two fans.

Continue working fans and then diamonds, alternating the half stitch and the honeycomb diamonds. Of course if you prefer there is no reason why you shouldn't work this bookmark with entirely honeycomb diamonds, or with eleven half stitch diamonds. You can also completely omit the gimp if you prefer, so from one basic pricking you can make quite a variety of bookmarks.

Left: Working diagram to show the start of the bookmark with fans, half stitch and honeycomb.

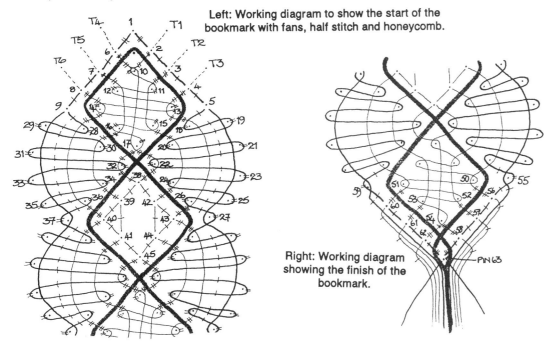

Right: Working diagram showing the finish of the bookmark.

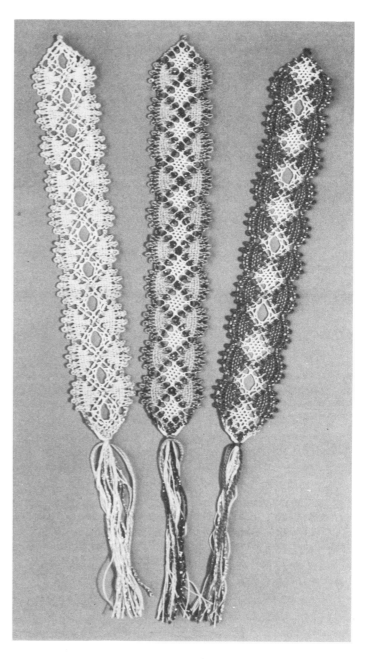

Above: Bookmarks with fans, half stitch and honeycomb.

When you reach the bottom of the bookmark complete the last diamond of half stitch and pass the gimp through the passives in the same way as usual. Cross the gimps at the point of the diamond. Now you are ready to work the final row of pinholes, so pick up the workers from pin 55 and cloth stitch them through the outside passive as usual, twist the workers once and then make a half stitch with the white passive pair from pin 50 at pin 56. Cover the pin with a second half stitch and add one extra twist to the worker pair. Make a similar stitch at pins 57 and 58 using the pair from pin 52 and the righthand pair from pin 54. Pass the righthand gimp through the worker pair and twist the worker pair twice more. Leave this pair of workers here whilst you do the same with the worker on the lefthand side at pins 60, 61 and 62. Again pass the gimp through the worker pair and twist the workers twice more. The two worker pairs now come together and work a half stitch, pin, half stitch at pin 63. Pass each gimp back through the worker pair closest to it so that the glittery threads are lying next to each other in the centre.

Remove the twist from all the white passive pairs and go back to the glittery edge passive from pin 55, twist it once and cloth stitch it through the three white passive pairs and the first worker pair from pin 63. Leave it here and go back to the white passive from pin 56. Twist it once and cloth stitch it down through the three pairs to its left finishing with the coloured worker pair. Do the same with the next white passive pair from pin 57, although this time there will be only two pairs to work through. Finally take the last white passive pair and make a cloth stitch with the coloured worker pair. Follow the same sequence on the other side of the finishing point, working each pair in turn towards the centre so that the coloured workers end up at the two outside edges. Remove the bobbins from these two pairs and tie a collecting knot with the double threads. Start with the first half of a reef knot, but add an extra 'over and under' so that it doesn't slip once you have tightened it. Now lift the other bobbins as a bundle and pass the righthand knotting threads to the left and vice versa, put the bundle of bobbins down and tie an ordinary reef knot on the top of them with the same double worker threads. Tension all the threads carefully and then remove all the bobbins and trim the ends to make a tassel 2-3" (5-8cm) in length. Your bookmark is now complete and can be slipped into a plastic cover, or mounted on a piece of ribbon.

DECORATED CHRISTMAS BALLS.

SCALLOPED BAND WITH BEADS TO DECORATE A CHRISTMAS BALL.

I have worked this design to fit Christmas balls of three different sizes. The basic pattern is very simple consisting of two cloth stitch trails. These two trails are connected with beads at the end of each scallop and it is here that you can enjoy experimenting with different combinations and types of beads.

For the small Christmas ball - approximately 1" (2.5cm) in diameter.
2 pairs of workers in 36/2 Brok or DMC 30 Brilliant. Cut 2 x 1½yd (135cm) lengths.
4 pairs of passives in 36/2 Brok, DMC 30 Brilliant or DMC Metallise. Cut 4 x 1yd (1m) lengths.

For the medium Christmas ball - approximately 1⅞" (4.75cm) diameter.
2 pairs of workers in 36/2 Brok, DMC 30 Brilliant, Mez Effektgarn, DMC Metallise or fine Madeira. Cut 2 x 3yd (2.75m) lengths.
4 pairs of passives in one of the threads listed above. Cut 4 x 1¼yd (110cm) lengths.

For the large Christmas ball - approximately 2¼" (6cm) diameter.
2 pairs of workers in DMC Fil a Dentelle. Cut 2 x 3yd (2.75m) lengths.
4 pairs of passives in DMC 8 Coton Perle. Cut 4 x 48" (120cm) lengths.

I have added beads between the trails at the end of each scallop. You can use a wide variety of plastic, metal or glass beads. For the samples of the smallest balls I used 8 small plastic beads in the shape of a flower. These are just under 2/10" (5mm) across, but if you prefer you can use two smaller beads which together will take up the same space. One of the samples I worked entirely in 36/2 Brok, the other had DMC 30 workers with DMC Metallise passives.

On the medium sized sample I used twenty four 2mm round pearly beads putting on two beads at the end of each scallop. I worked the lace entirely in DMC Metallise using pink passives and silver workers. This gave a very fine strip of lace which I think went well with the tiny pearl beads.

For the largest Christmas ball I used red for both workers and passives and linked the trails with two 2mm and one 3mm bead. Altogether you would need 24 of the smaller beads and 12 of the larger ones.

WORKING INSTRUCTIONS.

Before you start work on the lace you ought to check the circumference of the Christmas ball you plan to decorate. The easiest way to measure this is to take a piece of ribbon and wind it round the widest part of the ball. Mark the point of overlap with a pin, then place the ribbon at the side of your pricking, with the end of the ribbon level with the start of the pricking. The pin marking the circumference of the ball should then be fairly close to the end of the pricking. If it is more than 1/2" (1cm) either way then I would suggest that you ought to enlarge or reduce the size of the pricking to achieve a satisfactory fit. Minor adjustments should not mean that a change of thread will be necessary, but be prepared to put an extra twist on the workers at the centre of the trails, or perhaps to omit those twists altogether if you have had to make the pattern smaller. The pattern doesn't have to be too exact, you can make adjustments as you glue the lace onto the ball at the end.

The lace strip for all of the Christmas balls is worked in a similar way, the only variation being whether to twist the workers between the two pairs of passives to give a lighter, more open effect. For example on the two smallest balls the one I worked in white 36/2 Brok I added one twist down the centre of each trail, but when I used the 30 DMC with Metallise passives I wanted those glittery threads to cover the whole width of the trail rather than be broken up into two groups as I thought it would be more effective, so I omitted the centre twist on the workers. On the medium sized Christmas balls I worked the sample with solid, unbroken trails, but for the largest ball I did introduce two twists on the workers half way across each row as both threads were matt, rather than glittery, and I thought that the added twists would give just that little bit more interest to what would otherwise have been a rather dull solid trail. You must use your experience to judge whether the thickness of the threads allows for one or two central twists, and your discretion to decide whether the appearance would be improved by those extra twists.

I started the strip with the workers hung on pins 3 and 4 and one pair of passives hung on each of pins 1, 2, 5 and 6. Cloth stitch the workers from pin 4 through the two pairs of passives (remembering to put a twist on the workers between the two if you have decided to work the trails in that way), twist the workers twice and put up pin 7. Tension the pairs and continue working along that trail until you reach the circled hole on the outside edge at the end of the first scallop. Twist the inside passive pair once, then go across to the opposite trail and cloth stitch the worker from pin 3 out to pin 8, again twist the worker twice at the end of the row and continue working along the trail until you reach the circled hole. Leave the workers here whilst you add the first bead, but don't forget to add one twist to the inside passive pair.

To add the bead you can use a crochet hook (which must be fine enough to go through the beads you are using) or a 'lazy susan'. First thread the bead, or beads, onto the crochet hook then put the inside passive thread from the lefthand trail into the hook and sliding the beads off the hook, pull the thread through to form a loop. Enlarge this loop so that you can pass the inside passive thread from the righthand trail through it spangle first. Pull both threads away from each other and the beads will slide up to rest against the work.

If you are using a lazy susan (a fine beading needle mounted in a wooden handle so that the eye faces outward, which is threaded with a 12" (30cm) length of thin coloured sewing thread) then push the bead, or beads, onto the needle and slide them down so that they rest up against the wooden handle. Now ease the sewing thread away from the needle close to its eye and pass the first inside passive bobbin through the loop which you have created between the needle and the sewing thread. Keeping a firm hold on the sewing thread (by trapping it against the wooden handle with your thumb) you can slide the beads off the needle, and by continuing to pull, the passive thread is brought through the beads to make a loop. Once the loop is large enough to catch with your fingers, you can disengage the lazy susan and pass the second passive thread through that loop. Pull on both threads simultaneously and the beads will slide up the threads to the work.

Once the bead, or beads, are in place twist the inner passive pair of both trails once. You can then resume work on the trails, where the most important thing is to maintain a good tension so that they will be completely flat and smooth. There are no short cuts to a good tension, you must take the time at the end of every row to pull on the workers and then, whilst the workers are under tension, pull and stroke each passive thread individually until each is perfectly smooth and the cloth stitch rows of weaving show no sign of 'caterpillaring'! Once the workers reach the circled pinhole at the end of each scallop then leave them at that outside pin twist the inner passive pairs once and use the two innermost passive threads from each trail to fix the bead into position.

When the last bead is in place take the workers across and back to the very last pinhole on each trail and tie a reef knot around those pins with the worker threads. The four passive pairs are then tied off with similar reef knots. You can now remove your bobbins trimming the threads close to the reef knots, lift your pins and remove the lace from the pillow.

Below: Large ball with scalloped band.

I used small touches of glue behind the trails to attach the lace to the Christmas balls. You must start by gluing the finishing end with all its knots to the centre of the ball. If you can obtain the type of Christmas ball with the ridges on the surface it does make it very much easier to judge the centre and to fix the lace on so that it is perfectly level. Now glue the whole of the next scallop of both trails and press it into position. Give this a minute or two to set firmly then check the fit of your lace around the diameter of the ball. If the piece of lace is on the generous side you can ease the trails further apart, making the scallop deeper but shorter in length. On the other hand if it is not quite long enough then you can stretch each scallop a little. It is important to check the fit as you glue, as it is too late to make much adjustment if you've left it all until the last few scallops! The final scallops are glued into place so that the neater starting ends will overlap and completely cover the knots of the finishing ends. Use a leftover length of thread to make a hanging loop.

Below: Working diagram for start of band.

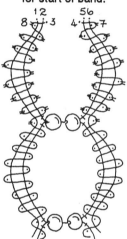

Above: Medium ball with scalloped band.

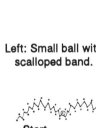

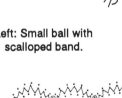
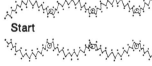

Left: Small ball with scalloped band.

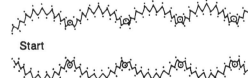

Start   Pricking for small scalloped band.

Start   Pricking for medium scalloped band.

Start   Pricking for large scalloped band.

85

TWO BANDS OF OPEN 'FANS'.

This pattern is very straightforward and quick to make. The pricking is the same as used for the small plastic ring with the bead drop, but instead of working the full circle of twelve repeats you work only ten.

1 pair of Twilley's Gold Dust or flat pack Madeira as 'fan' workers. Cut 1 x 3yd (3m) length.

4 pairs of DMC 30 Brilliante or equivalent as passives. Cut 4 x 1¼yds (110cm) lengths. If you choose to use DMC Metallise or the fine metallic Madeira cut 4 x 2½yd (225cm) lengths and fold each piece in half before winding it on to the bobbins.

1 Christmas tree ball 2¼" (6cm) in diameter.

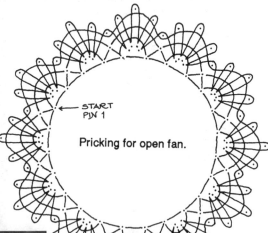

START PIN 1

Pricking for open fan.

Below: Large sized ball with two bands of open fans.

Right: Working diagram for open fans.

I worked the sample in green glittery Gold Dust with green DMC passives which looked very festive when mounted on a red silk covered ball. It would also be interesting to work it with passives which were the same colour as the ball the lace was to be mounted on, then the background threads would disappear making the worker 'fan' even more prominent.

WORKING INSTRUCTIONS.

Hang two of the passive pairs on pin 1 and interlink them. Twist the lefthand pair twice and the righthand pair three times. Hang another passive pair from T1 and use it to make a Torchon ground stitch (half stitch, pin, half stitch and twist) with the lefthand pair from pin 1, putting up pin 2. Remove pin T1 and tension both pairs. Take the righthand pair from pin 2 and make a similar Torchon ground stitch at pin 3. Add an extra twist to the righthand pair here to make a total of three. The pair at the inner edge of the circle must always be twisted three times in this way.

Hang the remaining passive pair from pin 4 and push it to the left. Hang the worker pair from the same pin and put it down to the right of the previous pair. Twist the centre two bobbins twice and then twist the outside passive pair once and the worker twice. Cloth stitch the worker through the passive pair from pin 2 and then twist the passive once and the worker twice. Cloth stitch the worker through the lefthand passive pair from pin 3, twist the worker twice and put up pin 5 but do not twist the passive at all. Tension the worker carefully and then work back towards the outside edge, cloth stitching the worker through each pair of passives and twisting the middle and the outside passive pairs once after each cloth stitch. The worker is twisted twice after each cloth stitch and at the end of the row. Put up pin 6. Repeat the last two rows until the worker reaches pin 12. The 'fan' is now complete.

Between each fan you must work three pinholes of ground (pins 13, 14 and 15), but first you must remember to twist the middle and inner passive pairs twice as they leave the 'fan'. The middle passive will already have one twist so just add one more, but the inner passive, being untwisted will need two twists at this point. Take the inner passive and make a ground stitch at pin 13, twist the inner pair once more to give it the usual total of three twists. Then bring the lefthand passive pair from pin 13 to make a ground stitch with the middle passive at pin 14. Make the final ground stitch at pin 15 using the inner edge pair and the righthand pair from pin 14. Again add an extra twist to the inside passive pair. The triangle of three ground stitches is now complete and you can work the next 'fan'.

When you have finished working the tenth 'fan' (leaving two 'fans' of the pricking unworked) carefully unpin all but the last three repeats and re-pin the first 'fan' you worked down onto the eleventh repeat, moving the bobbins to the outside of the pillow whilst you do so. Now join the inner edge passive to starting pin 1. The inner 'fan' passive will also be joined into pin 1 and tied off with a reef knot. The middle 'fan' passive will join into pin 2 and the worker must be joined into pin 4. The outside passive can be tied off without bringing it through a starting loop. Remove all the pins and trim off the ends.

Make a second piece of lace in exactly the same way. Both pieces are glued onto the ball using touches of glue behind the 'fan'. I used a ridged ball which allowed me to position the inner edge of the lace very accurately, it is more difficult to ensure that the edgings are glued on level without such a guide. To complete the project use a length of leftover worker thread to make a hanging loop.

CHRISTMAS TREE DECORATIONS IN RINGS.

TORCHON FAN AND GROUND.

This pattern is the same as the Simple Torchon Ground and Fan Christmas card, but I have enlarged it just enough to make it fit into a large sized metal bangle.

1 pair of fan workers in Twilley's Gold Dust. Cut 1 x 4½yd (425cm) length.
1 pair of passives for the outer edge of the fan in the same thread. Cut 1 x 1½yd (135cm) length.
1 pair of passives for the inner edge in the same thread. Cut 1 x ¾yd (70cm) length.
5 pairs of passives in DMC 80 Cordonnet Special. Cut 5 x 1½yd (135cm) lengths.
1 6.5cm metal bangle.

For the example shown I used gold Twilley's Gold Dust with white passives. If you prefer more colourful passives, then DMC Fil a Dentelle would be a satisfactory substitute.

Above: Torchon fan and ground Christmas tree decoration.

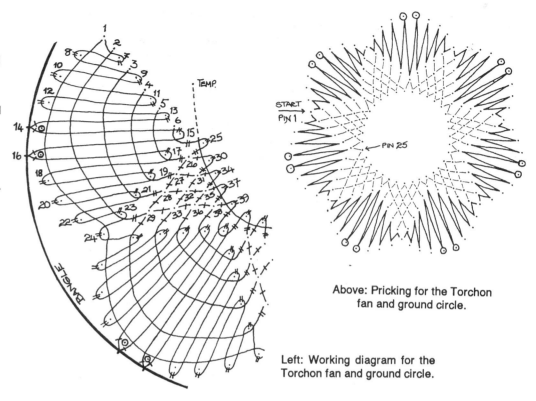

Above: Pricking for the Torchon fan and ground circle.

Left: Working diagram for the Torchon fan and ground circle.

WORKING INSTRUCTIONS.

Pin your pattern to the middle of the pillow and position a 6.5cm metal bangle on top of the pricking so that the circled pinholes on each fan are an even distance away from the ring. Although the exact size of the bangle may vary you should find that these circled pinholes are quite close to the inside edge of the ring. Pin the bangle into place by using three or four anchoring pins which are positioned inside the ring in the spaces between the fans. Do not use the circled pinholes as you will find that you have to remove these pins when you come to use those pinholes. If you place the anchoring pins at approximately equal distances around the inner edge of the ring you'll find that it holds the ring very firmly. You must push these pins well down into the pillow so that you can work without removing them, so it helps if you have chosen fairly large flat-headed pins for the job as the heads will project over the edge of the ring and prevent it from lifting off the pillow.

Follow the detailed instructions given for this piece in the Christmas card section. The pairs are hung on in exactly the same positions, the ground stitches and the fan are also worked in a similar manner, but there is just one very important difference. You will see that two of the pinholes at the edge of the fan are circled, and at these pins you must join the worker pair to the bangle. To do this work across the row as usual and put one twist on the workers at the end of the row. Now push the lefthand worker thread, which is nearest the ring, under the ring so that you can pull enough of that thread through to make a loop big enough to pass the other worker bobbin through (passing it through spangle first means that the thread is less likely to catch on the beads). Put up the pin in the circled pinhole and pull both threads tight. Twist the workers once and continue, making sure that you remember to link the workers to the ring again at the next outside pinhole, which is also circled.

You may find it helps to use a pin-lifter to push the thread under the ring. Make sure that there is plenty of slack on the worker thread and place it into the fork of the pinlifter, now simply push the toe of the lifter under the ring and you should be able to catch the thread with your finger nail, as when you withdraw the pinlifter, the thread is left behind. But one word of warning. If you do not make sure that the worker thread is slack, or if you use a very sharp edged pinlifter, there is a danger that you will cut straight through the thread as you push it under. So take care!

Don't worry if the ring pops off the anchoring pins as you push the thread under, just ease it back into place and re-position the anchor pins. You can also deliberately raise two or three of the anchoring pins when you come to link the workers to the ring. This will ensure that the ring stays in place, and yet allow it to lift as you push the worker thread through.

On completing the circle join the ends into the corresponding starting loops and tie off each pair with a reef knot. Trim off all the ends and remove the work from the pillow. Use a small length of the left over Gold Dust to make a hanging loop which should be attached to the ring at the centre of one of the fans between the two worker links.

SMALL RING WITH HOLLY LEAF CENTRE PIECE.

This fine edging forms a delicate trim for a very small plastic ring or without a ring it makes a lovely edging for a small picture or embroidery. The pinholes on the inner edge are quite close together so care must be taken not to miss any. The open fan is also a bit more tricky to work, but the end result is most rewarding.

1 pair of DMC Or Clair or Argent Clair, alternatively you can use a doubled length of DMC Metallise in which case you will need to cut your thread twice as long before folding it in half to wind your bobbins. You will need a working length of 1 x 3½yd (3.25m) as the workers for the fan.

1 pair of DMC 30 Brilliant as workers for the cloth stitch area. Cut 1 x 4½yd (4m) length.

5 pairs of DMC 30 Brilliant as passives. Cut 5 x 2yd (2m) lengths.

1 small plastic ring with an outside diameter of 4.5cm.

2 paper holly leaf triangles and 2 embroidered motifs or 2 ribbon roses to make the centre piece.

For one of the samples I used a gold Clair fan worker with red passives and a centre piece of gold holly leaves with red ribbon roses. The second has a silver fan worker with green passives and matching holly leaves trimmed with two embroidered motifs. For the Christmas card I used white passives with a sparkly, pearly white fan worker made from a doubled length of Metallise thread. The centre is a small piece of cross stitch embroidery.

WORKING INSTRUCTIONS.

First of all join the cloth stitch worker pair to the plastic ring by taking the centre of the thread between the two bobbins underneath the ring and up into the centre. Pass the bobbins through this loop spangle first. Pull the bobbins tight and position the ring in the centre of the pattern so that the loop attaching the thread to the ring is directly over the first of the pair of circled pinholes at the start. Put the pin into the circled pinhole so that it passes through the thread loop, preventing it from moving round the ring. Place three evenly spaced pins close against the inner edge of the bangle so that it is securely held in place. If you are working the edging without a bangle simply hang the cloth stitch workers from pin A.

Hang the fan worker on pin 6, now hang one each of the passive pairs on pins 1, 2, 3 and 4 which have been placed between the working pinholes of the cloth stitch triangle. The final passive pair is hung from pin 5.

Start the fan by making a cloth stitch with the fan worker and the first passive (from pin 1), twist both the worker and the passive pairs once. Continue with this cloth stitch and twist through the next three passive pairs hanging from pins 1, 2 and 3. At the end of this row add a further twist to the worker, giving it the usual total of two twists before putting up pin 7. Tension the workers and all four passive pairs, then work back across

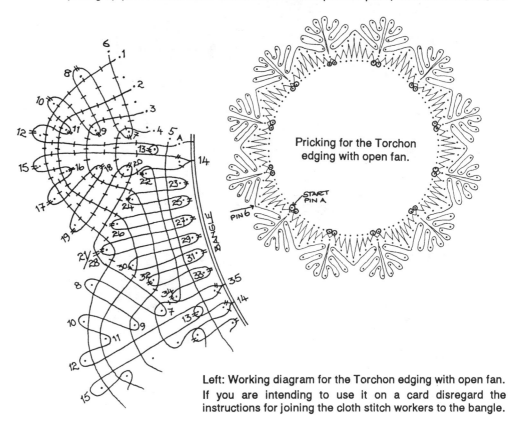

Pricking for the Torchon edging with open fan.

Left: Working diagram for the Torchon edging with open fan. If you are intending to use it on a card disregard the instructions for joining the cloth stitch workers to the bangle.

to pin 8 using a cloth stitch and twist for each stitch, don't forget to add an extra twist to the worker at the end of the row before putting up the pin and tensioning each pair. The next row of the fan will be shorter, so push aside the passive pair at the righthand end of the previous row (originally from pin 4) and work across to pin 9 with the usual cloth stitch and twist taking you through all three pairs of passives. Add an extra twist to the workers and put up pin 9, tension the pairs and work back across to pin 10 in exactly the same way. The next row of the fan will be even shorter, so once again push aside the pair at the righthand end of the previous row, so now there will be only two pairs of passives to work through to reach pin 11. Work back to pin 12 and tension each pair carefully, now using the usual cloth stitch and twist, work through all four pairs of passives straight down through the middle of the fan towards pin 13, but leave the workers with just the one twist as soon as they have worked through the fourth pair of passives.

Now pick up the worker from pin A at the inside edge. Cloth stitch it through the passive pair from pin 5 and then through the fan worker. Twist the ordinary worker (not the fan worker) twice and put up pin 13, cloth stitch it back across to pin 14 where it must be joined to the ring if you are working on a bangle, so push the nearer worker thread under the ring to make a loop and pass the other worker bobbin through that loop. Pull both tight, twist them once and put up pin 14 in the circled hole. Leave them here whilst you finish the fan.

To complete the fan swing the fan worker out of the cloth stitch triangle and twist it once before working back through the four pairs of passives with the usual cloth stitch and twist to pin 15. The first two rows of the fan will be very short, so you will only work through the first two pairs of passives for pins 16 and 17. This increases to three pairs for pins 18 and 19, and then to all four pairs for the final row which brings you to pin 21. Give the worker its extra twist and leave it here as you now need to return to the cloth stitch triangle.

Pick up the worker from pin 14 and cloth stitch it through the inner passive and the first passive to leave the fan and enter this cloth stitch area. Put two twists on the workers and put up pin 22. Cloth stitch back to pin 23 where the worker is twisted twice. The next row of cloth stitch is longer, so bring in the next pair from the fan before putting up pin 24. You will also increase the number of passives in the triangle as you work to pin 26, and then again as you work to pin 28. Here you will cloth stitch through the outside fan passive, twist the worker and slip it round the back of the pin (without taking the pin out) before working back across the row. This pin therefore doubles as both pin 21 and 28. The fan worker is simply left outside the pin at this point.

Continue with the triangle, but you must now remember to leave out one pair of passives from the lefthand end of each row - after pins 28, 30, 32 and 34. Take the workers back to pin 35 where they are joined to the bangle, and where you will leave them while you work the first half of the next fan. However before you return to the fan make sure that you remember to add one twist to each of the four passive pairs as they leave the cloth stitch triangle (after pins 28, 30, 32 and 34). Take care with your tensioning as the threads are quite tightly packed in the cloth stitch triangle and you must make sure that they are tensioned well if this area is to be nice and smooth. To start the next fan follow the instructions from pin 6. The metallic thread of the fan worker can be rather stubborn so you will need to take extra care when tensioning your fan. Don't forget to join the workers to the bangle at each of the circled pinholes along the inner edge, unless you are making an edging for a card, when obviously you can disregard those instructions.

Small rings with Torchon edging and holly leaf centre pieces.

As you work the second half of the final triangle of cloth stitch you must look carefully to make sure you are using the correct holes, remember that the starting pins for the four pairs of passives are placed between the working pinholes which you will now need to use to complete the final rows of cloth stitch. To make the finishing just a little bit easier I found that it was worth joining the passive pairs into their starting loops as I went along. So as soon as you have reached the equivalent of pins 29, 31, 33 and 35 leave the worker at the inner edge while you join the passive which has just been left out at the lefthand end of the previous row to its starting loop. So whilst the worker is at pin 29 you can join the fan workers to the starting loop at pin 6 and the outside passive to the loop at pin 1. After the next two rows you will join the second passive into the loop at pin 2, the next into pin 3 and finally the fourth into pin 4. The inner passive will join its starting loop at pin 5 and the worker will be knotted around the threads coming away from the ring at pin A.

Remove the pins and trim off all the surplus thread close to the reef knots, with the exception of the fan workers if you are making the Christmas tree decoration. I have used these to make the hanging loop, simply knotting them together 2" (5cm) away from the edge of the lace.

If you are using this piece to trim a Christmas card then you will need to cut a hole approximately 17/8" (a fraction under 5cm) in diameter if you wish the lace to come up to the edge of the hole. If you would like to make a small border between the lace and the circular cut out, then make the hole smaller. You can mount a picture from an old Christmas card, a photo or a small piece of embroidery in the centre. As I didn't have a commercial card mount with a cut out of the correct size I made my own by cutting a piece of card 105/8" x 45/8" (27cm x 11.5cm) Divide the longer side into three equal parts and score across to make a good sharp fold. Cut the circle out of the centre section so that one section can be glued down behind it to hide the back of the picture or fabric you have used behind the cut out. Glue the lace into place using a very small amount behind the dense cloth stitch areas. You can add a variety of accessories to give the finishing touch, so experiment with commercial paper greetings, ribbon bows or roses.

If you have made this piece for your Christmas tree then you can make a nice centre piece for the ring with two holly leaf triangles which are glued back to back. I found that as they weren't perfectly symmetrical the white backing showed in places, so before I glued them together I coloured the backing to match the green or gold finish on the right side. First of all take a 2" (5cm) length of DMC Perle to match the DMC Brilliant and loop this onto the ring at the base of the cloth stitch triangle which has the hanging loop coming from its point. Bring the two ends of the Perle towards the centre of the ring and glue the Perle onto the back of one of the holly triangles, glue the second holly triangle on top of the first, then add an embroidered motif or ribbon rose to the centre of each triangle and your decoration is ready for the tree!

Torchon edging with open fan used to decorate a Christmas card.

CHRISTMAS RING WITH TRAILS AND SNOWFLAKE CENTRE BEAD.

This is a very attractive tree decoration with two cloth stitch trails which are linked with alternate kisses and beads. A silver or gold snowflake bead is stitched into the centre once the piece is off the pillow.

2 pairs of workers in DMC 8 Coton Perle. Cut 2 x 3yd (3m) lengths.
4 pairs of passives in Twilley's Gold Dust. Cut 4 x 1yd (1m) lengths.
18 beads 3mm in diameter and 1 snowflake bead.
1 small 5.5cm metal bangle.

For the example I used green Perle and Gold Dust with a gold snowflake, small gold beads and a gold bangle.

WORKING INSTRUCTIONS.

One of the worker threads needs to be attached to the ring and the easiest way of doing this is to join the thread to the ring before you wind on the bobbins, so fold the thread in half, bring the looped end up through the ring, open the loop and pass the cut ends through the loop. Pull it tight and slide it round the ring until it sits over the join in the bangle. Now position the ring centrally over the pricking so that the worker thread is right over one of the circled edge pinholes. Put one of the anchoring pins through the loop of the worker thread into pinhole 1 so that both ring and thread are firmly held in place. Two more anchoring pins spread evenly round the inside of the bangle should keep the ring in position. Push the anchoring pins down, and wind on the two worker bobbins.

Below: Working diagram for the trails and snowflake bead Christmas ring.

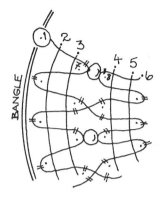

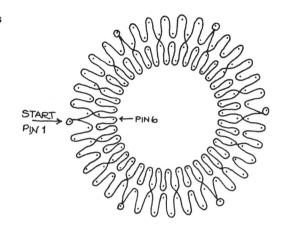

Above: Pricking for trails and snowflake bead Christmas ring.

Hang one passive pair on each of pins 2, 3, 4 and 5, and the second worker pair on pin 6. Cloth stitch the worker from pin 1 through the two pairs of passives to its right and twist the workers twice before putting up pin 7. Leave them here whilst you cloth stitch the workers from pin 6 to pin 8. Again twist the workers twice at the end of the row. You are now ready to add one of the small beads.

I have marked the pricking to show you the exact pathway which the workers will need to follow. Wherever there is a space between the two trails you must add a bead, and in between each bead you will see that I have worked a 'kiss'. To add a bead you will need a crochet hook or a Lazy Susan. If you have a fine hook you can thread one bead onto the hook and then bring one of the worker threads (I used the righthand worker from the outer trail) through the bead to form a loop. Now take the lefthand worker from the inner trail and pass it spangle first through that loop. Pull on both worker threads, swinging them apart as you do so and the bead will slide up into place. Alternatively thread the bead onto your Lazy Susan (a beading needle mounted eye-outwards in a wooden handle) which is threaded with a length of contrasting coloured thread. Now ease the thread away from the needle above the bead and make a loop big enough to pass the first worker bobbin through. Keeping the Lazy Susan thread firmly against its handle pull the bead off the needle and continue pulling to bring the worker thread through the bead. You can now pass the second worker bobbin through the loop formed by the first, and pull both tight to slide the bead up to the pins. Now continue the trails until your workers arrive at the inside pair of holes once more. This time you must do a kiss.

First make sure that both pins are in position at the end of the rows (pins 10 and 12) and that both worker pairs have been twisted twice as usual. Now make a cloth stitch with the two workers and twist both pairs twice once again. You can now resume work on the trails, but you will find that the worker from the outside trail is now the worker on the inner trail (and vice versa) until the next kiss when the workers will change trails yet again.

Continue in this way adding beads and linking the trails with a kiss at alternate pinholes. Watch out for the circled pinholes at the edge of the outside trail, this is where you must remember to join the outer worker pair to the bangle. So before you put up the pin slip the outside worker thread under the ring to make a loop and pass the second worker bobbin through this loop. Now place the pin in the circled hole and pull both threads tight, twist them once, and continue across the trail.

When the circle is complete the inside trail workers will be tied off into the starting loop at pin 6, the four passive pairs will be joined into their corresponding starting loops at pins 2, 3, 4 and 5, and the outside worker can be tied around the worker thread between pin 1 and the outside passive pair at pin 2. When the pins are removed trim off the surplus thread from pins 2, 3, 4, 5 and 6, but do not cut off the outside worker pair as this will form your hanging loop, just tie an overhand knot 2" (5cm) away from the ring and then trim off the extra thread.

All you need to do now is to stitch the snowflake bead into the centre. I used fine gold thread to match the snowflake and worked several stitches from the inner worker loop just to the right of the centre, through the bead, and back through the worker loop just to the left of the centre. Knot the thread off carefully and do the same through the bottom hole in the bead and the worker loops on each side of the centre to keep the snowflake steady. Your decoration is now complete.

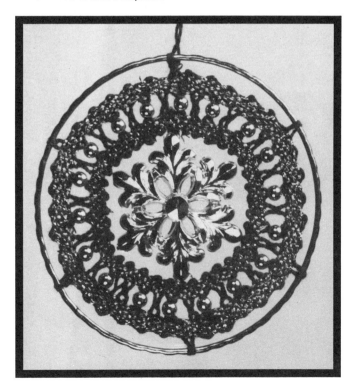

Christmas ring with trails and snowflake bead.

SNOWFLAKE TRAILS WITH OVAL AND ROUND BEADS.

This decoration is made up of two trails. The outer trail follows the shape of a hexagon and is linked to the circular inner trail by two different combinations of beads. This is a very simple project to make once you have mastered the art of attaching the beads!

1 pair of workers for the outer trail in DMC 30 Brilliante. Cut 1 x 4yd (4m) length.

1 pair of workers for the inner trail in the same thread. Cut 1 x 2yd (2m) length.

2 pairs of passives for the outer trail in Twilley's Gold Dust. Cut 2 x 1yd (1m) lengths.

2 pairs of passives for the inner trail in the same thread. Cut 2 x 1/2yd (50cm) lengths.

1 medium sized gold or silver metal bangle 6cm in diameter.

18 round beads 2mm in diameter to match 6 oval beads approximately 7mm long.

I worked two examples one in red thread with gold beads and the other in pink threads with pearl beads, but it would look equally attractive in different colour combinations. You should be able to find these beads in a white, pink or pale blue pearly finish as well as gold and silver. If you are unable to get beads of precisely this size then of course you could make up your own combinations, perhaps using a single 4mm bead in place of the pair of 2mm beads, and perhaps as many as three beads to cover the distance between the two trails at the point.

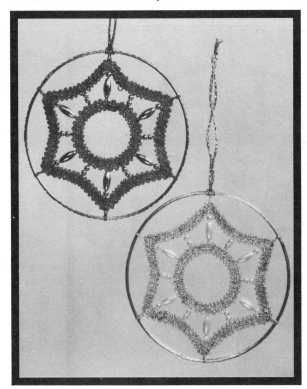

Christmas tree decorations with
snowflake trails and beads.

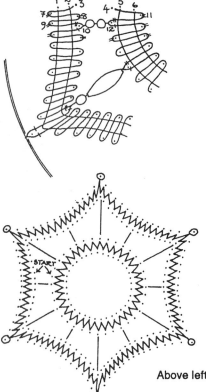

WORKING INSTRUCTIONS.

First of all you must anchor the ring to the pattern in the centre of your pillow, making sure that the pricking is exactly in the middle of the ring. Use at least three pins positioned inside the ring at regular intervals, but do not use pinholes which you will need to use for the outer trail. Push the pins down well.

It's best to start the trails for this project between the groups of beads, rather than at one of the points which would mean that your finish was complicated by trying to add beads and join threads together all in a very small area. You can see that I have marked the suggested start well away from the point of the hexagon and several pinholes before the first lot of beads. This will ensure that the trail is well and truly established before we have the added complication of beads!

Hang the workers for the outer trail on pin 3 and the inner trail workers on pin 4. Hang the outer passive pairs from pins 1 and 2, and the inner trail passives on pins 5 and 6. Work the trails in cloth stitch twisting the workers twice at the end of each row. When the workers arrive at pins 10 and 12 make sure both are twisted in the usual way and that both pins are in position. Now add two tiny round beads with the aid of a crochet hook or a Lazy Susan. If the holes in the beads are big enough thread two beads onto the crochet hook and bring the righthand worker thread from the outer trail through the beads to make a loop, now pass the lefthand worker thread from the inner trail through that loop and pull both workers tight, sliding the beads up to the pins. If the crochet hook is too big to go through the beads, use a Lazy Susan and thread both beads on to the beading needle, now pass the worker bobbin from the outer trail between the needle and the thread in the eye of the beading needle, slide the beads down the needle and pull through the worker thread to make the loop. Now you can complete the process in the usual way. Once the beads are in place twist both worker pairs once then continue with the trail.

Watch the pattern markings carefully as you work the trails, as it is these markings which will tell you when you need to stop and add the next set of beads. This will happen just before the point on the outer trail. This time you have to be a bit more careful, as unlike the previous pair of beads, these two are not identical, so it is very important to develop a system and to use exactly the same system each time if the oval bead is always to lie to the right of the tiny round bead. I threaded the oval bead onto the Lazy Susan first, followed by the little round bead, and I brought the righthand worker from the outer trail through the bead to make the loop, the lefthand worker from the inner trail being passed through that loop to secure the beads in place. So adopt a system and stick to it to avoid confusion!

Once these two beads are on, the outer worker cloth stitches across the trail to the point and here it must be linked to the ring in the usual way, pushing the lefthand worker thread under the ring to make a loop through which the other worker bobbin is passed, twist them once, put up the pin at the point and work back across the row. You must be very careful about your tensioning here as if you pull too firmly on the outside passive pair you'll find that it pulls away from the point. So either be very gentle with the outside passive here, or put in an extra support pin in the centre of the trail, between the two pairs of passives, so that the passive cannot be pulled too far over.

Above left: Working diagram for the start of the snowflake trails and beads decoration.

Left: Pricking for the snowflake trails and beads decoration.

Continue round the circle adding beads and linking the worker to the ring at the appropriate time. When complete, you must join each pair into its own starting loop and tie a neat reef knot with each one. Unwind the bobbins, remove the pins and take it off the pillow. Now you can trim off the surplus thread. Use a 4" (10cm) length of left-over Gold Dust to make the hanging loop which is attached to the ring at one of the points. Knot the ends of the hanging loop together and your project is complete.

MAGIC CHAINS AND SNOWFLAKE.

This Christmas tree decoration is made up of two trails, an outer circular trail which is linked at alternate pins to the outside metal ring, and a hexagonal shaped trail which fits inside it. The two trails are joined at each point of the hexagon, and are decorated with a 'magic chain' of two differently coloured thicker threads. A snowflake shaped bead is stitched into the centre when the piece is taken off the pillow.

1 pair of workers for the outer trail in DMC Fil a Dentelle. Cut 1 x 3yd (3m) length.
1 pair of workers for the hexagonal trail in the same thread. Cut 1 x 2yd (2m) length.
4 pairs of trail passives in DMC Coton Perle No 8 in the same colour as the workers. Cut 4 x 1yd (1m) lengths.
4 pairs for the 'magic chain' in Twilley's Gold Dust. Using two different colours will give you a more interesting effect than making them all the same. Cut 4 x 1yd lengths.
1 medium sized gold or silver metal bangle 6cm in diameter.

For the example I used green workers and Perle passives with a magic chain in red and gold. The snowflake in the centre is gold, but you could easily work out a colour scheme to take a silver snowflake for a change.

WORKING INSTRUCTIONS.

As usual, when working decorations inside a metal bangle you must position your pricking and then centre the ring around the pattern in the very middle of your pillow. Anchor the bangle down with three or four evenly spaced pins inside the ring, and push them right down into the pillow with their heads just overlapping the bangle.

It is best to start both trails a few pinholes before the outer trail is linked to the ring, and the two trails are joined together at one of the hexagon points. You can then get both trails established before carrying out the linking process. So hang the outer worker on pin 4 and the hexagonal trail worker on pin 8. The four pairs of Perle passives are hung on pins 1, 3, 5 and 7. Finally hang the Gold Dust pairs on pins 2 and 6, making sure that you use one of each colour at each pin and that the pairs are hung on 'open'. There's no need to worry about which colour is the outer pair and which is the inner pair at these pinholes as it's not really necessary for them to match.

Start the outside trail first by cloth stitching the worker from pin 4 through the passive from pin 3. Now lift the first of the Gold Dust threads and pass both of the worker bobbins underneath it. Keep both of the worker bobbins in one hand and lift them over the two centre Gold Dust threads, now lift the outside Gold Dust thread and pass the two worker bobbins underneath it. To complete the row make a cloth stitch with the workers and the final pair of Perle passives. Twist the workers twice and put up pin 9. You now repeat exactly the same sequence for the next row, starting with a cloth stitch, then passing the workers under the first, over the centre two and under the last of the Gold Dust threads, finish with a cloth stitch and two twists on the workers. Put up pin 10.

Now it is time to change the order of the Gold Dust threads to make the 'magic chain'. Simply pick up the two outer Gold Dust threads and lift them over, and put them down between, the two middle Gold Dust threads. So the two outside threads are now the new centre threads and vice versa. You can now work two more rows exactly as you did before with precisely the same lifting sequence for the Gold Dust threads, but you will notice that at the lefthand end of the next row you must link the worker to the metal ring. Just push the outer worker thread under the ring to make a loop and pass the other worker bobbin through that loop. Pull both tight, twist them once more and put up pin 11. Now work back across the row to pin 12. Leave the workers here because this is the pinhole at the point of the hexagon which has to be shared with the inner trail.

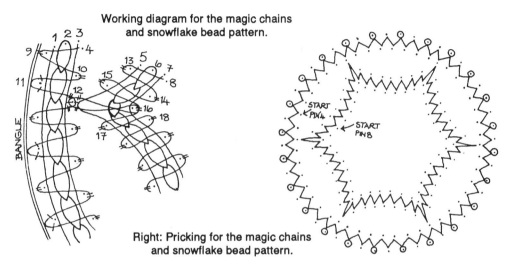

Working diagram for the magic chains and snowflake bead pattern.

Right: Pricking for the magic chains and snowflake bead pattern.

To start the inner trail work as far as pin 16 following exactly the same steps as the outside trail (from pin 4 to 9, 10, 11, [but ignore the instructions for linking the worker to the ring] and 12). Change the order of the Gold Dust threads and work across towards pin 12. Both workers should be twisted twice, now cloth stitch them together, twist both once and removing pin 12, replace it between the two pairs of workers. Cover the pin with a clothstitch, twist both pairs twice and resume work on the trails. As you bring the inner trail worker back across the row you will find that in order to follow the zigzag marking on the pricking you will need to use pin 16 a second time. There is no need to make a proper back stitch, you can simply lift the workers round the back of pin 16 and carry on, you will not need to take the pin out or reposition it in any way. The worker is twisted twice around this pin on both occasions.

Don't forget that every time your worker arrives at the righthand edge of the trail you must change the order of the Gold Dust threads. This rule is good for both the inner and the outer trail. Keep a close eye on your trails and if it looks as if the chains are suddenly twice as long as normal, it indicates that you have forgotten to change the order of the Gold Dust threads at the righthand end of the previous row and you must go back and put it right. By changing the order of these threads every two rows each chain should go over two worker rows throughout this project. The outer trail worker must be linked to the ring at every alternate pinhole. These pinholes are circled on the pricking to remind you. You will also need to link the two worker pairs around the shared pin at each point of the hexagon. Tension all the pairs carefully as you go along, but don't be too firm with the Gold dust threads, tensioning them more gently than usual will give you a nicer, more rounded 'chain stitch' effect.

Joining the two trails together at the end of your project is a bit tricky, so start off by tying the workers into their corresponding starting loops. You can do the same with the Perle passives. Now all you have to tackle are the Gold Dust 'magic chain' pairs and I found that the easiest way to get a neat finish was to remove the piece from the pillow and thread each one of those thicker glittery threads in turn in a needle which allows you to complete the magic chain sequence using embroidery rather than bobbins. Finish all the ends off neatly and securely and trim off all the surplus thread.

The next step is to add the snowflake and this I stitched into the centre using a piece of thread left over from the workers. The bead has a hole through two of its six points, so I attached it to the worker loops opposite the top and bottom hexagon points. Finally use a small piece of the left over Gold Dust thread to make a hanging loop.

Christmas tree decoration with magic chains and snowflake bead.

MAGIC CHAIN CIRCLE WITH PLAITS AND PICOTS.

This design consists of two circular trails, both of which have the added decoration of 'magic chains'. The outer trail is linked to the ring at all of the outside pinholes and the two trails are linked by a plait with two picots on each zigzag. A gold coloured metal motif is then sewn into the centre. It is a rather more challenging piece because of its plaits and picots, but any lacemaker who has covered the basic skills of Bedfordshire lace should enjoy working this piece.

2 pairs of workers for the two trails in DMC 30 Brilliante, or equivalent. Cut 2 x 2yd (2m) lengths.
2 pairs for the plaits in the same thread. Cut 2 x 2yd (2m) lengths.
4 pairs of passives in DMC Coton Perle No 8 in the same colour as the workers. Cut 4 x 1yd (1m) lengths.
4 pairs of passives for the 'magic chain' in Twilley's Gold Dust, using two different colours. Cut 4 x 1yd (1m) lengths.
1 medium sized gold or silver metal bangle 6cm in diameter.

I used green workers and outside passives for the trails. The 'magic chain' was worked in green and gold glittery threads.

WORKING INSTRUCTIONS.

Once again you must start by pinning your pricking and the metal bangle to the centre of your pillow. Now hang one of the workers on pin 4, one Perle passive on each of pins 1 and 3 and two contrasting coloured Gold Dust threads hung 'open' around pin 2. Cloth stitch through the first pair of passives, now follow the same sequence through the Gold Dust threads that you used in the previous project, lift the first thread and pass both workers underneath it, the workers now pass over the centre two Gold Dust threads, before being passed underneath the final thick glittery thread. Now make a cloth stitch to complete the row, add two twists to the worker and you are ready to link the workers to the ring by pushing the outer worker thread under the ring to make a loop. The second worker bobbin is then passed through the loop spangle first. Put up pin 9, pull both threads tight and add one more twist to the workers. You must now change the order of the magic chain threads as on the outer circle the Gold Dust threads are moved at the end of every row, so bring the two outside glittery threads into the centre by lifting them over, and then putting them down between the other two Gold Dust threads. You can then work the next row using the same under, over, under sequence with both workers through the Gold Dust threads. Twist twice as you have now reached the end of the row, and put up pin 10. Don't forget to change the Gold Dust threads at the end of the row, then work across to the outside of the trail and link the workers to the ring in the usual way at pin 11, change the Gold Dust threads and work back across the row leaving your workers 'parked' around pin 12, but do not twist them. Don't forget to change the order of the Gold Dust threads at this point, then they will be in the correct position when you return to this trail.

Now start the inner trail by hanging the worker on pin 8, the Perle passives on pins 5 and 7, and the two contrasting coloured pairs of Gold Dust on pin 6. Don't forget to hang these last two pairs 'open' around the pin. Work across the row to pin 13 and back again to pin 14 in precisely the same way as you worked the outside trail, but this time you will only change the order of the Gold Dust threads when your worker arrives at the righthand edge of the trail. Work back to pin 15 where you will need to add the two pairs to make up the plait.

Hang the two plait pairs open around a temporary pin positioned in the first of the picots pinholes (pin 21). Now cloth stitch the workers from pin 15 straight through the righthand pair only (there are no twists on the workers between the trail passives and this new pair). Twist the worker pair twice as it has now reached the end of this row, take out pin 15 and re-position it between the worker and the new pair it has just worked through. Work back across the row cloth stitching through the new plait pair and the trail passive pair before following the usual under, over, under sequence through the Gold Dust threads and making the final cloth stitch with the inside trail passive, twisting the worker twice and putting up pin 16.

Now push the plait pair (which was worked as a trail passive for the last two rows) to the left to meet up with the two bobbins hanging from pin 21, this temporary pin can now be removed. These four threads will make up the plait, so don't make the mistake of working them into the trail at this point. Before you start to make the plait you should work as far as pin 20 on the inner trail, but don't forget to change the order of the Gold Dust threads before you continue, and to do the same after pins 18 and 20. Now go back to the plait pairs waiting for you at pin 15.

Dust threads in the usual way. You will find that you are now using one of the plait pairs as your worker, the old worker is left behind to become part of the new plait. Link the workers to the ring at the outside pinhole (pin 23) and work back across to pin 24 twisting the workers twice and putting up the pin immediately after working through the inside Perle trail passive. The old trail worker and just one of the previous plait pairs are now ready to make the new plait. Before you continue with the plait it's a good idea to proceed just a little further with the outside trail linking the workers to the ring at pins 25, 27 and 29, and changing the order of the Gold Dust threads after every pin.

Leave the workers at pin 28 whilst you continue with the plait making picots at pins 29 and 30. Join the plait to the trail at pin 31 cloth stitching the worker straight through both incoming plait pairs, putting the pin up between those plait pairs, making a cloth stitch with the plait pairs to cover the pin and then continuing to work back across the row in the usual way. This exchange of workers and plait pairs will give you a nice sharp point where the plait changes direction so you'll have a very dramatic zigzag.

You can now repeat the instructions from pin 16 until you have completed the circle. The last plait will join into its starting loop around pin 15, bring two threads up through that loop and tie each one with one of the other plait threads in a nice neat reef knot. The trail workers and the four Perle trail passives are all joined to their own starting loop and tied off in the same way. The Gold Dust threads are joined as neatly as possible with a needle once the lace is off the pillow, and the ends are darned away. Trim off the surplus thread and use a piece of the left over glittery thread to make a hanging loop. To add the finishing touch I used a very delicate metal motif which was really intended for use by egg decorators! I simply stitched this into place through the top and bottom petal shapes.

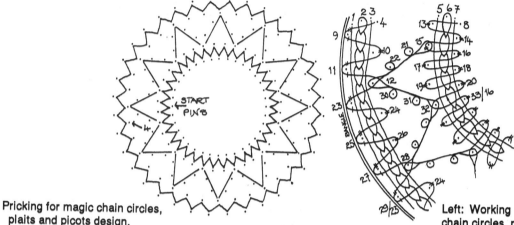

Pricking for magic chain circles, plaits and picots design.

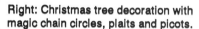

Left: Working diagram for the magic chain circles, plaits and picots design.

Start the plait with a cloth stitch in the usual way, tension it carefully and continue plaiting with a twist (bobbins 4 and 2 over the bobbins in position 3 and 1 respectively) and then a cross (bobbin in position 2 over the one in position 3) tension all four threads and repeat those two movements until your plait is just a fraction short of the first picot pinhole (pin 21) make a picot to the left of the plait (I twist the lefthand pair five times before placing the pin and twice afterwards). Restart the plait with a cloth stitch and continue plaiting, tensioning carefully as you go. You will make a second picot at pin 22, then plait on until you reach pin 12, where the worker from the outside trail is waiting. You must now link the plait to the outside trail.

Make sure that there are no twists on the workers and that you have remembered to change the order of the Gold Dust threads in the outer trail. Now cloth stitch that worker pair through both of the plait pairs, but do not twist the workers at all, remove pin 12 and put it up again between the two plait pairs (not between the workers and the plait pairs which might be your first inclination). Now make a cloth stitch with those two plait pairs to cover the pin, and continue cloth stitching back across the trail and through the Gold

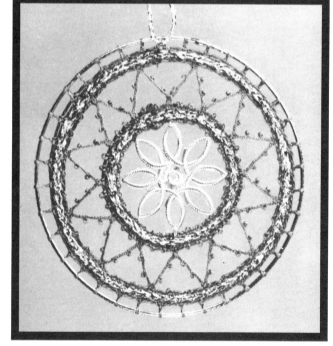

Right: Christmas tree decoration with magic chain circles, plaits and picots.

PLAIT, PICOT AND TRAIL EDGING FOR A BANGLE.

This design does require a knowledge of some of the basic skills of Bedfordshire lace. The plait, which is decorated with picots, passes through the trail using a Cluny crossing. The pattern is given in different sizes so that you can vary the size of the bangle used according to the decoration you plan to add to the centre of the ring.

For the small sized bangle:-

3 pairs of DMC Fil a Dentelle or DMC 30 Brilliante for the trail worker and plait pairs. Cut 3 x 2yd (2m) lengths.

2 pairs of Twilley's Gold Dust for the trail passives. Cut 2 x 1yd (1m) lengths.

For the medium sized bangle:-

3 pairs of DMC Fil a Dentelle for the trail worker and plait pairs. Cut 3 x 2yd (2m) lengths.

2 pairs of Twilley's Gold Dust for the trail passives. Cut 2 x 1 1/4yd (110cm) lengths.

For the large sized bangle :-

3 pairs of DMC Fil a Dentelle or DMC 30 Brilliante for the trail worker and plait pairs. Cut 3 x 2 3/4yds (2.5m) lengths.

2 pairs of Twilley's Gold Dust for the trail passives. Cut 2 x 1 3/4yd (160cm) lengths.

You can use any combination of the basic Christmas colours of red, gold, green and silver, choosing your threads to compliment the ornament to be hung in the centre. For the small bangle shown I worked the edging all in pink adding two small silver holly leaves and a spray of pink silk flowers to the top of the ring. I worked one medium bangle in red and gold adding a gold holly leaf 'star' with a red and gold tinsel trim to the centre. The other I worked in green and silver threads with a silver holly leaf 'star' decorated with red ribbon and a silver bell. The large size bangle I worked in red and silver hanging a silver tinsel star in the centre of the ring.

WORKING INSTRUCTIONS.

Before winding one of the Gold Dust threads onto the bobbins attach it to the bangle by folding it in half and bringing the centre fold up through the ring, widening the loop and passing the ends through that loop. Position the pattern in the centre of your pillow and pin it down. Now place your bangle in the middle of the pattern with the attached thread at the starting position on the outside edge of the bangle. Put three or four anchoring pins close against the inner edge of the ring to keep it in place, and push them right down into the pillow so that they don't get in your way. Put up pin 1 through the loop attaching the thread to the bangle and wind on the bobbins. Hang the other Gold Dust pair from pin 2 and one of the DMC pairs from pin 3, this will be your worker for the first few pinholes.

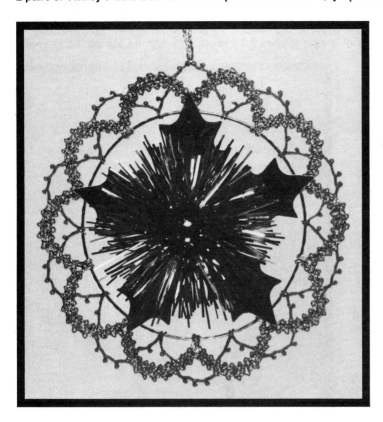

Left: Medium ring with plait, picots and trail edging.

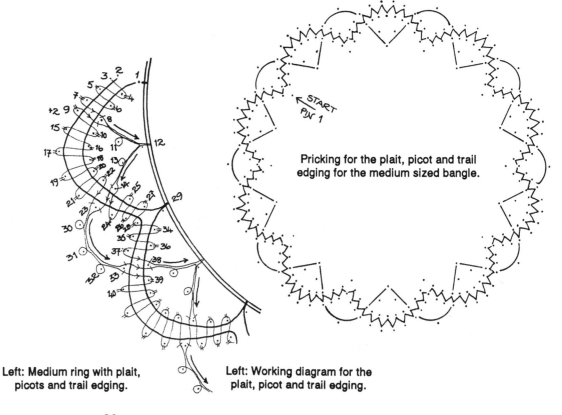

Pricking for the plait, picot and trail edging for the medium sized bangle.

Left: Working diagram for the plait, picot and trail edging.

Cloth stitch to and fro across the rows twisting the workers twice at the end of every row, putting up pins 4-8 in the usual way. Park the workers at pin 8 but only twist the workers once this time. Now add the remaining two pairs 'open' around pin 9 and put the bobbins down to the left of the other pairs. Twist either the pair to the left, OR the pair to the right of the pin twice. The righthand pair now cloth stitches across the trail and is twisted once ready to join the previous worker pair at pin 8 to make the plait, but first bring the pair remaining at pin 9 across the row and leave it at pin 10, this pair will be the new trail worker. Put an anchoring pin through the spangle of each of the bobbins at pin 10 so that you can make the plait which is joined to the ring at pin 12. Always start your plait with a cloth stitch and continue with a series of 'reversed' half stitches, i.e. twist and cross. Tension the threads well between each stitch and make a picot at pin 11

Medium ring with plait, picot and trail edging.

putting three twists on the lefthand pair if you are using Fil a Dentelle, and five if you are using 30 Brilliante, before putting up the pin. Add two more twists once the picots threads have been tensioned. Restart your plait with a cloth stitch and continue plaiting until you reach pin 12. Use only the righthand pair to join the plait to the ring, push the thread nearest the ring underneath it and make a loop in the centre of the ring, pass the other bobbin of this pair through the loop and pull up both threads tightly. Add one twist to this pair and put up the pin below all four plait threads. Now make a cloth stitch to start off the next plait. Make a picot at pin 13 and 'park' the plait at pin 14 with one pair on each side of it whilst you go back and pick up the worker from pin 10.

Work the trail in the usual way from pin 10-23. Leave the worker pair at pin 23 and only twist it once instead of the usual twice. Go back to the opposite side of the trail to pin 14 where the plait pairs are 'parked'. Twist both pairs once and then bring the pair nearest the trail (the lefthand pair) across the trail as your workers. Twist them once at the end of the row and push them to the left to join the previous worker pair. These two pairs will work the plait in a moment. Take the pair remaining at pin 14 as your new worker and continue until you reach pin 28. Leave the worker pair here and use the inner passive pair to link the work to the bangle at pin 29. Push the passive thread at the righthand end of the row underneath the bangle and make a loop in the centre of the ring, pass the next passive thread through this loop and tension both threads, twist them once and put up pin 29 in front of them both to stop the link sliding forward around the ring when you tension this passive pair as it rejoins the trail.

Before you resume work on the trail make the plait from pin 23 towards the three picot pins at 30, 31 and 32. Park the plait at pin 33 whilst you go back and pick up the trail worker from pin 29. Work pins 34-38 as usual, but remember to put only one twist on the worker pair at pin 38. Make sure the parking pin at 33 is correctly positioned and put one twist on each of the plait pairs. Now bring the nearest pair across the trail and twist it once before pushing it to the right to join the old worker pair at pin 38. These two pairs will make the next plait. The replacement worker is found waiting to the left of pin 33, so continue your trail as usual until the next plait needs to cross through the trail. If you're not too confident about Cluny crossings, then I hope the accompanying working diagram will help you follow things through, alternatively follow the instructions for pins 23 and 14 as the plait crosses through the trail from the centre of the ring towards the outside edge, and for pins 38 and 33 when it is coming in from the edge towards the ring.

Continue all the way round the bangle until you meet up with the start. The inner Gold Dust passive must be knotted around the starting loop at pin 1, the other trail passive is joined into its own starting loop at pin 2, and the worker pair into the loop at pin 3. The outside plait pairs having completed the final three picots are plaited to pin 9. At this pin bring two of those four threads through the worker loop and tie two reef knots using one thread from the starting loop and one from outside it for each knot. When all the threads are secured in this way you can remove all the bobbins, then the pins and lift your lace off the pillow. Trim the ends close to the reef knots and use a small length of the Gold Dust thread to make a hanging loop. This thread is too thick to pass through the centre picot on the plait, so fold the Gold Dust thread in half and bring the mid point up through the lace between the V of the trail and the outer plait. Pass the ends of the Gold Dust thread through the loop and tighten it so that the loop rests around that central picot. Tie the ends of the hanging loop together in an overhand knot.

Once your border is complete all you have to do is to decide on which ornament you would like to hang or glue in the centre of the ring. For the smallest ring I glued two small silver holly leaves on top of the scallop to each side of the hanging loop (it's best to put the glue on the right side of the cloth stitch trails and then press the leaves on to them). If you are worried about the leaves being white on the back you can either stick some silver paper-backed tinsel onto the reverse of the leaves, or you can colour them over with a silver felt tipped pen. I trimmed the stem of the flower spray to about 1/2" (1.5cm) and glued it onto the back of the leaves so that it hung down into the ring.

Both of the medium rings are decorated with a five-leafed 'holly star'. As there are ten scallops on this edging, the points of the leaves can be glued over the places where the trails (or the plaits if you prefer) are linked to the ring. As these holly stars are perfectly symmetrical you can cover the back with a second star. For a really stunning effect you can glue two of the commercial holly stars with tinsel centres back to back. You can if you wish add your own decoration to a holly star. I used two 15/8" (4cm) lengths of 1/4" (6mm) wide ribbon with Vs cut into both ends to form the cross. Across the middle I used a 4" (10cm) length overlapping the ends by 1/2" (1.5cm) behind the centre of the

Star template.

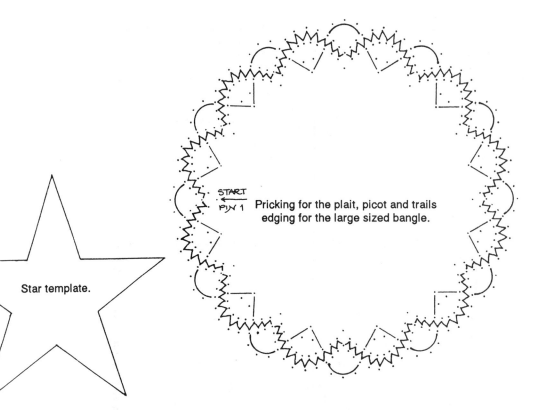

Pricking for the plait, picot and trails edging for the large sized bangle.

Left: Large ring with plait and picot trail edging.

'bow' which is 1 3/4" (4.5cm) wide overall. A piece of fine wire or strong thread can be wound around the centre and pulled tight to shape the bow. Glue the bow across the centre of the cross. I then added a silver bell with a 'clapper' which allowed the bell to move even when the knob at the top is glued securely onto the centre of the ribbon bow.

For the large ring I made a tinsel star decoration using a small length of garland tinsel and some thin silver card (also available in gold and copper finishes) purchased from our local artists' supplies shop. Cut out a paper or card template of the star and mark round it onto the back of the card with the metallic finish. Cut the stars out very carefully and glue two of them together back to back. Trim off any overlapping sections and to avoid white edges on your star you can run a gold or silver felt pen along the cut sides. I used the largest sized hole on a leather punch to make a hole in the centre of the star, but a paper hole punch will do the same job. Now cut into the hole from the V between two of the star points. Cut a 1" (2.5cm) piece of garland tinsel and roll it along its central stitching. Use a piece of fine wire or strong thread to secure the roll, now ease the slit in the star open, and slip in your roll of tinsel. I found that the edges of the star came back together again quite satisfactorily, but you can always use a couple of pieces of clear sticky tape to keep your star in shape if necessary. Fluff out your tinsel roll, make a hole in the tip of one point for a hanging loop which is then attached to the top of the ring. The star should be small enough to swing freely in a large size bangle, but the points will overlap the ring of a medium size bangle sufficiently to allow it to be glued into place.

Above: Small ring with plait, picot and trail edging.

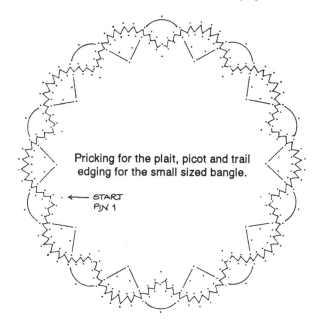

Pricking for the plait, picot and trail
edging for the small sized bangle.

← START
PIN 1

RING WITH FAN EDGING AND BEAD DROP.

This very simple edging makes a glittery trim for a small plastic ring. It is particularly effective if you work the fan in a thick metallic thread and the fine background threads in a dark colour which will then seem to disappear once the decoration is hung on a dark green Christmas tree making the glittery 'fan' threads stand out very vividly.

1 pair of Twilley's Gold Dust or flat pack Madeira as the workers. Cut 1 x 31/2yd (3.25m) length.

4 pairs of DMC 30 Brilliant as passives. Cut 4 x 11/2yd (135cm) lengths. You can use DMC Metallise or fine metallic Madeira but this will need to be used double so cut 4 x 3yd (2.75m) lengths and fold each piece in half before winding it on to the bobbins.

1 small plastic ring with an external diameter of 4.5cm.

1 bead, preferably glass, to hang in the centre.

1 ribbon bow.

I have worked several versions of this project, two with the bead drops in the centre and one with just a ribbon bow. I used an elongated red plastic bead for the centre of a red plastic bangle, using red passives and a gold worker for the lace. The crystal glass bead drop I used in a green bangle trimmed with green passive threads and a pearly white Madeira worker. The final version was worked entirely in pearly white threads with a white ribbon bow.

Small plastic rings with fan edging and bead drop.

99

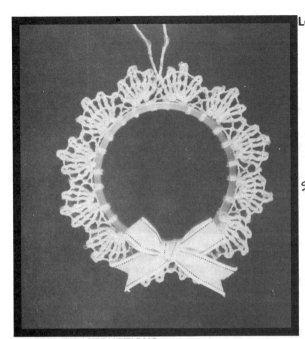

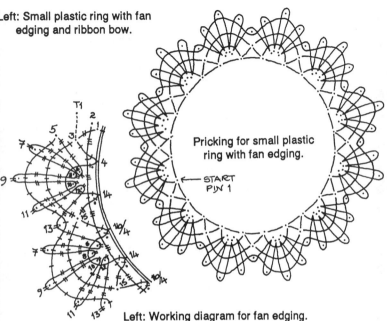

Left: Small plastic ring with fan edging and ribbon bow.

Pricking for small plastic ring with fan edging.

← START PIN 1

Left: Working diagram for fan edging.

Above: Small plastic ring with fan edging and bell motif.

WORKING INSTRUCTIONS.

Attach one of the passive pairs to the ring by bringing the half way loop up through the centre of the bangle and passing the bobbins through that loop spangle first. Pull the bobbins tight and position the bangle so that it lies exactly in the centre of your pricking which you must pin to the middle of your pillow. Place three or four anchoring pins close to the inner edge of the bangle so that when they are pushed down into the pillow the heads just overlap onto the edge of the ring, helping to keep it in place.

Slide the pair which is attached to the ring round the bangle until it is close to the start, put up pin 1 so that it goes through the loop attaching that pair to the ring, this will keep it firmly in place. Now hang the next passive from pin 2 and make a cloth stitch and twist with these two pairs. Add a second twist to the lefthand pair (originally from the ring) and two more twists to the righthand passive pair to make a total of three twists altogether. This pair will form the inner edge passive pair staying alongside the bangle all through the project.

Hang a third pair of passives from pin T1 and use it to make a Torchon ground stitch (half stitch, pin, half stitch and twist) at pin 3 with the passive pair immediately to its right. Remove the temporary pin from T1 and tension both pairs at pin 3, now take the righthand pair and cloth stitch it through the inside edge passive pair and twist both pairs once. Now push the nearest thread of the travelling passive pair under the ring to make a loop inside the bangle. Enlarge the loop so that you can pass the other bobbin of this pair through it. Pull both tight and twist them once. Put up pin 4 to the right of all the threads and cloth stitch through the inner edge pair. Twist the edge pair three times and the other passive pair twice. You'll notice that pin 4 is not 'covered' but by placing it 'underneath' the linking threads at this point you prevent the loops from sliding around the ring.

Hang the remaining passive pair on pin 5 and push it to the left. Hang the fan worker from the same pin and put it down to the right of the previous pair. Twist the centre threads twice to interlink them. Now twist the worker twice and the outside passive pair once. The worker will be twisted twice throughout the 'fan', the outside and middle passive pair will always be twisted once during the 'fan', and the inner passive will not be twisted at all until it leaves the 'fan'. So taking the worker from pin 5 cloth stitch it through the middle passive (from pin 3) and twist the worker twice and the passive once. Cloth stitch the worker through the inner passive pair (from pin 4) and twist the worker twice before putting up pin 6. Tension all the pairs and work back to the outside edge following exactly the same twist pattern. Put up pin 7 and tension each pair again. Continue working in this way until the worker arrives at pin 13. Tension all the passives particularly carefully at this point. The inner passive should lie as close to the inner row of pins as possible and the outer passive should lie close to the outer pins at the other end of the row. The middle passive should be positioned to follow a nice curve midway between the two.

Add a second twist to the middle fan passive and twist the inner fan passive twice. Now work the inner passive through the edge passive pair, twisting both pairs once before linking the old inner fan passive to the ring. Put up pin 14 and cloth stitch it back through the edge passive pair and twist it twice. The edge passive is twisted three times. Work a Torchon ground stitch at pin 15 and then take the righthand passive pair through the circle pair to link it onto the ring at pin 16. Work it back through the edge passive pair and add two twists to the ordinary passive and three to the inner edge passive. You are then ready to work the next 'fan' by repeating the instructions from pin 5.

100

Complete the edging and join each pair carefully into its starting loop. The inner passive pair will be joined to its starting loop at pin 2, the inner fan passive will join the starting loop around the ring at pin 1, the middle fan passive will join into pin 3, and the worker into the loop at pin 5. The outside passive pair can be tied off with a reef knot without being linked to a starting loop. The worker threads can be used to form the hanging loop from pin 5, and the two passive pairs which have just been joined into pins 1 and 2 can be used to attach the centre bead, the other threads can all be trimmed off close to the reef knots once the pins are removed and the piece is off the pillow.

To attach a bead to the centre bring the passive pairs from pins 1 and 2 into the centre of the ring and using a crochet hook take them through the hole in the bead. Now get a friend to help you by twisting those threads very tightly whilst you hold the bead and the ring quite firmly. You must hold the bead in the ring just a little below its final position. Your friend need only twist the first 4-6inches (10-15cm) of thread, then whilst you hold the bead she must bring the twisted threads back on themselves so that you can catch those threads against the ring with your thumb. Let the bead go and the threads will twist together. When you are satisfied that you have the bead hanging just where you want it, untwist the threads above your thumb and push them through to the other side of the ring taking one pair down on each side of the starting loop, you can then tie a reef knot with the threads to secure everything firmly and neatly. Trim off the ends, make your hanging loop and glue a small ribbon bow to the top of the ring.

As a variation you might like to work this decoration without the bead and to add the bow to the bottom of the ring so that it looks rather like a Christmas wreath.

Right: Shell edging for small sized bangle.

SHELL EDGING FOR A BANGLE.

This is a very simple edging which makes a very effective border for a ring. Again this pattern is given in several sizes to make it as versatile as possible.

For the small sized bangle:-
1 pair of Twilley's Gold Dust as the workers. Cut 1 x 3 1/2yds (3.25m) length.
3 pairs of DMC Fil a Dentelle as the passives. Cut 3 x 1 1/2yd (135cm) lengths.

For the medium sized bangle with 15 shells:-
1 pair of Twilley's Gold Dust as the workers. Cut 1 x 4yd (3.75m) length.
3 pairs of DMC Fil a Dentelle as the passives. Cut 3 x 1 3/4yd (160cm) lengths.

For the medium sized bangle with 18 shells:-
1 pair of Twilley's Gold Dust as the workers. Cut 1 x 5yd (4.75m) length.
3 pairs of DMC Fil a Dentelle as the passives. Cut 3 x 1 3/4yd (160cm) lengths.

For the large sized bangle:-
1 pair of Twilley's Gold Dust as the workers. Cut 1 x 5yd (4.75m) length.
3 pairs of DMC Fil a Dentelle as the passives. Cut 3 x 2yd (2m) lengths.

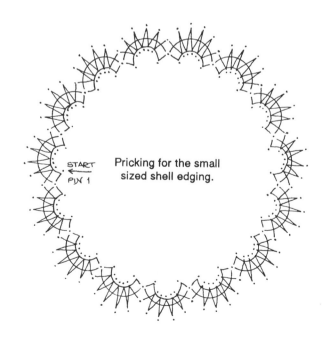

START
PIN 1

Pricking for the small sized shell edging.

If you are planning to hang this decoration on a green Christmas tree it is a good idea to use dark green passives for this design, then when it is hung against the dark background of the tree the passives will seem to disappear, leaving the glittery shell-shapes of the Gold Dust workers standing out very clearly. I worked three of my samples in this way. The small ring was worked in silver and green and trimmed with a green and silver tinsel 'holly star'. One medium ring was worked in gold with a matching gold tinsel star glued onto the bangle. The other was worked in pink and green with two silver bells and a silver bow providing the finishing touches. The largest bangle was worked in red and gold and trimmed with a small arrangement of leaves and flowers.

WORKING INSTRUCTIONS.

Before you wind one of the passive threads onto the bobbins attach it to the bangle by folding it in half and bringing that mid-point fold up through the centre of the ring, passing the ends through that loop and pulling them tight. Pin your pattern down to the centre of your pillow and place your bangle in the middle of the pattern. The inner row of pinholes should just be visible on the outside of the bangle and the thread you have just attached to it should be level with start pin 1. Place three or four anchoring pins at equal intervals around the inner edge of the ring to keep it firmly in place, press these pins down into the pillow so that they don't get in the way whilst you're working. Now wind the thread onto the bobbins and put up pin 1 through the loop joining that thread to the ring.

Hang the next passive pair from a temporary pin behind pin 2 (T1), you can use any of the higher pinholes for this as it will be removed very shortly. Make a Torchon ground stitch (half stitch, pin, half stitch and twist) with these two pairs at pin 2. Remove the temporary pin and tension it so that it slips down to rest around pin 2. The righthand pair is now linked to the ring at pin 3, so push the nearest thread under the bangle to form a loop in the centre of the ring, pass the other bobbin of this pair through that loop and pull them both tight. Add two twists to this pair and put up pin 3 in front of both threads to keep the link firmly in place. They are now ready to go back into the work as the inner passive pair in the Gold Dust 'shell'. The pair from pin 2 which also has two twists on it will enter this 'shell' as the middle passive pair.

Hang the third passive pair on pin 4 and push it a little to the left, hang the worker pair from the same pin and put the bobbins down to the right of the previous pair. Twist the centre two threads twice to interlink them and then twist both pairs once. Cloth stitch the workers through the middle passive pair (to their right) and again twist both pairs once. Cloth stitch the workers through the inner passive pair and twist the workers twice because it is the end of the row, but do not twist the passive pair at all. The pinholes are quite close together at this end of the row and there simply isn't room for a twist on the inner passive pair here. Put up pin 5, then work back to the outer edge twisting the worker once after each cloth stitch and twice at the end of the row. The middle and outer passive pairs are both twisted once after the worker has cloth stitched through them.

Below: Working diagram for shell edging.

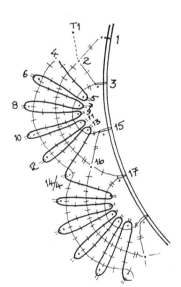

Pricking for the medium sized ring with 15 shells.

Above: Shell edging for medium sized bangle with 15 shells.

Shell edging for medium sized bangle with 18 shells.

On the smallest ring I glued a five-leaved holly star with a tinsel centre. There will be three 'shells' between each of the holly leaf points. You can either glue a second identical decoration to the back of the first, or you can just glue on a holly star without the tinsel centre, alternatively you can colour the back with a felt pen.

I made a gold tinsel star for the medium ring with fifteen shells. The star is fixed into position with a touch of glue on each point, placing it on the ring so that there are three 'shells' between each point. For the medium ring with eighteen shells I used two of the left over lengths of Gold Dust to hang two bells in the centre of the ring. First pass the thread through the loop of the bell and get a friend to help you twist the thread. When it is well twisted fold the thread in half and let it twist to form a nice cord. Tie the ends together in an overhand knot. Do the same for the second bell and then hang them from the top of the ring so that one is higher than the other. Tie the two cords together with another overhand knot so that the knot can be glued just above the bangle. Trim off the surplus twisted cord and cover the knot with a silver bow.

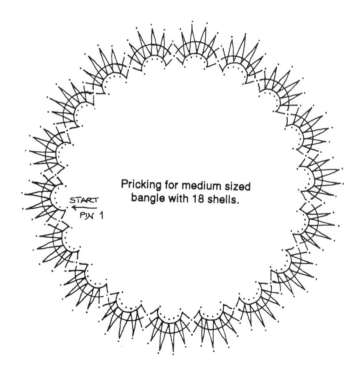

Pricking for medium sized bangle with 18 shells.

Keep working to and fro in this way until the worker reaches pin 14 at the end of the 'shell'. Add one more twist (to make a total of two) to the middle passive pair and twist the inner passive twice. Link the inner passive to the ring in the same way as you did at pin 3. Twist it twice after the link and use it to work a ground stitch with the middle passive pair at pin 16. The righthand pair from pin 16 is now joined to the bangle at pin 17. Don't forget to twist it twice after joining it to the ring so that it is ready to go back into the work as the new inner passive.

You are now ready to start work on the next shell, so repeat the instructions from pin 4. Continue around the circle until you reach the start once more. The inner passive will be twisted twice before being knotted around the threads which were attached to the ring at pin 1. The middle passive pair is also twisted twice before being joined to the ground stitch at pin 2. The worker is joined to its starting loop at pin 4 and then the outside passive can also be tied off with a reef knot. Once the lace is off the pillow you can trim off the passive threads close to the reef knots. The worker threads can be tied together in an overhand knot 2-3" (5-8cm) away from the finishing reef knot to make the hanging loop.

For the large ring I used two large green holly leaves, a white silk flower with pearl stamens, two red holly berries on string stems and a tiny fir cone on a wire stem. First of all you need to make your ribbon bow. For this it is best to use the very cheapest type of ribbon as the better quality taffeta or satin ribbon is too thick. I used an 11" (28cm) length. Fold it in half and pinch the fold to crease the ribbon. Fold this doubled length in half again, to make quarters, and once more press in a crease. Open the length out and place it right side down on the table. Bring one end and then the other over to make a cross with the two quarter folds on top of each other. Lift the halfway crease and place it behind the cross made by the quarter fold creases. Now wind a piece of fine brass wire, or fuse wire, twice around the centre. Trim the ends into nice Vs to complete the bow.

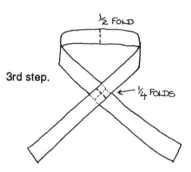

1st step.

2nd step.

3rd step.

Finished bow.

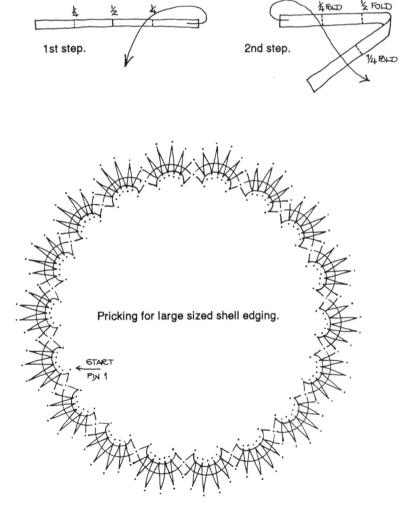

Pricking for large sized shell edging.

Shell edging for large sized bangle.

The leaves are arranged so that the bottoms of both leaves are level, on top of these you place the fir cone in the middle and a holly berry to each side. The white flower goes in the centre. When you are satisfied with your arrangement place the bow on top and use the wire holding the bow together to wind around the stems of the leaves, flower, berries and fir cone. Wrap the wire around the stems for approximately 1/2" (1.5cm). Trim off the remainder of the stems and glue the whole arrangement to the bottom of the ring. Now fold up the wire-wrapped stem so that it lies hidden behind the leaves. Your decoration is now complete.